The Values of Independent Hip-Hop in the Post-Golden Era

Christopher Vito

The Values of Independent Hip-Hop in the Post-Golden Era

Hip-Hop's Rebels

Christopher Vito
Southwestern College
Chula Vista, CA, USA

ISBN 978-3-030-02480-2   ISBN 978-3-030-02481-9 (eBook)
https://doi.org/10.1007/978-3-030-02481-9

Library of Congress Control Number: 2018958592

© The Editor(s) (if applicable) and The Author(s) 2019. This book is an open access publication.
Open Access This book is licensed under the terms of the Creative Commons Attribution 4.0 International License (http://creativecommons.org/licenses/by/4.0/), which permits use, sharing, adaptation, distribution and reproduction in any medium or format, as long as you give appropriate credit to the original author(s) and the source, provide a link to the Creative Commons license and indicate if changes were made.
The images or other third party material in this book are included in the book's Creative Commons license, unless indicated otherwise in a credit line to the material. If material is not included in the book's Creative Commons license and your intended use is not permitted by statutory regulation or exceeds the permitted use, you will need to obtain permission directly from the copyright holder.
The use of general descriptive names, registered names, trademarks, service marks, etc. in this publication does not imply, even in the absence of a specific statement, that such names are exempt from the relevant protective laws and regulations and therefore free for general use.
The publisher, the authors and the editors are safe to assume that the advice and information in this book are believed to be true and accurate at the date of publication. Neither the publisher nor the authors or the editors give a warranty, express or implied, with respect to the material contained herein or for any errors or omissions that may have been made. The publisher remains neutral with regard to jurisdictional claims in published maps and institutional affiliations.

Cover illustration: © Melisa Hasan

This Palgrave Pivot imprint is published by the registered company Springer Nature Switzerland AG
The registered company address is: Gewerbestrasse 11, 6330 Cham, Switzerland

For my mom.

Preface

I remember back in 2008 Lupe Fiasco released the song "Hip-Hop Saved My Life." He was telling a story of a rapper facing the everyday struggles of making it in hip-hop, getting out the hood, providing for a family, and ultimately growing as a person. Like Lupe's song, many messages in hip-hop gave me something to relate to growing up, facing many of the same struggles that a person of color in urban America faces today. But my story was also unique. As a first generation US-born Filipino in San Diego, CA, I grew up in a culture that either stereotypically envisioned us as smart and passive or just completely invisible. All the meanwhile, many Filipinos are just trying to get by, assimilating into a culture that has colonized them, and creating a different legacy for the next generation.

What I saw in hip-hop was a place where many voices and stories could be heard, including my own. I knew I did not have the skills or talent to become a musician, but I wanted to tell my story in a different way. At San Diego State University, I took an Introduction to Sociology course with Professor Jung Min Choi and it allowed me to connect the music I was listening to with what I was learning in the classroom. And thus, this project began.

I eventually obtained my M.A. in Sociology from SDSU and later published an article in the *International Journal of Cultural Studies* analyzing Immortal Technique's lyrics. I then obtained my Ph.D. from UC Riverside under the guidance of supportive professors such as Ellen Reese, who urged me to follow my interests. I am now a tenure-track professor in my hometown at Southwestern College trying to give back to my community. My goal in this book is to tell the story of the independent hip-hop culture that had such a profound influence on my life. But I am sure that this culture did not just impact myself, but many other artists, listeners, and fans of hip-hop. Thus, my intention is for this book to be read by a wide array of audiences ranging from independent artists themselves, hip-hop fans and listeners, academia, and students. I do not intend this book to be revolutionary or groundbreaking in its findings, but rather an accessible way to tell the story of independent hip-hop culture as told through their voices.

Ultimately, I hope this book reveals more about hip-hop culture, how it shapes society, and more importantly gives back to the culture that shaped me. Truly and wholeheartedly...*Hip-Hop Saved My Life*.

Chula Vista, USA   Christopher Vito

Acknowledgements

I would like to thank my family and friends for their endless love and support, my dissertation committee for their care and guidance, the editorial team for their countless hours, my colleagues for the smiles and laughs, my students for their passion, and everyone who has helped me along my path. I would also like to thank the Associated Student Organizations (ASO) of Southwestern College for partially funding this open access book. Most importantly I would like to thank hip-hop for saving my life.

Contents

1	Introduction	1
2	Just Say No to the Majors: Independent Hip-Hop Culture	45
3	Just Say No to 360s: Hip-Hop's Claim of Economic Exploitation	71
4	The Death of Indie Hip-Hop?: The Blurry Lines Between the Majors and Independent Hip-Hop	99
5	Conclusions and Implications	131
	Appendix A	145
	Appendix B	147
	Appendix C	151
	References	155
	Index	175

List of Figures

Fig. 1.1	Independent hip-hop album themes	30
Fig. 2.1	Blackalicious (Gift of Gab on left and Chief Xcel on right) (*Credit* Blackalicious.com)	49
Fig. 2.2	Immortal Technique (*Credit* Twitter @ImmortalTech)	58
Fig. 4.1	Carlos (Stagename: Mac Dirrty) (*Credit* Carlos Sanchez)	103
Fig. 4.2	Macklemore and Ryan Lewis' distribution model	122
Fig. 5.1	DJ Kuttin Kandi (*Credit* djkuttinkandi.com)	137
Fig. 5.2	Goodfellas Barbershop Shave Parlor (*Credit* Christopher Vito)	140

LIST OF TABLES

Table 1.1   List of independent hip-hop albums   27
Table 3.1   Record label expenses   79

CHAPTER 1

Introduction

Abstract To what extent and how does independent hip-hop challenge or reproduce US mainstream hip-hop culture and US culture more generally? This chapter attempts to address this age-old question. The author also reviews the history and literature on hip-hop culture, provides an overview of the underlying theory and methodology, and gives an outline of the remaining chapters. His research combines neo-Marxist, critical race, intersectional feminist, and queer theories, as well as Mansbridge and Morris' (Oppositional Consciousness: The Subjective Roots of Social Protest, University of Chicago Press, Chicago, 2001) concept of oppositional consciousness. The research design utilizes a mixed methods approach, which includes content analysis of twenty-five indie albums from 2000 to 2013 and interviews with forty-six members of the independent hip-hop community, to uncover the historical trajectory of independent hip-hop in the post-golden era and how it has affected the culture today.

Keywords Independent hip-hop · Mainstream hip-hop · Post-golden era · Race and class · Gender and sexuality · Oppositional consciousness

Hip-hop, or the cultural movement that developed during the late 1970s, and hip-hop music (aka rap music), or the aspect of hip-hop that focuses on the musical style where rhyming speech is done to the beat of music (Davey D 1984), have always faced a pull between "commercial vitality and its strivings to be a meaningful source of youth empowerment and social change" (Watkins 2005: 10). With the rise in popularity of hip-hop in the 1990s, large corporations began to invest in the culture and actively recruited musicians who fit the persona of a "gangster" to sell records. By 1998, hip-hop reached an impasse wherein sales reached its peak but also saw a majority of record sales under the creative control of major companies. More importantly, Watkins argues the pull between the two competing factors seemed to be swaying toward commercial vitality. As a response indie labels began to grow as there was push-back from artists and listeners who were concerned with the shift in the content of mainstream hip-hop culture and music, which was predominantly capitalistic, patriarchal, Eurocentric, heteronormative, and noncritical of social inequality (Dyson 2010; Ogbar 2007; Perry 2004; Rose 2008; Watkins 2005).

In 2012, Macklemore and Ryan Lewis' album *The Heist* reached critical acclaim as an innovative independent hip-hop album. Receiving national attention, it became a springboard that re-launched the duos' career. In their song "Jimmy Iovine" (2012), who is a music producer and chairman of Interscope Records, Macklemore and Ryan Lewis openly express their dissatisfaction with artists who get tricked into signing with major record labels. They cite problems with creative control, autonomy, and the ability to make profits from their music. Similarly, many independent artists have reflected in their lyrics concerns about the capitalist economy and its influence on the production and distribution of hip-hop music.

Thus, my book addresses an age-old question: To what extent and how independent hip-hop challenges or reproduces US mainstream hip-hop culture and US culture more generally in the post-golden era. In particular, I explore and analyze the historical trajectory of independent hip-hop in the post-golden era and how it has affected the culture today. I contend that indie hip-hop remains a complex contemporary subculture. While it consistently expresses grievances related to both race and class inequality, its gender and sexual politics are contradictory. Nonetheless, independent hip-hop expresses the oppositional consciousness of its artists and listeners as well as the limits of that consciousness (Harkness 2012; Kubrin 2005; Lena and Peterson 2008; Martinez 1997; Myer and Kleck 2007; Stapleton 1998).

Overview of Research

Harkness (2014) identifies three tiers of hip-hop music. Mainstream hip-hop music is defined as music produced and released by artists who are internationally established and connected to the three major record labels, which own or distribute more than 85% of the music globally (Universal Music Group, Sony Music Entertainment, and Warner Music Group) (Rose 2008). Conversely, underground hip-hop music broadly refers to any music created outside the commercial canon (Harrison 2006). The underground acts are often not signed to major labels and have not sold over 500,000 albums, but are trying to launch their career in the music industry (Oware 2014). This book focuses on the middle tier of hip-hop music, which is more specifically defined as music created by established independent labels and produced outside the confines of the three major record labels (Vito 2015). These performers are generally locally and regionally successful but operate without the aid of major corporations (Harkness 2014). Additionally, the terms mainstream, underground, and independent are not intended to be dichotomous, static, and reducible to a "set of sine qua non," but rather, a spectrum or continuum that is interrelated, overlapping, emergent, and discursively constructed (Harrison 2009; Terkourafi 2010; Vito 2015). As Oware (2014) points out, many musicians traditionally classified as underground or independent, such as Common or Talib Kweli, are not underground or independent according to the aforementioned criteria.

Independent hip-hop culture, or its values, beliefs, behaviors, and material objects, remains an important tool in the formation of resistance to oppression and domination by the ruling class. Nonetheless, in the USA it remains a severely understudied contemporary subculture (Perry 2004; Terkourafi 2010) despite studies on independent hip-hop that reveal a complex political discourse about the contradictions regarding issues of race, class, and gender within its music (Harkness 2012; Kubrin 2005; Lena 2006; Martinez 1997; Myer and Kleck 2007; Stapleton 1998). My work examines the politics of race, class, gender, and sexuality within independent hip-hop culture, as well as its ability to generate or express oppositional consciousness among its artists and listeners. I seek to build upon the existing scholarship on independent hip-hop (Alridge 2005; Asante 2008; Ball 2009; Bennett 1999a; Harrison 2006; Kitwana 2002; Maher 2005; Ogbar 2007; Smalls 2011) as well as the broader literature on music and culture.

My central research questions are: To what extent and how does independent hip-hop challenge or reproduce mainstream ideologies, which include ideologies of race, class, gender, and sexuality, within US hip-hop culture and US culture more generally? Does independent hip-hop express and inspire among its artists and fans oppositional consciousness, defined as an empowering mental state that prepares members of an oppressed group to undermine, reform, or overthrow a dominant system (Mansbridge and Morris 2001)? How do artists and fans navigate the changing meanings of independent hip-hop culture, particularly in response to changes in technology and media? How do artists' social locations of race, class, gender, and sexuality shape the kinds of messages they produce? How do fans' social locations of race, class, gender, and sexuality relate to their understanding of the messages within independent hip-hop?

My research design utilizes a mixed methods approach. First, I analyze the lyrics of independent hip-hop albums through a content analysis of twenty-five independent albums from 2000 to 2013. I uncover the dominant ideologies of independent hip-hop artists regarding race, class, gender, sexual orientation, and calls for social change. This is unique in that there has not been a comprehensive study of independent albums within the USA over this period of time. By systemically analyzing the content of the lyrics in these post-golden era albums, I uncover the salient grievances of the independent hip-hop community and how they vary across artists to uncover the historical trajectory of independent hip-hop and how it has affected the culture today.

For example, I find that the messages of independent hip-hop artists are vexed and contradictory. Consistent with Balaji (2010), I find that much of independent hip-hop of this genre is largely produced by straight, male, working-class youth of color. Similar to Oware (2014), I also find that while musicians often challenge dominant beliefs about race and class relations, they sometimes reinforce traditional views of gender and sexuality. There are exceptions to such trends, of course. Some artists, namely queer and female ones, do challenge traditional views about gender and sexuality, but they tend not to be the most popular and well-known acts in this time period.

Second, I examine interviews with forty-six members of the independent hip-hop community who are self-defined listeners and active fans. I explore the meanings that they associate with hip-hop culture and how technological changes have altered their understanding of the culture from 2000 to 2013, and whether and how this shapes their engagement with oppositional consciousness. I further examine the complex and contradictory cultural politics of independent music in the post-golden era, which includes the fluid and blurry lines between mainstream and indie labels, and how hip-hop challenges or reinforces dominant ideologies about race, class, gender, and sexuality.

Similar to the results from content analysis, I find that while much of the culture elucidates the experiences of heterosexual black and Latino men, it often denigrates or neglects other racial and ethnic minorities, women and lesbian, gay, bisexual, transgender, and queer (LGBTQ) groups. This is likely to both shape and limit the oppositional consciousness that it inspires among its listeners as straight, male, working-class youth of color remain the majority and are provided more privilege in claiming authenticity within independent hip-hop culture. In addition, my findings show that there are fluid and blurry lines between mainstream and indie as many performers attempt to retain economic and creative freedom while still attempting to become economically successful. My findings also reveal that acts remain intensely intertwined with major companies in old and new ways to utilize their marketing and distribution channels. Yet while these contradictions exist, interviews determine if hip-hop fans and listeners gain messages that spur them to oppositional consciousness.

My research aims to address a gap in the literature that has traditionally focused either myopically on mainstream hip-hop (Kelley 1994; Perry 2004; Rose 1994), local underground hip-hop (Ball 2009; Harrison 2006; Wang 2014), or the appropriation of US hip-hop in the global sphere (Androutsopoulos and Scholz 2003; Bennett 1999b; Mitchell 2003). This has left independent hip-hop culture in the USA an understudied topic of research, particularly in regard to artists and listeners of the current generation.

Specifically, scholars fail to systematically study independent hip-hop in the post-golden age and its effects on the culture today. I address this gap in the literature by identifying three key themes found in indie hip-hop albums and interviews with independent hip-hop community listeners. First, I focus specifically on the cultural grievances against mainstream culture and major corporations, as well as their support for an alternative indie movement, that acts express in song lyrics during the post-golden era. Second, I examine the claim that major labels profit at the expense of artists, which include economic and political aspects such as forwards, copyright, artist repertoire, touring, merchandising, and press. In addition, I analyze the argument within musicians' lyrics that independent labels help mitigate economic exploitation and corporate control. Third, I explore via interviews how listeners interpret and navigate the changing technological and economic landscape of hip-hop and its influence on mainstream and independent subcultures, particularly in relation to race, class, gender, and sexuality. The book concludes with a chapter on the ramifications of the study, recommendations for readers and the independent hip-hop community, and future research.

Theoretical Framework

My research combines insights from neo-Marxist, critical race, intersectional feminist, and queer theories. In what follows, I critically review each of these theories as well as Mansbridge and Morris' (2001) concept of oppositional consciousness. I then discuss how these theories have informed my research on hip-hop culture.

Relations of Domination and Culture

Frankfurt School Marxists, such as Theodor Adorno and Max Horkheimer (1969), focus on how culture and class relations interact, rejecting vulgar Marxist theories which view culture simply as a by-product of the dominant mode of production. They believe that popular culture produced by the "culture industry" reinforces capitalism through the types of messages that it produces. The culture industry refers to the capitalist and bureaucratic structure that disseminates modern popular culture. Similarly ,Gramsci (1971) argues that the dominant classes maintain control of the proletariat through both physical force (coercion) and consent achieved through the dissemination of hegemonic ideas that suggest elites serve their best interests.

Drawing insights from the Frankfurt School, Shusterman (1992) states that mainstream hip-hop represents an "administered culture" created by the ruling class to reinforce hegemonic ideas and prevent the masses from challenging the status quo. Blair (1993) also states that hip-hop artists were not only forced into becoming corporatized but also willingly supported the status quo by reproducing the hegemonic practices of major record labels.

While the Frankfurt School emphasized the importance of culture, they failed to adequately address various social locations. Racial formation and intersectional feminist theory suggest that hegemony is shaped by multiple relations of domination. Omi and Winant (1994) argue that race is socially constructed and shaped by cultural, economic, and political factors. Extending Gramsci's insights, they argue that racial domination is reinforced through coercion and consent by the masses. They also suggest that race relations and ideologies change over time in response to the struggle among racial groups.

Intersectional feminist theorists, such as Collins (Collins 2005), highlight the interlocking nature of race, class, and gender relations. According to Collins (2005), one's social location within multiple relations of domination interacts simultaneously to shape one's consciousness and understanding of the world. Additionally, Connell (1995) defines "hegemonic masculinity" as the dominant form of masculinity within the gender hierarchy that keeps minority males and women in positions of subordination. It is essentially a configuration of race, class, and gender that promotes an ideal type of white masculinity and denigrates all races and genders that do not uphold it. Hegemonic masculinity is upheld through the physical embodiment of an ideal masculinity, social dominance of hegemonic males over others, and heterosexual prowess over women in all social life ranging from school, sport, and popular culture (Connell and Messerschmidt 2005).

Further, queer theory and other critical theories of sexuality argue that our society upholds patriarchal heteronormativity, which is based on a male/female dichotomy wherein males are seen as innately superior to women. Heteronormativity subsequently presumes a heterosexual/homosexual dichotomy wherein heterosexuality is seen as normal and superior. As a result, LGBTQ lives are marginalized socially, culturally, and politically in a myriad of ways. Among LGBTQ groups there remains heterogeneity in their experiences, and thus various versions of queer theory emphasize the need to incorporate the insights of intersectional theory (Hammonds 1994; Ferguson 2004). They argue that intersectional theory is necessary because it elucidates the lack of queer colored images in the media and emphasizes the need to rearticulate queer theory to account for race and class dominance (Cohen 1997). N. Sullivan (2003) highlights the importance of "queering" cultural practices to transform traditionally heterosexual artifacts and performances to include the experiences of non-gender conforming modes of sexuality and subjectivity.

Hip-hop scholars have similarly argued that the fomentation of resistance to social domination requires addressing multiple relations of domination and subordination (Alridge 2005; R. Sullivan 2003). Alridge (2005) states that hip-hop culture is an important site of racial formation in the USA (Omi and Winant 1994). Hip-hop reinforced the gains of racial and ethnic minorities made through the Civil Rights Movement, but has ultimately been limited by the white hegemonic structure that promotes racist ideologies and the consent of artists adhering to it. In contrast, Adams and Fuller (2006) emphasize the salience of gender in their analysis of the underrepresentation, objectification, and marginalization of women in the industry. Balaji (2010) incorporates an intersectional feminist approach (Collins 2005) to argue that black women in hip-hop are often portrayed by male performers as sexually aggressive and promiscuous, which is in contrast to white women who are often portrayed as sexually revered and sacred. Drawing insights from Connell (1995), scholars highlight the importance of hegemonic masculinity as a tool to subordinate other masculinities, as well as women within hip-hop (Iwamoto 2003). For example, black males in hip-hop are expected to exhibit hyper-masculinity in order to be viewed as legitimate. Conversely, because hegemonic masculinity places white men as superior they can incorporate themselves into the culture as color-blind individuals who are not complicit in reproducing the current unequal racial hierarchy.

Hip-hop scholars, building insights from queer theory, have criticized heterosexism within hip-hop and demonstrated how queer hip-hop has remained at the margins. Queer hip-hop artists have nonetheless challenged the predominant views of homosexuality in mainstream culture (N. Sullivan 2003). Hernandez (2014) highlights queer feminist hip-hop practices that challenge heterosexism by discussing the emancipation of coming out of the closet. In doing so, it can be used as a tool for disenfranchised communities who consume and contribute to the culture, particularly queer communities of color and of the working class (Crenshaw 1991). While the social locations of race and class are salient, Harkness (2012) states that hip-hop is no longer shaped by a monolithic black male culture (Dyson 2010; Rose 1994) but is becoming increasingly heterogeneous (Harkness 2012) and must address multiple social locations which include women and LGBTQ groups as well as other racial and ethnic minorities.

Oppositional Consciousness and Social Movement Activism

Mansbridge and Morris (2001) define oppositional consciousness as "an empowering mental state that prepares members of an oppressed group to undermine, reform, or overthrow a dominant system" (4). This occurs when members of a group have been treated as subordinate or deviant, and thus claim an oppositional consciousness that: (1) utilizes their subordinate identity as a positive identification, (2) identifies injustices done to their group, (3) demands changes in society, and (4) sees other members as having a shared interest in rectifying the injustices. Collins (2005) adds that these subordinated identities cannot be analyzed in isolation, but rather through a complex interplay between race, class, gender, and sexuality both individually and through broader social structures. In doing so, oppositional consciousness can foment oppositional cultural resistance and practices that include creating "free spaces," or physical spaces to communicate and share perceptions of their experiences with relatively little interference from the dominant group. It can be used for the elaboration and testing of ideas and conscious creativity by activists drawing on experiences from everyday life. For instance, the Disability Rights Movement was able to create images, slogans, literature, humor, rituals, and other cultural expressions in a free and safe space to build a collective identity drawn from their everyday experiences (Mansbridge and Morris 2001).

Neo-Marxist theorists (Freire 1970; Gramsci 1971) emphasize the importance of intellectuals and artists in the formation of critical thinking and oppositional consciousness. Gramsci (1971) argues that organic intellectuals (which include musicians), or those belonging to the working class, are not firmly bound by the hegemonic order, and thus can openly challenge hegemonic ideas and practices. Freire (1970) similarly argues that intellectuals need to develop a relational knowledge with the masses to help them become self-reflective and engage in critical thinking. When critical thinking and oppositional consciousness are created, Mansbridge and Morris (2001) state that it can help inspire social movement activism to change the current hegemonic social order.

Can independent hip-hop foster critical thinking among its fans about existing relations of domination and ultimately spread oppositional consciousness? Morgan and Bennett (2011) argue that hip-hop culture encourages and integrates innovative practices that aid in the development of oppositional consciousness regarding issues of race, class, gender and sexuality through artistic expression, knowledge production, social identification, and even political mobilization. In addition, hip-hop cultivates organic intellectuals (Gramsci 1971) who can act as intellectual leaders for the community in which they are embedded (Forman 2000; Morgan and Bennett 2011). Artists can act as organic intellectuals because they are produced by a similar economic, social, cultural, and educational environment and share similar life experiences with the masses. They can engage in critical thinking that challenges dominant culture and help spread oppositional consciousness, while not being controlled by or reproducing dominant ideologies. Finally, Clay (2006) argues that members of the hip-hop community have played an important role in supporting and reinforcing broader social movements such as the Civil Rights Movement and the Occupy Wall Street Movement.

Overall, previous research suggests that hip-hop both reproduces and challenges mainstream culture (Rose 1994), and thus engages in a complex process of negotiation between multiple social locations (Balaji 2010) and the fomentation of oppositional consciousness (Forman 2000; Morgan and Bennett 2011). Yet scholars have not systematically explored independent hip-hop culture, and thus, I add to the current literature and empirically determine if recent independent hip-hop culture reproduces or challenges dominant ideologies that uphold various relations of domination and subordination.

Previous Research on the History of Hip-Hop Culture

Chang (2005) writes that hip-hop's origins can be traced to a tiny seven-mile circle in the South Bronx. It stems from the vocal and musical expression of culture from African-American, Afro Caribbean, and Latino men in the 1970s. The formation of alternative local identities was represented through rapping, DJing, breakdancing, and graffiti. Rap, which is often used interchangeably with hip-hop music, is rooted in African oral traditions such as boasting, testifying, and signifying (Forman 2010; Oware 2016). Hip-hop's origins were a form of expression that reflected the economic and social hardships as the "throwaways of America's capitalism" (Au 2005; Forman 2000; Morgan and Bennett 2011; Pough 2004; Stapleton 1998). Alridge (2005) additionally argues that early hip-hoppers offered a form of social critique against racism that supported the goals of the Civil Rights Movement.

Since its inception, hip-hop has faced the concomitant struggle between maintaining its spontaneity and locality in New York with further commodification and cooptation (Pough 2004). As previously mentioned, on the one hand, the culture has been able to address numerous social issues ranging from the prison industrial complex to political movements involving the Black Panthers and the Young Lords. On the other hand, the rise of new technologies, ranging from cassettes, CD players and burners, the Internet, and social media, has allowed for a much easier flow of information and music production that spurs commodification (Dennis 2006; Harrison 2006). Commodification has helped hip-hop move from the margins to the mainstream music industry based on large conglomerates that homogenize music production, the distribution process, and the means of consumption (Rose 2008).

Hip-hop scholars (Watkins 2005) have attempted to understand its complex, multifaceted, politically conflicting, and consistently debated history. The challenge has been to create a dialogue and vocabulary to bridge the culture in the streets and academia. Presented below are the major areas of debate and contestation in the hip-hop literature.

Politics of Hip-Hop Culture

Perkins (1996) argues that before 1979, hip-hop remained a key component of the flourishing underground culture in the Bronx and upper Manhattan. Boasted by griots, ciphers, and dance battles hip-hop became a breeding ground for discussion and debate on salient social issues. But post-1979 its popularity garnered attention from the mainstream music industry. As George (2005) finds, independent black music has traditionally been an untapped space for growth by corporate labels. Myer and Kleck (2007) and Johnson (2008) add that historically popular music is driven by indie music. Indie labels were the key in finding what audiences wanted to hear by feeling the "pulse" of the public. Large corporations would then use sophisticated modes of production and distribution to take advantage of consumer tastes in order to make a profit. They ultimately mimic popular independent music until music sales declined, and then move on to the next proven commodity in the indie scene to maintain record sales.

The Fall of the Golden Era

In the case of hip-hop, the 1990s became an important decade marked by a distinct shift in the culture. Johnson (2008) believes that in the "Golden Era," from 1979 to the mid-1990s, there was lyrical mastery, innovation in beat production, diversity in style and content, and a subsequent meteoric rise of hip-hop music in the mainstream media (Johnson 2008). Myer and Kleck (2007) argue that the extraction from the underground into the mainstream reached a peak in the post-golden era in the late 1990s where the corporatization of the culture, or the full immersion of corporations in the creation of the music, decreased the diversity and cultural influences of the underground. As Rose (2008) points out, by 1998 81 million hip-hop records were sold but 70% of purchases were made by whites in mainstream culture.

Myer and Kleck (2007) find that since its corporatization there has been a decrease in one hit wonders. As corporations invested more and more money in artists and albums, they secured their investments by standardizing music to increase record sales and profits. The model allowed companies to buy out indie labels with little risk to boost record sales. For example, Bad Boy Records was bought out by Sony BMG once they obtained enough capital and parity to contend with larger corporations for record sales. In addition, major companies bought out radio stations and flooded the market with musicians they chose through the "pay for play" system. Ball (2009) finds that the average cost to get a song played on the radio is now up to $1000 per song per station. Thus, independent artists have historically had a difficult time getting "spins" on the radio, which pushed them toward signing with major labels to obtain financial support.

Rose (2008) points out that this corporatization had deleterious effects for the hip-hop community. For example, copyright ownership transfers ownership of rights from the artist to the studio to sell, promote, and benefit from those copyrighted materials. Thus, the power of ownership becomes more concentrated in the hands of the few, which is best represented by elite white men. As Myer and Kleck (2007) uncover, white males in the music industries' three major record labels are overrepresented in managerial and ownership positions. Within the industry, scholars have pointed to the infiltration and subsequent ownership of major hip-hop labels by whites dating back to the 1970s with white executives such as Malcolm McLaren, Rick Rubin, and Tom Silverman(Chang 2005; George 2005). This very small segment of society occupies multiple positions of power in the music industry. It becomes more salient given that three companies either own or distribute more than 85% of the music distributed globally (Rose 2008).

Resistance from the Underground

Since hip-hop's rise in 1979, there have been two dominant themes (Lena 2006, 2013; Lena and Peterson 2008; Tickner 2008). First, "conscious rap" was associated with the representation of experiences from a marginalized, subordinated, and discriminated population and was geared toward building a sense of activism among its constituents rather than reproducing stereotypical racial and economic tropes of mainstream society. In particular, these musicians emphasized the local environment and the hostility from corporate America. Second, "gangster rap" portrayed the same representations of the ghetto but upheld values of consumerism and patriarchy. They also blended "street" credibility with commercial success as a hustler "protagonist."

While these two themes are not mutually exclusive, gangster rap became mostly associated with mainstream hip-hop while conscious rap was predominantly produced in the underground (Oware 2014). Yet the mainstream can encompass both gangster rap and conscious rap, and underground and independent hip-hop can have themes of gangster rap. Harrison (2006) clarifies what is meant by underground, stating that while it encompasses a wide variation of topics, it is the hip-hop community closer to the end of the popularity spectrum where audiences consist largely of friends, family, and other associates. As underground artists gain more notoriety, their fan base extends further outside their circle and they gain access to new processes such as record label formations and documentation of album sales. Performers often face a crossroads in deciding to remain underground, signing with or creating an indie label, or signing with a large corporation.

During the post-golden era, the dominant model used by major corporations was gangster rap. Gangster rap emphasized the nihilistic, macho, and violent side of ghetto life. Ironically, its originating impulse was its disgust with the hypocrisies of mainstream culture. For example, Wells-Wilbon et al. (2010) analyze the life of Tupac Shakur to show his long-standing legacy in popular culture, which was filled with both radical critiques of mainstream culture and the reproduction of dominant cultural depictions of gangsters in urban neighborhoods. Hip-hop mirrors the values, violence, and hypocrisy of modern culture and represents some "ugly truths about everything society is and is not" (Taylor and Taylor 2007). Thus, Rose (2008) states that it is vitally important to address issues of cooptation within the mainstream.

Conversely, conscious rap has traditionally thrived in the underground and independent scene. In the post-golden era, underground and independent hip-hop act as a tool to both legitimize the authenticity of mainstream culture by pulling some of its artists and culture, but simultaneously counteracts it by distancing itself away from commercialization (Maher 2005; Rose 2008). Morgan and Bennett (2011) point out commercial hip-hop only represents a fraction of artistic production and performance. In this alternative underground space, there is more room to critically challenge the norms of traditional mainstream hip-hop and distinguish itself from mainstream culture. As Harrison (2006) states, the underground can be united in embracing progressive politics of subcultural inclusion and resisting cooptation by large corporations.

Moreover, Ball (2009) analyzes the importance of other material conditions salient to music creation and production. In order to understand the politics of the culture, scholars must analyze the politics by which underground and independent hip-hop navigates corporatization by major companies. For instance, resistance to major record sales comes from mixtapes that are released through means outside corporate distribution. This includes handing out music in person on the streets, airtime at clubs and independent radio stations, and the spread of music through online Web sites and social networks. Ball looks specifically at FreeMix Radio, which is a freely distributed monthly radio program spread through compact disk and acts as an alternative means of expression free from the filters of mainstream media. Harkness (2012) similarly explores the Chicago underground hip-hop scene by analyzing how it can remove itself from corporate infrastructure through self-production. Maher (2005) also analyzes the importance of self-production with indie rappers Dead Prez and finds that they can act as intellectuals freely speaking on their ghettocentric (i.e., their experiences in urban low-income neighborhoods) and Afrocentric (or experiences revolving around being African-American) experiences.

Scholars (Ogbar 2007; Adams and Fuller 2006) argue that hip-hop negotiates a complex cultural and political landscape in its search to create a sense of identity. It is not monolithic and unitary, but rather diverse and highly dependent upon historical context and the ways in which the hip-hop community experience and understand life. This is most salient in the relationship between the mainstream and the independent. For example, Karubian (2009) states that big labels sign fewer acts today and instead focus on signing established independent acts looking to break into the mainstream. Many artists may treat the independent and underground scene as a "waiting station or the minor leagues" until they achieve more popularity and sign lucrative contracts with major labels (Oware 2014). Conversely, some acts such as MF Doom (Hess 2012) began their careers signing with a larger label but have since dropped them to obtain successful careers as indie artists (Oware 2014). In essence, many musicians negotiate terms for mutually beneficial outcomes to generate profits (Ostrove 2014).

Similar to punk rock (Hesmondalgh 1999), independent hip-hop has seen periods of commodification and resistance (Lopes 1992). Suhr's (2011) findings highlight a recent period of commodification in the music industry as major and independent labels have converged despite their consistently changing relations of tension and compatibility. As a result, Oware (2014) contends that we cannot view these two subcultures with reinforced and restricted boundaries, but rather as a fluid continuum by which many musicians and fans continuously define and navigate. Thus scholars (Dyson 2010; Hess 2012 ; Hill 2009; Oware 2014) argue that it is necessary to study both mainstream and independent hip-hop culture and acknowledge the complex and contested site for both resistance and domination.

The Role of Race and Gender in Hip-Hop

While underground and independent hip-hop can be unified in their attempts to resist corporate domination in the post-golden era, Asante (2008) argues it still has the potential to reproduce racist ideology and unequal gender relations. Scholars (Harkness 2012) have thus focused on the resistance and complicity of the culture along various intersecting axes of domination such as race, class, and gender.

Racial Inequality and the Perpetuation of Racial Stereotypes
Hip-hop's origins offered a social critique of racism similar to Civil Rights activists. While largely being devoid of a sound intellectual activist foundation, the culture still engaged in resistance to racist policies in the USA and offered a hidden political discourse for African-Americans

to engage, negotiate, and interpret their identities (Alridge 2005; R. Sullivan 2003).

As hip-hop spread from the margins to the mainstream, African-American culture had to negotiate the struggle between remaining directly tied to the experiences of blacks in search of alternatives to white mainstream culture (McCall 1994) and appeasing the broader audience to sustain its growth and record sales (McLeod 2005). Perry (2004) states that hip-hop became a public discourse reflecting both the good and bad of American society through the lens of black America.

In the post-golden era large corporations have manipulated the images of hip-hop to appease a larger audience enthralled with violence and poverty. As R. Sullivan (2003) finds, African-Americans were more likely to state that hip-hop is a reflection of societal reality. But for outside consumers, this gritty portrayal of urban life was highlighted as a "black culture" immersed in crime, violence, drug use, and gang-related activity. Reyna et al. (2009) find that these negative images of blacks were primarily attributed to individual problems of the black community in the USA. Rebollo-Gil and Moras (2012) remind readers that the commodification of black sexuality is a major component in recreating a system of institutionalized racism in America.

As a response, hip-hop has faced critiques from white critics and politicians who blamed it for violence and gang activity in the USA (Rebollo-Gil and Moras 2012). For example, Vice President Dan Quayle attacked Tupac Shakur's lyrics, President G. H. W. Bush criticized Ice-T's image, and President Bill Clinton blamed Sister Souljah for promoting violence. Even notable African-American figures such as Deloris Tucker and Reverend Calvin Butts have criticized hip-hop. R. Sullivan (2003) points out that as hip-hop has become "wider and whiter," messages of antiracism have decreased in favor of messages of gang activity and drug use. Nonetheless the counter-knowledge, or knowledge that challenges dominant ideologies (Gosa 2011; Kelley 1994), produced by performers such as Immortal Technique and Mr. Life still remains and provides opportunities to challenge race relations despite cooptation by major corporations in twenty-first-century America (Williams 2008). Obama's recent administration has allowed performers, particularly millennials (Gosa 2010), to utilize mixtapes and Internet spaces to address issues of race and class in a post-Civil Rights America (Forman 2010).

What Is "Real" Hip-Hop?
As hip-hop continued to spread, it faced cultural appropriation by non-blacks and non-Latinos who engaged in the culture and attempted to gain entry into it. This raises the issue of authenticity in American hip-hop, as it is necessary for artists to establish credibility and identify boundaries among the broader community (Clark 2013; Hess 2005; McLeod 1999). Harkness (2012) shows that different facets of authenticity (such as being black, male, hard, and from the streets) are enforced and maintain boundaries of realness.

Conversely, women, whites, suburban blacks, and other minorities are often deemed as inauthentic and even "posing." Dimaggio (2010) articulates how other minorities, such as second-generation Arab Americans, Asian-Americans, Cuban Americans, and Indian Americans, have used hip-hop as a form of art to navigate their experiences as minority groups in the USA. Similarly, Fraley (2009) shows that white rappers negotiate and rearticulate whiteness to gain authenticity via alternative means. They must make the claim that artists and fans should not look at race but at rap skills and remaining "true to the game" (Hodgman 2013). Usually, entrance by whites such as Eminem and Esoteric requires reinforcing and exaggerating images of masculinity and working-class background to obtain acceptance among mainstream culture (Fraley 2009; Hodgman 2013; Oware 2014).

The entrance of whites has two primary complications. First, hip-hop culture becomes more complex as whites now produce and consume the culture while simultaneously reproducing values of sexism and material wealth (Tickner 2008). White artists entering into the culture strengthens the power of white ownership to dictate the social norms of the hip-hop community and broader society. Also, the entrance of white performers replaces racially coded messages with color-blind ones (Rodriquez 2006). White rappers' claim at participation and subsequent authenticity via "rap skills" engages in color-blind racism by denying the existing of power relations by whites.

Another Claim at Authenticity via Glocalization
Numerous artists (Harkness 2012) and scholars (Perry 2004) argue that hip-hop is a black form of culture and music. Concordantly, race is treated as a fixed category that acts as the ultimate arbiter of authenticity. This presents a problem for scholars who see the appropriation of hip-hop by other racial and ethnic groups in the US underground (Kubrin

2005); most notably Filipino youth in the Bay area who engage in DJing and dancing (Wang 2014). This viewpoint also presents a problem for a growing body of literature that focuses on the cultural appropriation, via diaspora, into new communities globally while simultaneously focusing on local issues (Bennett 1999a; Mitchell 2000).

Androutsopoulos and Scholz (2003) argue that while hip-hop has moved from the margins to the mainstream, it has become a site of cultural appropriation in which hip-hop music has been used in new social and linguistic environments. Numerous studies have demonstrated that this process has reached every corner of the globe. Dennis (2006) shows through ethnographic research of Choc Quib Town and Voodoo SoulJahs to show how Afro-Colombians have appropriated the culture to rework traditional concepts of race and ethnicity. In particular, he finds that they challenge the superiority of mestizos and bring questions of racism to the epicenter of society. Omoniyi (2006) looks at Nigerian hip-hop song lyrics to find a similar process in which Nigerian musicians utilize hip-hop culture with significant variants such as phonological variation, codeswitching (language changing), cross-referencing, nicknaming, colloquialisms, and reinterpretation. Further, Lin (2006) finds that independent Hong Kong hip-hop performers challenge the capitalist practices of the pop culture music industry and produce music within niche spaces for both cultural survival and innovative cultural production. Other works focus on the importance of the culture in Australia (Maxwell 1994; Morgan and Warren 2011; Warren and Evitt 2010), Europe (Delamont and Stephens 2008; Hesmondhalgh and Melville 2002; Mitchell 2000), and Tanzania (Clark 2013).

Global hip-hop is best explained through the process of glocalization, or the simultaneous interaction between global and local dynamics that takes a double-helix form (Smith 1997; Tickner 2008). This is important because local groups can appropriate the culture to address a wide range of issues ranging from the individual, local, and global (Baker 2005; Bennett 1999a). In essence, global hip-hop is translocal because it represents complex cultural dialogues between local innovations in diverse forms, transcultural interactions outside the USA, and interactions between the USA and local spaces (Morgan and Bennett 2011).

Forman and Neal (2004) point out the persistent theme of authenticity in hip-hop culture. Within the USA, this is complicated as traditionally those who are "real" encompass men of color, while those considered to be "fake" are associated with whites, females, and the upper class. Yet with cultural appropriation Harkness (2012) shows that a situated authenticity, wherein outsiders emphasize certain categories and deemphasize those that are fixed, better elucidates how malleable the term authenticity is. As such, the concept of authenticity is socially constructed and consistently contested (McLeod 1999). For example, in the USA a poor white male may be more "authentic" than a Japanese middle-class male, but still less authentic than any black male artist. Outside the USA, the idea of cultural appropriation again brings into question the notion of authenticity (Hesmondhalgh and Melville 2002; Mitchell 1996). As Pennycook (2007) and Tickner (2008) point out, the relocation of hip-hop to other contexts contradicts the traditional notion of "keeping it real" in the USA. Nonetheless, while the process of glocalization has allowed for the destabilization of the term authenticity in regard to race, women of color are still often left in a marginalized and precarious situation (Dennis 2006).

Is It an All-Male World?
Authenticity is traditionally embodied by black male rappers who engage in hyper-masculinity to establish their dominance over women. The literature analyzing authenticity in hip-hop must address social positions of race, class, gender and the intersections between them (Jeffries 2011). As Iwamoto (2003) shows, Tupac Shakur challenged the current class and racial structure but still embodied the hyper-masculinity of African-Americans in American culture. Iwamoto (2003) cites Tupac's use of the "cool pose," his affirmation of "thug life," and his persona as a "ladies man" to explicate how hip-hop mirrors the larger social structure of patriarchy and sexism. Ironically, due to the complex nature of intersectional theory, Iwamoto also finds that Tupac simultaneously reproduces the objectification of women and creates messages valuing women in society as equals. Alim et al. (2010) ultimately argue that the constructions of blackness and masculinity help performers create and negotiate their identities, but simultaneously may support dominant racial and gender hierarchies within broader society.

While notions of hegemonic masculinity in hip-hop both hurt men who do not fulfill expectations of masculinity and help men maintain a patriarchal structure, women remain in a subordinated and marginalized position wherein their voices are actively silenced (Rebollo-Gil and Moras 2012). Using content analysis, Weitzer and Kubrin (2009) determine that hip-hop reproduces "essential" genders and concordant conduct norms of the broader society. They find five gender-related themes: (1) naming/shaming, or songs aimed at degrading women, (2) sexual objectification, or the notion that women are only good for sex, (3) distrust of women, or the suspicion of women who are prone to betray men, (4) legitimating violence, or violent punishment toward women, and (5) prostitution and pimping, or women as subordinates to men who are pimps. Similarly, Tanner-Smith et al. (2006) analyze the content of *Radio and Records* magazine to determine that women in hip-hop are portrayed as vulnerable, domestic, and subordinate sex objects. Within hip-hop videos from 2007 to 2008, Hunter (2011) finds that performers merge ideals of a successful rap mogul with strip club culture to create a gendered relationship based on sexual transaction.

More specifically, hip-hop serves to support the ideological and social systems that have placed African-American women at the bottom of the social ladder. Compared to white women who are portrayed as sexually empowered and liberated, black women are portrayed as embodying a primitive sexuality (Balaji 2010). African-American rappers also often fit one of the following stereotypes: the queen mother who is the intellectual matriarch, the sistah with attitude who is aggressive and defiant, the fly girl who is hypersexual and independent, or the lesbian. Adams and Fuller (2006) add that African-American women are objectified through stereotypes such as the "Sapphire," an overweight and dark-skinned asexual, or a "Jezebel," a loose sexually aggressive woman. In hip-hop's language, the Jezebel is referred to as the "ho" or the "bitch." These preconceived categories reduce women to objects and expendable beings (Adams and Fuller 2006; Harkness 2012) .

The dialectical nature of hip-hop has had contradicting effects for women in the culture (Adams and Fuller 2006. On one hand, the culture exploits black women's sexuality, denigrates black womanhood, and endangers the lives of young black girls (Pough 2004). On the other hand, it has opened a space for women to determine for themselves the image they want to portray (Balaji 2010; Collins 2005; Emerson 2002), and even use that space to create economic opportunities in the marketplace that challenge hegemony by industry elites and take back their sexuality (Miller-Young 2008; Stapleton 1998; Tanner-Smith et al. 2006). Most notably, an analysis of Brooklyn based female rapper Jean Grae elucidates the ways in which her music interrupts notions of black heteronormative sexuality (Smalls 2011). Gupta-Carlson (2010) similarly highlights how female hip-hop dancers in Seattle use their cultural space to create political messages and generate audience responses to call attention to the gendering of hip-hop's spaces.

Further, hip-hop has profound influences regarding religion (Morgan and Bennett 2011) and sexuality (Ogbar 2007). For example, women in the global Muslim hip-hop movement challenge broader stereotypes of Muslim culture and universal misogyny. Also, the LGBTQ movement, which started among early hip-hoppers who supported gay and lesbian movements, has formed a growing following in underground and independent movements aimed at raising awareness and promoting equality for LGBTQ groups in the USA.

Oppositional Consciousness

Kanye West's lyrics demonstrate hip-hop's ability to simultaneously point out his addiction to money and his resistance to racism. Maher (2007) argues that West's lyrics teeter between uncritical (reflecting the status quo) and critical (challenging the status quo) consciousness, which can be both a source of oppression and liberation. These contradictions are found throughout the culture's history as it engages in both resistance and complicity with relations of domination (Mitchell 1996). Ultimately, hip-hop can create an invaluable tool for creating definitions and conceptualizing terms such as race, class, and gender, as well as transcend these boundaries to create social consciousness, resistance, and even potentially inspire social activism (Ogbar 2007; Martinez 1997).

The Message in the Music and the Formation of Oppositional Consciousness

The dialectical nature of hip-hop allows for artists and listeners to create and interpret meaning from music. These interpretations and meanings can simultaneously promote dominant ideologies and resist them. It is thus important for scholars to elaborate on the importance of performers' messages, the interpretations of the listeners, and the messages and meanings of the music itself.

Artists are in a unique position to have visibility in the hip-hop community through various outlets such as ciphers (or freestyles among groups of rappers), live performances, recorded music, and social media (Newman 2005). They are essentially celebrities of varying degrees whose voices can be heard by the public and concordantly be scrutinized or praised for their messages (Ferris 2007). Because of this visibility, rappers such as Eminem and MF Doom (Hess 2005) are able to create hidden transcripts, or encrypted messages understood by the hip-hop community, that can act as a form of resistance, or what Stapleton (1998) terms "play-as-resistance." These messages exemplify the multiplicity of language which can both be used both as a tool of resistance and as a means of creating and recreating meaning (Potter 1995).

Hip-hop culture also acts as an important tool for listeners to express and reflect on their lived experience (Sanchez 2010; Tickner 2008). In particular, this is salient for the poor and marginalized youth to express their dissatisfaction with mainstream culture and society. Alim (2007) argues that hip-hop takes on its own language and form of communication that is distinctly different from the current hegemonic sociolinguistic order, or the dominant modes of reading, writing, and speaking. It often takes the form of "real talk" or "straight talk," and can be used by listeners to navigate the social world and act as a means of resisting and combating mainstream ideology and culture.

Finally, hip-hop acts as a means of expression both for individual artists and listeners and collective groups with similar critical observations of society (Au 2005; Jenkins 2011). Once created, it can serve as the impetus for oppositional consciousness (Mansbridge and Morris 2001), which is fueled by discontent among groups who suffer from subordination and also have a shared interest in ending or diminishing their subordination. It can be enabled by an oppositional culture, such as hip-hop, that provides ideas, rituals, and long-standing patterns of interaction that can be refined and developed to maintain and spur oppositional consciousness. Furthermore, it can be led by organic intellectuals (Gramsci 1971) from the community who are directly affected by similar grievances and develop a vested interest in changing the current social order. Within the culture's potential is the power to redefine history, create a sense of community, and form an oppositional consciousness (Decker 1993).

What Can the Message Do for You?
Hip-hop's potential for oppositional consciousness needs to be fostered through critical thinking. Scholars (Akom 2009; Dimitriadis 2009; Hill 2009) thus engage in analyses that understand how the hip-hop community promotes a mental state that encourages critical thinking, identity formation based on their social location, and resistance to domination (Freire 1970).

KRS-ONE advocates for a Critical Hip-Hop (Akom 2009) that calls out practices which create conforming listeners who do not question social reality. Instead, he argues that it must provide a foundation for critical learning about issues such as racism, police brutality, incarceration, and poverty. As a medium of expression, it can provide a means of "knowledge building" that is applicable to a specific population that has been marginalized. It can occur in a wide variety of levels ranging from primary texts such as lyric writing with a "pen and paper," secondary texts such as the music on the radio or television, and tertiary texts such as ciphers or spoken word poetry groups (Akom 2009; Au 2005; Gosa 2011; Low 2010).

At the core of critical thinking is the formation of identities based on a shared recognition of an oppressed social position. Leard and Lashua (2006) demonstrate through ethnographic research of listeners the ability of hip-hop to express ideas from a disenfranchised social location through a culture and knowledge outside mainstream society, which has two profound consequences. First, it allows for a collective process in which lyrics provide an alternative outlet for the hip-hop community to effectively express their grievances. Second, urban youth of color use these texts to construct locally validated selves and create a sense of community linked to what it means to be marginalized in the USA and around the world. It is in essence an alternative "lived" curriculum to teach important lessons about how to survive in the world and understand how it works (Dimitriadis 2009; Söderman and Folkestad 2004).

Hill (2009) argues that an effective medium for engaging in alternative methods of critical thinking among working-class students of color at the margins of the educational system occurs when hip-hop is incorporated into the classroom. This is particularly salient for students who: (1) believe that the school system does not understand or accommodate their social position, and (2) believe that the school system has failed them. Hip-hop artists and listeners interpret music and integrate its messages into their everyday lives. Connecting hip-hop to education helps them better navigate the learning process by mediating it with their personal experiences, creating an opportunity to build common bonds and a shared community, and developing an alternative curriculum that better accommodates their needs (Petchauer 2010; Stovall 2006).

Hip-Hop Activism
Hip-hop's artists and community members have had a long history of political activism in social movements ranging from the Civil Rights Movement in the 1960s to the South African apartheid resistance

movement in the 1980s (Alridge 2005; Chang 2005). Yet hip-hop itself has also faced less success in their own battles for class and racial equality despite sharing similar desires for social change and ending a long legacy of oppression and domination. This may be attributed to the nature of the culture in which artists and listeners are not trained or inclined to be social activists, but rather are subject to market demands, corporate executives, and acceptance from the public (Maher 2005; George 2005). Nonetheless, Kitwana (2002) argues that hip-hop can spark debate and challenge mainstream thought and cannot be disengaged from political action.

Watkins (2005) writes that hip-hop activism, or addressing social issues both in the hip-hop community and broader social life, draws upon the social experiences and harnesses the energy of disenfranchised populations. Hip-hop activism can range from actions focused on the micro-level, such as posting videos and lyrics on Internet Web sites, to broader macro-level activism such as protests, sit-ins, and rallies. Within hip-hop activism, there are two dialectical processes. First, it can exhibit both push and pull factors upon society (Trapp 2005). It can push political systems and mainstream culture into addressing issues of a subgroup that they previously had been unable to accommodate such as African-American youth. It can also pull actors together from the hip-hop community and foment action for social change. For example, rappers rejected the conservative nature of the government wherein Ronald Reagan blamed the poor for their deteriorating values and laziness and instead adopted a critical stance toward the government. Second, the hip-hop community can act as both the mirror and engine of a social movement. Contrasting the works of two prominent musicians, Trapp (2005) shows, through analyses of Queen Latifa's and Tupac Shakur's portrayals of women, that they can reflect reality, while simultaneously influencing social movement participants and leaders in the Civil Rights Movement and the Black and Third Wave Feminist Movement.

Activism in hip-hop is most poignantly seen in the creation of oppositional culture from African-Americans, as well as American Indians and Mexican Americans, who use their own cultural resources to resist oppression under internal colonialism (Mansbridge and Morris 2001). Martinez (1997) shows through content analysis of hip-hop music lyrics how political and gangster rappers in the late 1980s and early 1990s provided key themes of anger and resistance toward a racist and discriminatory society. This resistance culminated in the heralded 1992

Los Angeles riots that expressed messages of resistance, empowerment, and social critique against a racist police department and legal system. Nielson (2012) claims that while this creates messages of resistance, it also creates further responses of enhanced pervasive surveillance and pressure by police institutions. Clay (2006) similarly finds activism through ethnographic fieldwork within the San Francisco Bay Area's youth of color in their attempts to create youth empowerment and political activism through breakdancing. Globally, Forman (2010) highlights community organizing and civic engagement spreading from USA to cities such as London, Paris, Frankfurt, and Rio de Janeiro. Dedman (2011) also finds social activism among independent UK hip-hop's grime scene through ethnographic fieldwork, which appropriates hip-hop into a subculture of resistance and social activism against mainstream's commodification of culture.

The Future of Hip-Hop?

Hip-hop's engagement with mainstream media has led to the fall of a golden era to commodification by major corporations. Hip-hop has also been accused of reproducing racial and gender inequality. As McWhorter states, it ultimately holds blacks back and in the end it "creates nothing" (McWhorter 2003). Thus the notion of hip-hop being important in creating social change is still highly contested and is subject to debate. But alternative literature has also explicated how hip-hop can be used to criticize race and gender relations. Other subordinate social groups have also appropriated the culture, such as LGBTQ groups and minority groups outside the USA. Scholars have thus highlighted the ability of hip-hop music to express and foster critical thinking and form an oppositional consciousness, which has the potential to result in social activism and social change (Akom 2009; Dimitriadis 2009; Hill 2009).

DATA AND METHODOLOGY

The methodology for my research includes a content analysis of independent hip-hop lyrics and semi-structured interviews with self-identified independent hip-hop listeners and community members. Hill (2009) advocates for a three-pronged approach to understanding hip-hop culture: (1) political culture, (2) textual analysis, and (3) audience reception. Similarly, Griswold (1987) argues that an analysis of a cultural object addresses artists' creative intentions, the circumstances of time and location underlying its production, the comprehension of the lyrics by both artists and listeners, and an explanation of the interpretation of the lyrics via social groups and communities. Following these approaches, my research considers the sociopolitical context when analyzing the lyrics of performers and how the audience interprets their lyrics. My method is appropriate given a research question that addresses the meanings embedded within artists' lyrics and the meanings received by listeners, as well as the fomentation of independent hip-hop as a potentially oppositional culture.

Content Analysis of Independent Hip-Hop Lyrics

To examine key themes in independent hip-hop lyrics, I identified a sample of twenty-five albums (412 tracks) that meet the criteria for independent hip-hop albums produced between 2000 and 2013. Each album was produced by US artists and released by a record company not affiliated with the three major record labels. While these albums only analyze a specific point in time, the artists chosen for this study have released albums predominantly on independent record labels and have stated their desire to remain independent from 2000 to 2013. Presented in Table 1.1 are the twenty-five albums chosen for this study.

Independent hip-hop labels are not affiliated with the three major record labels, which are Universal Music Group, Sony Music Entertainment, and Warner Music Group. Yet they require a trademarked name and must be legally filed for business status. The record company must also have obtained a retail merchant's license to legally distribute sellable goods to the public. Once the album meets these criteria, it is ensured that these labels possess no direct financial connection to the "Big Three" record labels at the time of the album's release.

Hip-hop's inception began in the 1970s and shifted into more corporatized models in the mid to late 1990s. Concordant with Kubrin (2005: 367), "the year 2000 represents a turning point in the music industry whereby production values more clearly addressed commercial competition," and thus the salience of an alternative form of creative expression in the production and reproduction of music waned. Thus, my analysis focuses specifically on albums from 2000 to 2013, which has not been systematically studied.

Table 1.1 List of independent hip-hop albums

1. Aesop Rock-Labor Days (2001, Definitive Jux): 14 tracks
2. Atmosphere-God Loves Ugly (2002, Rhymesayers/Fat Beats): 18 tracks
3. Binary Star-Masters of the Universe (2000, Subterraneous Records): 24 tracks
4. Blackalicious-Blazing Arrow (2002, MCA Records): 17 tracks
5. Blu and Exile-Below the Heavens (2007, Sound in Color): 15 tracks
6. Blue Scholars-The Long March (2005, Massline): 9 tracks
7. Brother Ali-Us (2009, Rhymesayers Group): 16 tracks
8. Cakes the Killa-The Eulogy (2013, Mishka Records): 12 tracks
9. Cunninlynguists-A Piece of Strange (2006, QN5/L.A. Underground): 16 tracks
10. Hieroglyphics-Full Circle (2003, Hieroglyphics Imperium Recordings): 16 tracks
11. Immortal Technique-Revolutionary Vol. 2 (2003, Viper Records): 18 tracks
12. Jean Grae-The Evil Jeanius (2008, Babygrande Records): 10 tracks
13. Jedi Mind Tricks-Violent by Design (2000, Superegular Records): 25 tracks
14. KRS-ONE-Hip-Hop Lives (2007, Koch Records): 18 tracks
15. Macklemore and Ryan Lewis-The Heist (2012, Macklemore LLC-ADA): 15 tracks
16. MadVillain-Madvillainy (2004, Stones Throw): 22 tracks
17. MF Doom-Born Like This (2009, Lex): 17 tracks
18. MURS-3:16 The 9th Edition (2004, Definitive Jux): 10 tracks
19. Mykki Blanco-Bettie Rubble: The Initiation (2013, UNO Records): 8 tracks
20. People Under the Stairs- OST (2002, Om Records): 20 tracks
21. Rapsody-The Idea of Beautiful (2012, Jamla): 16 tracks
22. Sage Francis-Li(f)e (2010, ANTI-/Epitaph): 12 tracks
23. Swollen Members-Monsters in the Closet (2002, Battle Axe): 20 tracks
24. Tech N9ne-Killer (2008, Strange Music): 32 tracks
25. Yonas-The Proven Theory (2011, City of Dreams): 12 tracks

Utilizing this approach to selecting independent albums allows this study to address a glaring gap in the literature. Other studies use comprehensive studies of hip-hop lyrics (Kubrin 2005; Lena 2006; Martinez 1997; Weitzer and Kubrin 2009) but solely focus on mainstream albums that are documented, or tracked by sales, by the Recording Industry Association of America or Billboard. Conversely, determining a sample of independent hip-hop albums considered to be influential in the hip-hop community requires a more nuanced method of identifying albums that meet these criteria since many albums obtain popularity via alternative means such as social media, bootlegging, illegal downloading, and file sharing.

The twenty-five independent hip-hop albums were determined by the number of appearances on Web sites that reflect hip-hop music and their total record sales. First, online Web sites that I am familiar with, that have been recommended to me by independent listeners, and that were identified using a Google search were used to identify albums that are considered foundational, well known, and successful among independent hip-hop Web sites. The Web sites identified through a Google search were subject to an inspection to ensure their validity. The Web sites chosen include: www.worldstar.com, www.hiphopdx.com, www.hotnewhiphop.com, www.allhiphop.com, and www.undergroundhiphop.com. Second, a Google search was conducted to find various online lists using phrases such as: "the greatest independent hip-hop albums of all time," "influential independent hip-hop albums of all time," and "classic independent hip-hop albums of all time." These lists were used only if the Web site could be verified as a reliable source representing the hip-hop community via daily hits/visits and message boards. The message boards were analyzed to determine if the lists created were well received by public users and additional contributions to the list were used to finalize my sample. Third, newer albums were included in the sample to gain heterogeneity in representation for younger artists, women, LGBTQ members, and other racial minorities. Google searches included: "best new independent hip-hop artists," "best female independent hip-hop artists," "greatest female independent hip-hop artists," "LGBTQ independent hip-hop artists," "queer independent hip-hop artists," and "Latino and Asian independent hip-hop artists." Finally, all albums were re-inspected to ensure that albums chosen: (1) were from hip-hop artists who have remained independent between 2000 to 2013, (2) have documented record sales to determine their popularity and financial success, and (3) appeared most frequently on various lists through the methods mentioned above.

The unit of analysis is bars, which is loosely defined as a line in a rap verse. While Shusterman (1992) argues that it is also important to study beats in addition to lyrics, my research will focus on the content of the lyrics. Therefore, each song was recorded by various lyric Web sites. The primary site chosen for transcribing lyrics is www.genius.com for its popularity among the hip-hop community. I listened to each song, while simultaneously reading the lyrics to ensure accuracy. In instances where the Web site may be inaccurate, the author referred to the alternative sites to verify the correct lyrics. The lyrics were then placed in NVivo, a qualitative program to help store and code the data.

Unlike Oware's (2014) work that analyzes five predetermined categories in the lyrics of underground acts, I use a modified grounded theory approach to identify recurrent themes (Charmaz 1983; Lio et al. 2008; Strauss and Corbin 1994). Grounded theory approaches traditionally identify themes from an analysis of the data without reference to categories derived from theory. Like thematic analysis, I used deductive, focused coding techniques (Charmaz and Belgrave 2012) to record bars that are aligned with the theories discussed above in an iterative method of constant comparative analysis. I also paid attention to other possible emergent and recurrent themes that may go beyond the thematic categories derived from my theoretical perspective. Next, the data was re-examined to determine the key themes and subthemes and to identify the relations both within and between them. Bars were re-coded as necessary to address potential issues of double entendres, or meanings only understood within a broader social context. Finally, my analysis was guided by my ethnographic notes from personal experiences at hip-hop shows, music festivals, and other interactions relating to the culture. I was also informed by my examination of various media sources such as YouTube videos, online interviews, and artist/label Web sites. Ultimately, a modified grounded theory approach aims at developing substantial theories of independent hip-hop culture derived from a holistic understanding and interpretation of the data.

Presented in Fig. 1.1 are the major themes uncovered from the twenty-five indie albums chosen for the study.

Themes of independent hip-hop music appeared in 297 bars, which were reanalyzed to determine two major categories: culture and economics. Bars were again reanalyzed to compose subcategories. Three subcategories regarding culture were uncovered: (1) a resistance to major corporations, (2) an emphasis on independence, and (3) the creation of an alternative culture. Three subcategories related to economics were found: (1) economic exploitation, (2) specific forms of economic exploitation such as 360-degree contracts and advances, and (3) economic resistance. The categories were additionally studied in conjunction with the other overlapping themes such as capitalism and economy to provide the basis for Chapters 2 and 3.

Interviews with Independent Hip-Hop Listeners

To examine the ways in which independent hip-hop community members and listeners interpret and use hip-hop lyrics, I interviewed forty-six self-identified independent hip-hop listeners and fans within

Independent Hip-Hop Album Themes																											
Theme:	Album #	1	2	3	4	5	6	7	8	9	10	11	12	13	14	15	16	17	18	19	20	21	22	23	24	25	Total
Capitalism and Economy		33	17	2	11	6	16	1	0	4	1	12	2	6	1	3	2	1	7	0	0	3	4	0	0	2	134
Critical Thinking/Conscious		16	9	8	11	2	9	2	0	6	6	13	7	5	9	3	2	0	6	2	6	4	3	5	0	14	148
Drugs		0	0	0	2	4	1	4	0	2	0	2	1	1	0	1	1	0	3	0	0	0	0	0	0	0	21
Education/Knowledge		2	0	0	2	3	13	3	0	1	0	0	3	1	0	2	0	0	2	0	0	1	2	0	0	2	37
Gender and Sexuality		1	16	3	5	13	3	9	14	2	4	7	8	8	1	7	6	4	8	12	3	12	2	3	15	3	169
Government and Politics		7	1	0	3	0	3	0	0	3	1	19	2	8	1	0	1	1	2	0	0	0	5	0	1	2	60
Independent Hip-Hop		33	27	43	12	23	4	9	1	2	16	26	9	0	9	15	5	5	10	2	9	13	1	9	9	5	297
Mass Media		0	0	1	0	1	0	0	0	4	0	8	2	0	0	0	0	0	2	0	0	2	2	0	0	1	24
Military		0	0	2	2	0	0	0	0	0	0	1	0	0	0	0	0	1	0	0	0	1	1	0	0	0	11
Police		1	3	0	1	0	3	0	0	2	0	1	5	2	6	0	0	4	4	0	0	0	2	2	0	2	38
Poverty and Struggle		0	0	2	2	12	6	9	0	9	1	3	4	0	0	2	2	0	4	0	3	12	6	1	3	6	85
Prison		1	1	7	0	0	0	1	0	3	0	4	5	1	1	0	0	1	3	0	0	0	1	0	1	1	33
Race and Ethnicity		1	2	2	6	5	8	14	1	7	0	15	3	2	2	5	1	9	4	12	0	4	0	0	3	1	95
Religion/Spirituality		5	3	3	7	7	0	1	2	2	1	0	9	4	4	1	0	1	2	3	0	2	7	0	6	3	70
Social Change		18	7	0	8	8	13	3	0	2	4	11	4	0	7	2	2	0	3	0	4	4	1	1	0	3	101
Total		117	85	73	73	85	79	57	18	48	33	131	57	37	39	43	22	27	61	16	21	58	37	21	38	47	1323

Fig. 1.1 Independent hip-hop album themes

Southern California. The participants were identified through a snowball sample. I recruited from my own personal networks in San Diego, as well as at UC Riverside and San Bernardino Valley Community College to find students who meet the criteria. Open advertisements at college campuses were also given to reach local community members who are familiar with independent hip-hop. Respondents took an initial survey to determine if they qualify for this study given two parameters (see Appendix A): they were insiders who participated in and listened to hip-hop music and also appeared to incorporate hip-hop culture into their lifestyle (Rodriquez 2006). They were first asked to identify their familiarity with independent hip-hop, the artists they listen to, and their activity within the independent hip-hop community. To qualify as informants who are fans of indie hip-hop, respondents must have adequately demonstrated their interest and familiarity with at least ten of the twenty-five independent hip-hop albums identified in the content analysis. They also showed active participation within the hip-hop community through participation in at least five hip-hop related events, which can range from attending concerts, talks by hip-hop artists, or parties where hip-hop music is played within the past three years.

Like previous studies (Jeffries 2011; Rodriquez 2006), I stratified my interview sample in order to make comparisons across various social locations. As described in Appendix B, I have a diverse sample with regard to race/ethnicity, gender, social class, educational attainment, sexual orientation, political orientation, and age. First, I interviewed participants primarily from the following racial/ethnic groups to reflect Southern California's demographics in the hip-hop community: African-American (18%), Asian-American (28%), and Latino (46%). I also conducted interviews with a handful of whites (4%) and biracial individuals who were White/Asian and Black/Asian (4%). Previous reports (Burgess 2012) have argued that whites make up nearly 80% of hip-hop listeners, but further analysis of the statistic uncovers sampling bias as many albums are not purchased legally, not documented via SoundScan, or do not fall along "mainstream" hip-hop categorizations. Thus, my study interviewed hip-hop listeners from various racial and ethnic backgrounds. Second, I interviewed about equal numbers of men (25) and women (20) within each racial group, with one respondent identifying as gender fluid (1).

Third, I stratified my sample by class using three different indicators: (a) employment status, (b) income, and (c) self-defined social class. A majority of respondents reported working full time (52%), while some claimed part-time status (35%) or being unemployed (13%). Of those interviewees who stated they were employed an overwhelming majority reported earning less than $50,000 a year (93%), with only a few respondents earning $90,000 or more annually (7%). Concordantly, a majority of my sample consisted of self-identified working-class individuals (74%), with some identifying as middle class (15%) and upper class (11%). Fourth, participants showed to have various educational attainment rates with (11%) completing high school, (6%) obtaining an Associate's Degrees, (37%) currently at a four-year university, (35%) earning Bachelor's Degree, and (11%) receiving a Master's Degree. Fourth, my sample aimed to be representative of the US population with regard to sexual identity: (87%) heterosexual respondents, (9%) bisexual respondents, and (4%) homosexual respondents. Fifth, my sample was skewed in regard to political orientation. Many respondents (48%) reported not having strong political orientations/affiliations, but suggested that they took various positions based on the issue. Conversely, (43%) of interviewees identified as liberal or radical and (9%) identified as conservative.

Finally, I interviewed hip-hop listeners between the ages of 18–35. Klatch (1999: 72) argues that between the ages of 18–25 (30 respondents) is an important time in the formation of one's political ideology. She claims that high school students are exposed to teachers, books, and school activities that may precipitate critical thinking in the future. I have extended the age limit to 35 to include listeners who were within the age of 18–25 in 2000 (16 respondents) to account for the previous generation of hip-hop listeners. Ultimately, my study explores how people's exposure to independent hip-hop may relate to their social consciousness and political activity.

Despite its small sample size, my research method was appropriate because of its heterogeneous population representative of the diversity among independent hip-hop listeners. An additional strength of my sample was obtaining two San Diego hip-hop artists, one of which created his own label and the other is independent/unsigned. My limitations are twofold: (1) my sample is geographically limited to Southern California residents, and (2) limited to the hip-hop generation associated with baby boomers and millennials born in the 1980s–1990s.

The interviews were conducted in one of two ways. A public space at the respondent's convenience was chosen. They were approximately one to two hours in duration and were recorded using an audio device upon verbal agreement. The interview utilized an open-response format, but engaged in questions directly related to the experiences of the listeners with independent hip-hop music, the meanings they obtain from the music, and the concordant actions they engage in or participate in due to the music they listen to. The questions asked were directly related to the salient issues that appeared in the content analysis of the twenty-five independent hip-hop albums. If respondents were not able to meet in person a Skype interview was conducted either via video chat or direct messaging. The same open-response format was used during the one to two hour interview. Attached in Appendix C is my interview guide. Once completed, the data was coded in NVivo based on the respondents' responses to determine the primary themes presented in the interviews, using the modified grounded theory approach described above. Results presented in Chapter 4 are based on common themes among respondents within the major subtopics on the interview guide in Appendix C: (1) definitions of independent hip-hop, (2) the messages within independent hip-hop music, (3) the politics of independent hip-hop, (4) issues of race, class, and gender, and (5) social change.

Overall, I am well fit for this project as I have been embedded in the culture and have direct ties with the local scene. My content analysis and participant interviews are informed from my long-time experiences as an avid listener and active participant in hip-hop, allowing me to develop a thick, rich, and holistic understanding of the hip-hop community. My position as an "insider" (a fan) enables me to better understand the complexities of the culture. Merton (1972; Simmel and Wolff 1950) states that insiders are in a position to understand the experiences of groups of which they are members, and can be used to gather a richer set of data (Dwyer and Buckle 2009; Kerstetter 2012). Similarly, DeVault (1999) writes that insider status allows for enhanced access and rapport, but more importantly allows for the possibility of active attention and analysis of social locations.

Previous research has used insider status to obtain ethnographic data, ranging from San Francisco's underground hip-hop scene (Dimitriadis 2009) to evening education programs utilizing hip-hop pedagogy in Philadelphia (Hill 2009), that would otherwise be inaccessible to mainstream researchers. As Low (2010) states, hip-hop insiders hold a precarious position of trust within the community, which allows for access to information and resources unattainable by outsiders whom they may perceive as inauthentic, ingenuous and ultimately incapable of understanding their social position. My insider status is thus highlighted by my ability to access online materials, new music, concerts, and events, as well as access to initial contacts within the hip-hop community who know and trust me. Finally, the hip-hop community may face scrutiny from outsiders for their beliefs, ideas, and actions. While I consider myself to be an insider as a fan and as man of color from a working-class background, I simultaneously face the problem of being an outsider for some fans as an academic and because of my particular race, gender, and sexual orientation (a Filipino-American heterosexual male). In my research I am attuned to my outsider status and aware of reflexivity regarding race, class, gender, and sexuality.

Overview of Major Findings

My findings document the claims of independent hip-hop culture from 2000 to 2013 and highlight the vexed and contradictory nature of the politics of independent hip-hop. Chapter 2 aims to uncover how independent hip-hop in the post-golden era challenges or reproduces cultural ideologies within US mainstream hip-hop culture and US culture more generally. Based on my content analysis of artists' lyrics, I identify three recurrent themes among albums by twenty-five independent hip-hop artists. First, these acts resist the majors in three ways: (1) mainstream artists, (2) large radio stations, and (3) major record labels. Second, they reject the corporatization and commodification by major record labels and mainstream culture in favor of independently owned companies. Third, they advocate for an independent culture based on alternative cultural ideals, and thus socially construct and advocate for a brand of authenticity rooted in hip-hop's origins.

Chapter 3 focuses on how independent hip-hop artists in the post-golden era resist economic exploitation from mainstream culture and major corporations in various ways. Indie musicians make the grievance that major labels benefit at the expense of performers and hence are highly exploitative. Their unfair treatment is predominantly reflected in the contracts acts sign with major labels. This has repercussions for artists in numerous facets of the music industry: (1) advances/forwards, (2) control of copyrights, (3) artistic direction and relations with A&R,

(4) touring, merchandising, and advertising deals, and (5) radio stations, media, and press. Finally, some hip-hop artists make the claim that creating and maintaining independent record labels helps mitigate economic exploitation, controls record label oversight, and serves for the betterment of the hip-hop community.

Chapter 4 utilizes forty-six interviews with self-identified independent hip-hop listeners to navigate the changing meanings of independent hip-hop in the post-golden era. The chapter elaborates on listener's definitions of independent and mainstream hip-hop. It also analyzes their interpretations of race, class, gender, sexual orientation, and the fomentation of oppositional consciousness. Listeners suggest that independent hip-hop often focuses on race and class but often ignores issues of gender and sexuality. Among my informants, I find that female and queer listeners are more conscious of this omission than male and straight listeners, despite a current push toward female and LGBTQ representation in hip-hop's mainstream. Also, interviews indicate that there remains a blurry line between independents and majors that many artists navigate as they attempt to retain economic and creative freedom while still attempting to become financially successful. Technological shifts and advances have further exacerbated these blurry lines. For instance, my findings reveal that artists remain intensely intertwined with major companies in old and new ways to utilize their marketing and distribution channels. In essence, the culture is not viewed as binary oppositions but rather as fluid and constantly changing in the ways that they are complexly intertwined.

Chapter 5 recapitulates the key findings. I also connect my research to broader societal implications and show how my work is salient to the current body of literature. Currently, it fills two large gaps in the literature. Most works tend to focus on mainstream hip-hop (Kelley 1994; Perry 2004; Rose 1994), disparate underground groups (Ball 2009; Harrison 2006; Wang 2014), or global hip-hop (Androutsopoulos and Scholz 2003; Bennett 1999b; Mitchell 2003), leaving a large portion of the culture in the USA understudied. Also, a majority of hip-hop (Kelley 1994; Perry 2004; Rose 1994) focus on "old school" hip-hop culture, leaving a plethora of research uncovered regarding younger artists and listeners in the present. The major implications of my research are threefold: (1) it aims to better understand the politics of independent hip-hop culture through the lens of artists and listeners in the post-golden era, (2) it adds to the current scholarship by giving a voice to the new generation in the hip-hop community concerned with issues of race, class, gender, sexuality, and oppositional consciousness, and (3) it understands the complexity and changing nature of the culture. Future research needs to be done to understand the current state of hip-hop and its relationship to the broader community in order to anticipate future directions in society. Artists' and listeners' grievances are changing, especially as independent hip-hop artists and listeners are becoming more diverse in terms of their gender, sexuality, and racial and ethnic makeup, a new generation of artists and listeners is emerging, technological and media changes are shifting the boundaries between independent and major, and the political and economic context is shifting. All of these changes are likely to have important implications for the potential of independent hip-hop to inspire oppositional consciousness among its listeners.

References

Adams, Teri, and Douglas Fuller. 2006. "The Words Have Changed but the Ideology Remains the Same: Misogynistic Lyrics in Rap Music." *Journal of Black Studies* 36 (6): 938–957.

Adorno, Theodor, and Max Horkheimer. 1969. *The Dialectic of Enlightenment*. New York: Continuum.

Akom, Antwi. 2009. "Critical Hip Hop Pedagogy as a Form of Liberatory Praxis." *Equity & Excellence in Education* 42 (1): 52–66.

Alim, Samy. 2007. "Critical Hip-Hop Language Pedagogies: Combat, Consciousness and the Cultural Politics of Communication." *Journal of Language, Identity & Education* 6 (2): 161–176.

Alim, Samy, Jooyoung Lee, and Lauren Mason Carris. 2010. "'Short Fried-Rice-Eating Chinese MCs' and 'Good-Hair-Havin Uncle Tom Niggas': Performing Race and Ethnicity in Freestyle Rap Battles." *Journal of Linguistic Anthropology* 20 (1): 116–133.

Alridge, Derrick. 2005. "From Civil Rights to Hip Hop: Toward a Nexus of Ideas." *The Journal of African American History* 90 (3): 226–252.

Androutsopoulos, Jannis, and Arno Scholz. 2003. "Spaghetti Funk: Appropriations of Hip-Hop Culture and Rap Music in Europe." *Popular Music and Society* 26 (4): 463–479.

Asante, Molefi Kete. 2008. *It's Bigger Than Hip Hop: The Rise of the Post-Hip-Hop Generation*. New York: St. Martin's Press.

Au, Wayne. 2005. "Fresh Out of School: Rap Music's Discursive Battle with Education." *The Journal of Negro Education* 74 (3): 210–220.

Baker, Geoffrey. 2005. "Hip Hop Revolucion! Nationalizing Rap in Cuba." *Ethnomusicology* 49 (3): 368–402.
Balaji, Murali. 2010. "Vixen Resistin': Redefining Black Womanhood in Hip-Hop Music Videos." *Journal of Black Studies* 41(1): 5–20.
Ball, Jared. 2009. "FreeMix Radio: The Original Mixtape Radio Show: A Case Study in Mixtape 'Radio' and Emancipatory Journalism." *Journal of Black Studies* 39 (4): 614–634.
Bennett, Andy. 1999a. "Hip Hop Am Main: The Localization of Rap Music and Hip Hop Culture." *Media, Culture & Society* 21 (1): 77–91.
Bennett, Andy. 1999b. "Rappin' on the Tyne: White Hip Hop Culture in Northeast England—An Ethnographic Study." *The Sociological Review* 47: 1–24.
Blair, Elizabeth. 1993. "Commercialization of the Rap Music Youth Subculture." In *That's the Joint! The Hip-Hop Studies Reader*, edited by Murray Forman and Marc Anthony Neal, 493–504. New York: Routledge.
Burgess, Omar. 2012. "Today's Mathematics: How Hip-Hop Measures Commercial Success." Retrieved April 15, 2016. http://hiphopdx.com/editorials/id.2023/title.todays-mathematics-how-hip-hop-measures-commercial-success.
Chang, Jeff. 2005. *Can't Stop Won't Stop: A History of Hip-Hop Generation*. New York: St. Martin's Press.
Charmaz, Kathy. 1983. The Grounded Theory Method: An Explication and Interpretation. In *Contemporary Field Research: A Collection of Readings*, edited by Robert Emerson, 109–126. Boston: Waveland.
Charmaz, Kathy, and Liska Belgrave. 2012. Qualitative Interviewing and Grounded Theory Analysis. In *The SAGE Handbook of Interview Research: The Complexity of the Craft*, edited by Jaber Gubrium, James Holstein, Amir Marvasti, and Karyn McKinney, 2nd ed., 347–366. Thousand Oaks, CA: Sage.
Clark, Msia Kibona. 2013. "The Struggle for Hip Hop Authenticity and Against Commercialization in Tanzania." *The Journal of Pan African Studies* 6 (3): 5–21.
Clay, Andreana. 2006. "All I Need Is One Mic: Mobilizing Youth for Social Change in the Post Civil Rights Era." *Social Justice* 33 (2): 105–121.
Cohen, Cathy. 1997. "Punks, Bulldaggers, and Queens: The Radical Potential of Queer Politics?" *GLQ: A Journal of Lesbian and Gay Studies* 3 (4): 437–465.
Collins, Patricia Hill. 2005. *Black Sexual Politics: African Americans, Gender, and the New Racism*. New York: Routledge.
Connell, Raewyn. 1995. *Masculinities*. Berkeley: University of California Press.
Connell, Raewyn, and James Messerschmidt. 2005. "Hegemonic Masculinity: Rethinking the Concept." *Gender & Society* 19 (6): 829–859.

Crenshaw, Kimberle. 1991. "Beyond Racism and Misogyny: Black Feminism and 2 Live Crew." *Boston Review: A Political and Literary Forum* 16 (6): 30–33.
Davey D. 1984. "What Is Hip Hop?" Retrieved January 1, 2018. http://www.daveyd.com/whatishipdav.html.
Decker, Jeffrey Louis. 1993. "The State of Rap: Time and Place in Hip Hop Nationalism." *Social Text* 34: 53–84.
Dedman, Todd. 2011. "Agency in UK Hip-Hop and Grime Youth Subcultures—Peripherals and Purists." *Journal of Youth Studies* 14 (5): 507–522.
Delamont, Sara, and Neil Stephens. 2008. "Up on the Roof: The Embodied Habitus of Diasporic Capoeira." *Cultural Sociology* 2 (1): 57–74.
Dennis, Chrisopher. 2006. "Afro-Columbian Hip-Hop: Globalization, Popular Music and Ethnic Identities." *Studies in Latin American Popular Culture* 25: 271–295.
DeVault, Marjorie L. 1999. *Liberating Method: Feminism and Social Research*. Philadelphia: Temple University Press.
Dimaggio, Paul. 2010. *Art in the Lives of Immigrant Communities in the United States*. New Brunswick, NJ: Rutgers University Press.
Dimitriadis, Greg. 2009. *Performing Identity/Performing Culture: Hip Hop as Text, Pedagogy, and Lived Practice*. New York: Peter Lang.
Dwyer, Sonya, and Jennifer Buckle. 2009. "The Space Between: On Being an Insider-Outsider in Qualitative Research." *International Journal of Qualitative Methods* 8: 54–63.
Dyson, Michael Eric. 2010. *Know What I Mean: Reflections on Hip-Hop*. New York: Basic Civitas.
Emerson, Rana. 2002. "Where My Girls At?: Negotiating Black Womanhood in Music Videos." *Gender and Society* 16 (1): 115–135.
Ferguson, Roderick. 2004. *Aberrations in Black: Toward a Queer of Color Critique*. Minneapolis: University of Minnesota Press.
Ferris, Kerry. 2007. "The Sociology of Celebrity." *Sociological Compass* 1 (1): 371–384.
Forman, Murray. 2000. "Represent: Race, Place, and Space in Rap Music." *Popular Music* 19 (1): 65–90.
Forman, Murray. 2010. "Conscious Hip-Hop, Change, and the Obama Era." *American Studies Journal* 54: 1–20.
Forman, Murray, and Marc Anthony Neal. 2004. *That's the Joint! The Hip-Hop Studies Reader*. New York: Routledge.
Fraley, Todd. 2009. "I Got a Natural Skill…Hip-Hop, Authenticity, and Whiteness." *Howard Journal of Communication* 20 (1): 37–54.
Freire, Paulo. 1970. *Pedagogy of the Oppressed*. New York: The Continuum International Publishing Group.
George, Nelson. 2005. *Hip-Hop America*. New York: Viking.

Gosa, Travis. 2010. "Not Another Remix: How Obama Became the First Hip-Hop President." *Journal of Popular Music Studies* 22 (4): 289–415.
Gosa, Travis. 2011. "Counterknowledge, Racial Paranoia, and the Cultic Milieu: Decoding Hip-Hop Conspiracy Theory." *Poetics* 39: 187–204.
Gramsci, Antonio. 1971. *Selections from the Prison Notebooks*. New York: International Publishers.
Griswold, Wendy. 1987. "A Methodological Framework for the Sociology of Culture." *Sociological Methodology* 17: 1–35.
Gupta-Carlson, Himanee. 2010. "Planet B-Girl: Community Building and Feminism in Hip-Hop." *New Political Science* 32 (4): 515–529.
Hammonds, Evelynn M. 1994. "Black (W)holes and the Geometry of Black Female Sexuality." *Differences* 6 (2): 126–145.
Harkness, Geoff. 2012. "True School: Situational Authenticity in Chicago's Hip-Hop Underground." *Cultural Sociology* 6 (3): 283–298.
Harkness, Geoff. 2014. *Chicago Hustle & Flow: Gangs, Gangsta Rap, and Social Class*. Minneapolis: University of Minnesota Press.
Harrison, Anthony Kwame. 2006. "Cheaper than a CD, Plus We Really Mean It: Bay Area Underground Hip Hop Tapes as Subcultural Artefacts." *Popular Music* 25: 283–301.
Harrison, Anthony Kwame. 2009. *Hip Hop Underground: The Integrity and Ethics of Racial Identification*. Philadelphia: Temple University Press.
Hernandez, Jillian. 2014. "Carnal Teachings: Raunch Aesthetics as Queer Feminist Pedagogies in Yo! Majesty's Hip-Hop Practice." *Women and Performance: A Journal of Feminist Theory* 24 (1): 88–106.
Hesmondhalgh, David. 1999. "Indie: The Institutional Politics and Aesthetics of a Popular Music Genre." *Cultural Studies* 13 (1): 34–61.
Hesmondhalgh, David, and Caspar Melville. 2002. "Urban Breakbeat Culture—Repercussions of Hip-Hop in the United Kingdom." In *Global Noise: Rap and Hip Hop Outside the USA*, edited by Tony Mitchell, 86–110. Middletown, CT: Wesleyan University Press.
Hess, Mickey. 2005. "Metal Faces, Rap Masks: Identity and Resistance in Hip-Hop's Persona Artist." *Popular Music and Society* 28 (3): 297–311.
Hess, Mickey, 2012. "The Rap Career." In *That's the Joint: The Hip Hop Studies Reader*, edited by Murray Forman and Marc Anthony Neal, 634–654. New York: Routledge.
Hill, Marc Lamont. 2009. *Beats, Rhymes, and Classroom Life: Hip-Hop Pedagogy and the Politics of Identity*. New York: Teachers College Press.
Hodgman, Matthew. 2013. "Class, Race, Credibility, and Authenticity Within the Hip-Hop Music Genre." *Journal of Sociological Research* 4 (2): 402–413.

Hunter, Margaret. 2011. "Shake It, Baby, Shake It: Consumption and the New Gender Relation in Hip-Hop." *Sociological Perspectives* 54 (1): 15–26.
Iwamoto, Derek. 2003. "Tupac Shakur: Understanding the Identity Formation of Hyper-Masculinity of a Popular Hip-Hop Artist." *Black Scholar* 33 (2): 226–252.
Jeffries, Michael. 2011. *Thug Life: Race, Gender, and the Meaning of Hip-Hop*. Chicago: University of Chicago Press.
Jenkins, Toby. 2011. "A Beautiful Mind: Black Male Intellectual Identity and Hip-Hop Culture." *Journal of Black Studies* 42 (8): 1231–1251.
Johnson, Christopher. 2008. "Danceable Capitalism: Hip-Hop's Link to Corporate Space." *The Journal of Pan African Studies* 2 (4): 80–92.
Karubian, Sara. 2009. "360 Deals: An Industry Reaction to the Devaluation of Recorded Music." *Southern California Interdisciplinary Law Journal* 18: 395–462.
Kelley, Robin. 1994. *Race Rebels: Culture, Politics, and the Black Working Class*. New York: Free Press.
Kerstetter, Katie. 2012. "Insider, Outsider, or Somewhere in Between: The Impact of Researchers' Identities on the Community Based Research Process." *Journal of Rural Social Sciences* 27 (2): 99–117.
Kitwana, Bakari. 2002. *The Hip-Hop Generation: Young Blacks and the Crisis in African-American Culture*. New York: Basic Civitas.
Klatch, Rebecca. 1999. *A Generation Divided: The New Left, the New Right, and the 1960s*. Berkeley: University of California Press.
Kubrin, Charis. 2005. "Gangstas, Thugs, and Hustlas: Identity and the Code of the Street in Rap Music." *Social Problems* 52 (3): 360–378.
Leard, Diane, and Brett Lashua. 2006. "Popular Media, Critical Pedagogy, and Inner City Youth." *Canadian Journal of Education* 29 (1): 244–264.
Lena, Jennifer. 2006. "Social Context and Musical Content of Rap Music, 1979–1995." *Social Forces* 85 (1): 479–496.
Lena, Jennifer. 2013. "Authenticity and Independence in Rap Music and Other Genre Communities." In *Explorations in Music Sociology: Examining the Role of Music in Social Life*, edited by S. Horsfall, J. M. Meij, and M. Probstfield, 232–240. Boulder, CO: Paradigm Publishing.
Lena, Jennifer, and Richard Peterson. 2008. "Classification of Culture: Types and Trajectories of Music Genres." *American Sociological Review* 73: 697–718.
Lin, Angel. 2006. "Independent Hip-Hop Artists in Hong-Kong: Cultural Capitalism, Youth Subculture Resistance, and Alternative Modes of Cultural Production." *Mobile and Popular Culture* 1: 1–18.
Lio, Shoon, Scott Melzer, and Ellen Reese. 2008. "Constructing Threat and Appropriating 'Civil Rights': Rhetorical Strategies of Gun Rights and English Only Leaders." *Symbolic Interaction* 31 (1): 5–31.

Lopes, Paul. 1992. "Innovation and Diversity in the Popular Music Industry: 1969–1990." *American Sociological Review* 57 (1): 56–71.
Low, Bronwen. 2010. "The Tale of the Talent Night Rap: Hip-Hop Culture in Schools and the Challenge of Interpretation." *Urban Education* 45 (2): 194–220.
Macklemore, and Ryan Lewis. 2012. "Jimmy Iovine." *The Heist*. Macklemore LLC-ADA.
Maher, George Ciccariello. 2005. "Brechtian Hip-Hop: Didactics and Self-Production in Post-Gangsta Political Mixtapes." *Journal of Black Studies* 26 (1): 129–160.
Maher, George Ciccariello. 2007. "A Critique of DuBoisian Reason: Kanye West and the Fruitfulness of Double Consciousness." *Journal of Black Studies* 39 (3): 371–401.
Mansbridge, Jane, and Aldon Morris. 2001. *Oppositional Consciousness: The Subjective Roots of Social Protest*. Chicago: University of Chicago Press.
Martinez, Theresa. 1997. "Popular Culture as Oppositional Culture: Rap as Resistance." *Sociological Perspectives* 40 (2): 265–286.
Maxwell, Ian. 1994. "True to the Music: Authenticity, Articulation and Authorship in Sydney Hip Hop Culture." *Social Semiotics* 4 (1–2): 117–137.
McCall, Nathan. 1994. *Makes Me Wanna Holler: A Young Black Man in America*. New York: Vintage Books.
McLeod, Kembrew. 1999. "Authenticity Within Hip-Hop and Other Cultures Threatened with Assimilation." *Journal of Communication* 49 (4): 134–150.
McLeod, Kembrew. 2005. "MP3s Are Killing Home Taping: The Rise of Internet Distribution and Its Challenge to the Major Label Music Monopoly." *Popular Music and Society* 28 (4): 521–531.
McWhorter, John. 2003. "How Hip-Hop Holds Blacks Back." *City Journal* 13 (3) (Summer): 66–75.
Merton, Robert. 1972. "Insiders and Outsiders: A Chapter on the Sociology of Knowledge." *American Journal of Sociology* 78: 9–47.
Miller-Young, Mireille. 2008. "Hip-Hop Honeys and Da Hustlaz: Black Sexualities in the New Hip-Hop Pornography: Feminism, Race, Transnational Feminism, Race Transnationalism." Special Issue. *Meridians* 8 (1): 261–292.
Mitchell, Tony. 1996. *Popular Music and Local Identity: Rock, Pop and Rap in Europe and Oceania*. Leicester: Leicester University Press.
Mitchell, Tony. 2000. "Doin' Damage in my Native Language: The Use of "Resistance Vernaculars" in Hip Hop in France, Italy, and Aotearoa/New Zealand." *Popular Music and Society* 24 (3): 41–54.
Mitchell, Tony. 2003. "Australian Hip-Hop as a Subculture." *Youth Studies Australia* 22 (2): 40–47.

Morgan, George, and Andrew Warren. 2011. "Aboriginal Youth, Hip Hop and the Politics of Identification." *Ethnic and Racial Studies* 34 (6): 925–947.

Morgan, Marcyliena, and Dionne Bennett. 2011. "Hip-Hop & the Global Imprint of a Black Cultural Form." *Dædalus: The Journal of the American Academy of Arts & Sciences* 140 (2): 176–196.

Myer, Letrez, and Christine Kleck. 2007. "From Independent to Corporate: A Political Economic Analysis of Rap Billboard Toppers." *Popular Music and Society* 30 (2): 137–148.

Newman, Michael. 2005. "Rap as Literacy: A Genre Analysis of Hip-Hop Cyphers." *Text* 25 (3): 399–436.

Nielson, Erik. 2012. "'Here Come the Cops': Policing the Resistance in Rap Music." *International Journal of Cultural Studies* 15 (4): 349–363.

Ogbar, Jeffrey. 2007. *Hip-Hop Revolution: The Culture and Politics of Rap*. Lawrence: University Press of Kansas.

Omi, Michael, and Howard Winant. 1994. *Racial Formation in the United States: From the 1960s to the 1990s*. New York: Routledge.

Omoniyi, Tope. 2006. "Hip-Hop Through the World Englishes Lens: A Response to Globalization." *World Englishes* 25 (2): 195–208.

Ostrove, Geoffrey. 2014. "The Political Economy of Financially Successful Independent Artists." *Class, Race and Corporate Power* 2 (1): 1–22.

Oware, Matthew. 2014. "(Un)Conscious (Popular) Underground: Restricted Cultural Production and Underground Rap Music." *Poetics* 42: 60–81.

Oware, Matthew. 2016. "'We Stick Out Like a Sore Thumb …': Underground White Rappers' Hegemonic Masculinity and Racial Evasion." *Sociology of Race and Ethnicity* 2 (3): 372–386.

Pennycook, Alastair. 2007. "Language, Localization, and the Real: Hip-Hop and the Global Spread of Authenticity." *Journal of Language, Identity, and Education* 6 (2): 101–115.

Perkins, William. 1996. *Droppin' Science: Critical Essays on Rap Music and Hip-Hop Culture*. Philadelphia: Temple University Press.

Perry, Imani. 2004. *Prophets of the Hood: Politics and Poetics in Hip Hop*. Durham, NC: Duke University Press.

Petchauer, Emery. 2010. "Sampling Practices and Social Spaces: Exploring a Hip-Hop Approach to Higher Education." *Journal of College Student Development* 51 (4): 359–372.

Potter, Russell. 1995. *Spectacular Vernaculars: Hip-Hop and the Politics of Postmodernism*. Albany: State University of New York Press.

Pough, Gwendolyn. 2004. *Check It While I Wreck It: Black Womanhood, Hip-Hop Culture, and the Public Sphere*. Boston, NH: Northeastern University Press.

Rebollo-Gil, Guillermo, and Amanda Moras. 2012. "Black Women and Black Men in Hip Hop Music: Misogyny, Violence and the Negotiation of (White-Owned) Space." *The Journal of Popular Culture* 45 (1): 118–132.

Reyna, Christine, Mark Brandt, and Tendayi Viki. 2009. "Blame It on Hip-Hop: Anti-Rap Attitudes as a Proxy for Justice." *Group Processes and Intergroup Relations* 12 (3): 361–380.

Rodriquez, Jason. 2006. "Color-Blind Ideology and the Cultural Appropriation of Hip-Hop." *Journal of Contemporary Ethnography* 35 (6): 645–668.

Rose, Tricia. 1994. *Black Noise: Rap Music and Black Culture in Contemporary America*. New York: Wesleyan University Press.

Rose, Tricia. 2008. *The Hip Hop Wars: What We Talk About When We Talk About Hip Hop—And Why It Matters*. New York: Basic Civitas.

Sanchez, Deborah. 2010. "Hip-Hop and a Hybrid Text in a Post-Secondary English Class." *Journal of Adolescent & Adult Literacy* 53 (6): 478–487.

Shusterman, Richard. 1992. "Challenging Conventions in the Fine Art of Rap." In *That's the Joint! The Hip-Hop Studies Reader*, edited by Murray Forman and Marc Anthony Neal, 459–480. New York: Routledge.

Simmel, Georg and Kurt Wolff. 1950. *The Sociology of George Simmel*. New York: Free Press.

Smalls, Shante Paradigm. 2011. "The Rain Comes Down: Jean Grae and Hip Hop Heternonormativity." *American Behavioral Scientist* 55 (1): 86–95.

Smith, Christopher. 1997. "Method in the Madness: Exploring the Boundaries of Identity in Hip-Hop Performativity, Social Identities." *Journal for the Study of Race, Nation and Culture* 3 (3): 345–374.

Söderman, Johan, and Goran Folkestad. 2004. "How Hip-Hop Musicians Learn: Strategies in Informal Creative Music Making." *Music Education Research* 6 (3): 313–326.

Stapleton, Katina. 1998. "From the Margins to Mainstream: The Political Power of Hip-Hop." *Media, Culture & Society* 20: 219–234.

Stovall, David. 2006. "We Can Relate: Hip-Hop Culture, Critical Pedagogy, and the Secondary Classroom." *Urban Education* 41 (6): 585–602.

Strauss, Anselm, and Juliet Corbin. 1994. "Grounded Theory Methodology: An Overview." In *Handbook of Qualitative Research*, edited by Norman Denzin and Yvonna Lincoln, 273–285. Thousand Oaks, CA: Sage.

Suhr, Hiesun. 2011. "Understanding the Hegemonic Struggle Between Mainstream vs. Independent Forces: The Music Industry and Musicians in the Age of Social Media." *International Journal of Technology, Knowledge and Society* 7 (6): 123–136.

Sullivan, Nikki. 2003. *A Critical Introduction to Queer Theory*. New York: New York Press.

Sullivan, Rachel. 2003. "Rap and Race: It's Got a Nice Beat, but What About the Message?" *Journal of Black Studies* 33 (5): 605–622.

Tanner-Smith, Emily, Damian Williams, and Denise Nichols. 2006. "Selling Sex to Radio Program Directors: A Content Analysis of *Radio and Records Magazine*." *Sex Roles* 54 (9/10): 675–686.

Taylor, Carl, and Virgil Taylor. 2007. "Hip-Hop Is Now: An Evolving Youth Culture." *Reclaiming Children and Youth* 15 (4): 210–213.

Terkourafi, Marina. 2010. *Languages of Global Hip Hop*. London: Continuum International Publishing Group.

Tickner, Arlene. 2008. "Aqui en el Ghetto: Hip-Hop in Colombia, Cuba, and Mexico." *Latin American Politics and Society* 50 (3): 121–146.

Trapp, Erin. 2005. "The Push and Pull of Hip-Hop: A Social Movement Analysis." *American Behavioral Scientist* 48 (11): 1482–1495.

Vito, Christopher. 2015. "Who Said Hip-Hop Was Dead?: The Politics of Hip-Hop Culture in Immortal Technique's Lyrics." *International Journal of Cultural Studies* 18 (4): 395–411.

Wang, Oliver. 2014. *Legions of Boom: Filipino American Mobile DJ Crews in the San Francisco Bay Area*. Durham, NC: Duke University Press.

Warren, Andrew, and Rob Evitt. 2010. "Indigenous Hip-Hop: Overcoming Marginality, Encountering Constraints." *Australian Geographer* 41 (1): 141–158.

Watkins, S. Craig. 2005. *Hip Hop Matters: Politics, Pop Culture, and the Struggle for the Soul of a Movement*. Boston, MA: Beacon Press.

Weitzer, Ronald, and Charis Kubrin. 2009. "Misogyny in Rap Music: A Content Analysis of Prevalence and Meanings." *Men and Masculinities* 12 (1): 3–29.

Wells-Wilbon, Rhonda, Nigel Jackson, and Jerome Schiele. 2010. "Lessons from the Maafa: Rethinking the Legacy of Slain Hip-Hop Icon Tupac Amaru Shakur." *Journal of Black Studies* 40 (4): 504–526.

Williams, Paul. 2008. "Twenty-First-Century Jeremiad: Contemporary Hip-Hop and American Tradition." *European Journal of American Culture* 27 (2): 111–132.

Open Access This chapter is distributed under the terms of the Creative Commons Attribution 4.0 International License (http://creativecommons.org/licenses/by/4.0/), which permits use, duplication, adaptation, distribution and reproduction in any medium or format, as long as you give appropriate credit to the original author(s) and the source, a link is provided to the Creative Commons license and any changes made are indicated.The images or other third party material in this chapter are included in the work's Creative Commons license, unless indicated otherwise in the credit line; if such material is not included in the work's Creative Commons license and the respective action is not permitted by statutory regulation, users will need to obtain permission from the license holder to duplicate, adapt or reproduce the material.

CHAPTER 2

Just Say No to the Majors: Independent Hip-Hop Culture

Abstract This chapter aims to uncover how independent hip-hop in the post-golden era challenges or reproduces cultural ideologies within US mainstream hip-hop culture and US culture more generally. Based on a content analysis of artists' lyrics, the author identifies three recurrent themes found in albums by twenty-five indie hip-hop artists. First, these acts resist the majors through mainstream artists, large radio stations, and major record labels. Second, they reject the corporatization and commodification by major record labels and mainstream culture in favor of independently owned companies. Third, they advocate for an indie culture based on alternative cultural ideals. They instead socially construct and advocate for a brand of authenticity rooted in hip-hop's origins.

Keywords Independent hip-hop · Authenticity · Corporatization and commodification · Mainstream hip-hop · Major record labels · Independent record labels

Immortal Technique's song, entitled "One Remix" (2003a), emphasizes the sentiments of many independent artists who believe that hip-hop needs to continue to be free from economic and cultural control by large corporations who dominate mainstream culture. As Rose (2008) states, three record labels nicknamed the "majors" (Universal Music Group, Sony Music Entertainment, and Warner Music Group) distribute more than 85% of the music globally in the industry. Conversely, independent

© The Author(s) 2019
C. Vito, *The Values of Independent Hip-Hop in the Post-Golden Era*,
https://doi.org/10.1007/978-3-030-02481-9_2

hip-hop focuses on music created by established indie labels and produced outside the confines of the three major music labels (Vito 2015). While these terms are not binary or dichotomous as independent and major label artists often mediate both realms, they provide an important framework for indie musicians to make economic and cultural grievances toward major corporations and mainstream culture.

With this demarcation by artists who have willingly chosen to remain independent, they make similar claims regarding class relations within the music industry that also reflect broader class relations in the USA. While these claims remain heterogeneous and fall along a broad spectrum, similar underlying themes can be found within their lyrical content. Thus, this chapter discusses three recurrent themes found in albums by twenty-five independent hip-hop artists in the post-golden era from 2000 to 2013. First, these acts resist the majors in three ways: (1) mainstream artists, (2) large radio stations, and (3) major record labels. Second, they reject the corporatization and commodification by large record companies and mainstream culture in favor of independently owned companies. Third, they socially construct and advocate for independent hip-hop based on alternative cultural ideals.

Resistance to the "Majors"

Independents often criticize major record label culture, citing the commodification, exploitation, and corporatization of hip-hop as major problems. In particular, the artists studied express resistance: (1) to mainstream artists who "sell out," (2) to large radio stations, and (3) to major record label control of music.

Resistance to Mainstream Artists Who "Sell Out"

The fall of the golden era in the 1990s was spurred on by the extraction of artists into the mainstream by major record labels looking to capitalize on hip-hop's emergence. Johnson (2008) believes that during this time, there was a significant decrease in lyrical mastery, innovation in beat production, and diversity in style and content. This shift was caused by the desire of large corporations to secure their investments by standardizing the music creation process and creating a market aimed at homogenization (Myer and Kleck 2007).

Indies express grievances toward major label musicians who have been complicit in this process of homogenization in hip-hop culture. For example, Subterraneous' Binary Star rap in "Masters of the Universe" (2000a): "subtle, anonymous, rap hippopotamus, milk homogeneous." Their album, which was produced with a very limited budget and a small market, garnered rave reviews for its varied beats and rhymes as an alternative to many mainstream acts during the time (Mills 2000). Similarly, Hieroglyphics Imperium's Hieroglyphics Crew writes in "Let it Roll" (2003a): "an exception to the mediocrity, monotony and hypocrisy, That hip hop is weak." Both groups write about the music industry catering to the needs of the masses through standardization and thus minimizing the importance of the creativity, heterogeneity, and innovation exhibited during the golden era.

In addition, they argue that major label artists have utilized two tropes of hip-hop culture to make music that is repetitive in theme (Watkins 2005). Indies criticize acts from major labels that utilize the "gangster rap" phenomena to objectify street culture as a means to be successful. Also, they reject hip-hop that focuses solely on making money and "getting rich."

During the first period of the post-golden era, the dominant model used by large corporations was gangster rap, which emphasized nihilism, machismo, and violence (Rose 2008; Taylor and Taylor 2007; Wells-Wilbon et al. 2010). While these tropes of gangster rap resembled street culture, corporations have ossified these tropes into albums to be created and consumed by the masses. Independent performers add that many rappers today often talk about being hardcore and gangster because that appeals to whites in the mainstream. Concurrently, they claim that these acts are not "hard" but rather create a façade to sell records. As Binary Star raps in "Honest Expression" (2000b), "I ain't hardcore...most of y'all gangsta rappers ain't hardcore neither." "Honest Expression" (2000b) picks up on the same themes, asking "what makes you think you're hardcore, cause you was raised in the projects?" For Binary Star mainstream acts and major corporations corroborate to create stereotypical images embedded within urban culture simply to make a profit.

Much of hip-hop is also marred by the trope of the "bling bling" era. Many acts uphold the stereotype that urban culture is dominated by the consumption of material goods such as money, jewelry, and cars. This materialism permeates into the lyrical content of the majors. Binary Star asks in "Binary Shuffle" (2000c) "do you want to hear about the money we got? (oh no), talk about the people we shot? (oh no), bragg on the clothes we wear? (oh no)." Their lyrics object to music focused on money, gang violence, and material consumption as the basis for lyrical content. KRS-ONE adds that this trope of materialism gives many musicians entering the game the wrong idea about the industry in "Nothing New" (2007). KRS-ONE raps that the industry has changed since the golden era, facing increased corporatization and homogenization into a bling-bling genre. New acts coming into the industry believe that it always opens gateways to wealth and fame, but are mistaken as hip-hop is still dominated by large corporations who control the culture and its profits. In essence, many musicians are led to believe and even reinforce the cultural ideologies of materialism in their lyrics, which in turn is reproduced by listeners and broader mainstream culture.

Further, these complaints have led indie artists to argue that many acts signed to the majors have sold out by creating a formulaic package with similar messages to attract large audiences to their music, sacrificing the art of hip-hop culture. The increase of homogenization, the commodification of gangster rap, and the ideology of materialism have led them to conclude that hip-hop has been jeopardized by sell outs. Bay Area rap duo Blackalicious reiterates these sentiments in "Purest Love" (2002): "how can I rap, if I ain't thugged out pimpin', flossin' my ice, packin' a gat," stating that they do not want to "sell (their) soul and front inside of mainstream's eyes" (Fig. 2.1).

Many musicians argue that rappers have sold out in two ways: (1) they merely act as puppets following orders from major labels and (2) becoming successful by creating a worn down and noncreative product that large companies want. As puppets, mainstream acts have been accused by the hip-hop community as being sell outs who have given in to the ideologies of the corporations to get their cut of the profits in the industry. For instance, in Hieroglyphics' "Prelude" (2003b), they claim that they have stayed true to hip-hop, while many rappers are just "parrots" who do what they are told in order to get rich. Sound of Color's duo of Blu and Exile rap in "Simply Amazin" (2007a) "fuck you sold-soul rappers, after diamonds and pearls." Binary Star reiterates these sentiments

2 JUST SAY NO TO THE MAJORS: INDEPENDENT HIP-HOP CULTURE   49

Fig. 2.1 Blackalicious (Gift of Gab on left and Chief Xcel on right) (*Credit* Blackalicious.com)

in "Indy 500" (2000d): "they pay your dumb ass…to get rich." In these songs, they denigrate rappers who sold out for the money and who do not care about the music and the message. Instead, these rappers homogenize the sound and play on tropes of minority communities at the request of the major companies and at the expense of the culture.

Independent musicians also make the claim that many artists create a worn down product that is noncritical and noncreative. Binary Star writes in "Honest Expression" (2000b) that "every gold record don't glitter that's for damn sure." Similarly, Viper Records' Immortal Technique raps on "Industrial Revolution" (2003b) "if you go platinum…it just means that a million people are stupid as fuck." Both acts make the argument that financial and commercial success does not translate into quality music production. Instead, it shows that they can create a product that has traditionally been successful and can capitalize on the tastes of the broader market. Ultimately, indies claim that mainstream hip-hop culture is homogenized, reproducing and recreating gangster rap and bling-bling tropes to achieve commercial success despite selling out on hip-hop.

Resistance to Major Radio Stations

After hip-hop's meteoric rise in America, large companies such as Cumulus Media and iHeartMedia (formerly Clear Channel) have used their control of major radio stations to flood the market with musicians they support. While the practice of payola, or paying radio stations for airplay, is illegal in the USA, many corporations have found loopholes through independent promoters to maintain dominance of the airwaves. For example, it may cost up to $1000 to play one song per station in the USA (Ball 2009). This has led to the cultural practice of favoring the majors rather than the independents. Many indie acts have thus rejected the cultural practices of large radio stations and mainstream media outlets. They argue that radio stations actively cooperate with the large corporations to create, promote, and maintain homogeneity in mass media simply to get paid. Concurrently, this also means that indies have a hard time getting "spins" from large radio outlets and mainstream media sources because they lack the cultural capital, as well as economic capital (see Chapter 3), to get "love" from the big outlets. In turn, this creates feelings of marginalization as they are forced to live in the underground.

Independent hip-hop remains at the margins of the major radio stations and thus has remained a niche market predominantly spurred on by local radio stations. Yet the cornering of the radio market by iHeartMedia (formerly Clear Channel) has worsened the marginalization independent musicians experience as their opportunities have diminished. Binary Star raps in "Honest Expression" (2000b) that radio stations play "nonsense." It's A Wonderful World Music Group's Rapsody raps in "Kind of Love" (2012a) that this change has diminished and tarnished hip-hop culture: "kind of love uncommon nowadays, Used to Love Her on my radio waves." In the verse, Rapsody references Common's song "Used to Love Her," reiterating his sentiments that hip-hop has changed in the face of corporatization and commodification by mainstream radio.

Indies have also had a hard time getting love from other media outlets. Rapsody writes in "The Cards" (2012b) about her struggles to get major airplay on MTV and BET. She claims these are not an anomaly, but rather indicative of the market as local DJs and musicians have a hard time getting brand recognition without the social, cultural, and economic capital of the large labels. Further, Rapsody argues that there is no space to make grievances about major radio's cultural practices as the corporate executives suppress their complaints. In "Believe Me" (2012c), she raps "complaining bout radio, my nigga, got no room, cause niggas wit opinions don't support you on iTunes." Indies understand that major radio stations and media outlets align themselves with the interests of the majors, which makes it difficult for them to obtain a larger share of the radio waves in the hip-hop industry.

Rejection of Interactions with Record Labels

Rose (2008) contends that the corporatization of hip-hop has had deleterious effects for hip-hop culture and its community. For example, corporatization has created an overrepresentation of white, upper-class males in positions of power in the music industry who control the direction of the culture (Myer and Kleck 2007). As a result, mainstream acts are forced to adopt the ideologies and practices of large corporations in order to be successful. Independents have alternatively developed negative views of the majors as they have been culturally marginalized in the industry.

In particular, they make three main grievances toward major corporations. First, indies voice their negative experiences with the majors when negotiating their behavior, ideas, and creative direction in their music. Second, they argue that the large companies are willing to pull artists and their culture from the underground to commodify them into a product when they are failing. Finally, indie artists who consider being part of a large label face the problem Immortal Technique (2003d) calls being "stuck on a shelf," or being "shelved." He argues that many artists have their music stuck in limbo and sometimes never even being released. In essence, they believe that indies are treated poorly if they are part of the underground circuit until the majors pull them from the underground when necessary. Once they are pulled from the underground, the culture of objectification has led many to be unsuccessful and treated as expendable workers for the industry.

Indies express their hesitation and distrust of the major record labels. As Sound of Color's Blu and Exile write in "Soul Amazing" (2007b), "I give a fuck about a pro hire." Blu and Exile describe their distrust of pro hires, or professional hiring companies focused on marketing and distribution, and the importance of remaining with smaller labels. Much of their distrust stems from negative experiences with the majors when negotiating their behavior, ideas, and creative direction in their music.

Lex Records' MF Doom raps on "Gazillion Ear" (2009): "once sold an inbred skinhead a nigga joke." In the verse, he is referring to the release of the album *Black Bastards* by KMD, a rap group that included MF DOOM. The album was canceled by Elektra Records, a subsidiary label owned by Warner Music Group, because of its controversial cover depicting a black Sambo figure being lynched. They cited the cover as depicting racist stereotypes, despite KMD's history of racially conscious lyrics and satirical artwork. KMD was subsequently released from Elektra despite KMD member DJ Subroc being killed in a car accident shortly before the album's completion (Ducker 2014). After retreating from hip-hop for years, MF DOOM resurfaced onto the indie scene. In his lyrics, he states his desire to stay away from labels such as Elektra Records as he feels that they limit his ability to speak on race relations and that many performers face detrimental consequences for criticizing or bringing attention to racism and racial problems.

Strange Records' Tech N9ne writes of his displeasure with the major record labels in "Like Yeah" (2008a): "the industry's still punks, that's why they real slump…all our records we will dump." On the track, he raps of his distrust of the industry, emphasizing the need to thrive on his own label. This stems from his negative experiences with Warner Bros in the 1990s. Tech N9ne fell out of favor with Quincy Jones and the label because he did not fit their artistic mold (Greenburg 2013a). He was eventually released from his deal as the company cites that Tech N9ne's hardcore rap "just wasn't working." He later formed Strange Records with partner Jimmy Gunn and openly stated that he would never go mainstream (Tucker 2015). The experiences of MF DOOM and Tech N9ne resemble the experiences of many indies that tried to make it in the game and were marginalized by the labels because they did not fit their cultural schema.

Indies have also made the grievance that companies pull from the underground and independent scene when they need a new source of innovation. Once indie musicians and their styles are commodified by mainstream labels, they exploit this innovation for their own profit without consideration for the artist. As Rhymesayer's Atmosphere points out in "God Loves Ugly" (2002a), "everybody gathers around…so they can steal each others' sound." They have additionally claimed that many acts are viewed as fads by companies, which leads them to often be stuck trying to survive in the larger market without much support. In "One of a Kind" (2002a), Atmosphere continues to spit: "switch up my styles… but see which kids next year sound the same as me." Indies such as Atmosphere believe that corporations pull acts from the underground as a form of cheap labor to produce fads and trends with no concern for the negative short-term and long-term consequences.

Further, independents have complained about the phenomenon of being "shelved," or having their music be stuck in limbo and sometimes never even being released (Platon 2017). A number of situations can contribute to an act's lack of success in the industry. For example, musicians are often bound by contracts and can be shelved if they encounter conflicts with upper management (Michaels 2010). A young MF Doom, as part of rap group KMD, had their album *Black Bastards* shelved by Elektra in 1993 due to disputes over album cover art featuring a Sambo figure being lynched (Steiner 2014). Their album was not released until 2001 under Ready Rock Records. In addition, the preponderance of signings by major labels is astoundingly high considering the small number of artists they actually promote each year. Many acts have thus complained that musicians signed in-house to these labels must fight with one another for scant access to resources and the opportunity to be successful in the market (Zafar 2013). Macklemore LLC's Macklemore and Ryan Lewis write in "Jimmy Iovine" (2012a): "CDs boxed in cardboard, artists that flopped, that got dropped and never got to be sophomores." The practice of shelving has led many to rot away in the music game without ever having an opportunity to release their songs to the public. During their music careers, many get stuck in different phases such as recording, distribution, and even touring. Underlying the majors' actions are the justification that signing many musicians keeps competition high, and thus acts are willing to take less in profits and resources. Many companies have also kept artists on the shelves at record stores and big-box chains to fill the shelves with acts that they know will flop or not sell (Lindvall 2010; Zafar 2013). This is done to keep shelf space full and divert attention to albums that the record company is pushing. Even with the decline of physical records, major record labels are still known to shelve musicians by signing them, recording their music, and then refusing to release it digitally. This creative marketing tactic is used at the expense of many musicians whom never get a full opportunity to let their work be put on the market. Many complain that major record labels keep acts metaphorically and physically shelved as objects that are exploited in the industry.

Ultimately, they are weary of the culture of objectification and expendability in the mainstream. Rap duo Binary Star writes of the lack of concern for artists in "Indy 500" (2000d). They spit: "and if that shit don't hit, the next day you're gone." Their lyrics reveal the nature of the "beast" in the industry. Musicians are generally seen by large corporations as employees who produce a commodity. When they are unable to make the company profitable, they are seen as expendable and replaceable regardless of its effect on their livelihood, family, friends, and community. The problem of commodification has ultimately left independents weary of major record labels and their cultural practices in the music industry.

Fighting Back Against the Majors

Hip-hop has consistently faced the problematic pull between commercial vitality and a meaningful source of youth empowerment and social change (Watkins 2005). As a result of commercialization in the post-golden era, independent labels began to grow again as a push-back from artists and listeners who were concerned with hip-hop's shift toward capitalistic, patriarchal, Eurocentric, heteronormative, and noncritical culture (Dyson 2010; Ogbar 2007; Perry 2004; Rose 2008; Watkins 2005). Thus, indies have made the claim, albeit with heterogeneous themes, that they need to create and maintain a niche market predicated upon independent labels and culture (Drake 2015). Their argument, based on their lyrics, appear in two differing ways: (1) the need to create independent companies to maintain a niche culture in the music industry and (2) the need to question, reject, and rebel against major record labels and mainstream culture. Both make the assertion that independent companies need to remain a subculture that allows for more cultural freedom and creative expression.

Creation of Independent Labels and Culture

Ball (2009) emphasizes the importance of material conditions in music creation and production. In order to understand hip-hop one must examine the creation of independent hip-hop companies and culture. Previous research (Berger and Peterson 1975) states that competition, diversity, and resistance (Hesmondhalgh 1999) in the music industry historically occurs following periods of homogeneity, which mirrors the rise of independent labels in the post-golden era. For instance, indies remove themselves from the corporate infrastructure through DIY (Do It Yourself) ethics (Moore 2007), or self-production (Harkness 2012), which allows for more cultural and economic freedom (Maher 2005). They can also look for alternative means of press through independent radio outlets, Web sites, and social networks with the rapid rise of music technology (Ball 2009; Jones 2002). This is epitomized in the creation and success of hip-hop record labels operating outside of major record label's mainstream culture.

Independents believe that the industry needs to be predicated upon the creation of companies that are predominantly interested and invested in the musicians' best interests. They contend that acts can be successful in the music industry while simultaneously being free from corporate control and creating their own culture. For example, rap collective Hieroglyphics writes in "Powers That Be" (2003c) "and the industry could never jail us, all my niggas free to be ourselves and our records still sell." Their album, *Full Circle*, was released in 2003 to positive reviews from critics and successful record sales in the independent album category (Bush 2003). They achieved financial and commercial success despite being a collective of artists who were deemed not commercial enough for many major labels. Viper Records' Immortal Technique echoes those sentiments by writing on "The Message and the Money" (2003c): "you don't own me, and none of you niggas ever will." In an interview with Immortal Technique, he reiterates these statements by claiming that his music is 100% independent, which he characterizes as owning your own masters, publishing, and creative control (The NE Hip-Hop 2013). Both acts emphasize the value of being free from major records' label control through the creation of independent companies and remaining outside of the mainstream market. As a result, they experience less direct oversight by corporate producers and can create their own niche culture and brand of music.

Rejection and Rebellion Against the Majors

The dialectical nature of hip-hop also allows for artists and listeners to create and interpret meaning from music, which can simultaneously promote dominant ideologies and resist them (Watkins 2005). These modes of resistance can be present in ciphers (freestyles among rappers), live performances, recorded music, and social media (Newman 2005). They often operate as hidden transcripts, or encrypted messages understood within the hip-hop community, that act as a form of resistance and a means of opening dialogue among artists and listeners (Ferris 2007; Hess 2005; Potter 1995). Indies in particular produce hidden transcripts regarding their experiences as marginalized actors dissatisfied with their position in mainstream culture and society. As KRS-ONE points out, hip-hop is in a unique position to critique society, which includes topics of racism, police brutality, incarceration, and poverty (Akom 2009; Au 2005; Dimitriadis 2009; Hill 2009). Their music also acts as a means to resist and rebel against the corporatization and commodification of hip-hop's culture by major record labels. In certain instances, these themes of resistance and rebellion create a collective identity predicated upon a shared recognition as working-class people of color (Leard and Lashua 2006). Within my sample, collective grievances appear in lyrics emphasizing their ability to speak freely regarding political and cultural ideologies and lyrics calling for resistance and rebellion against the majors and mainstream culture.

Independent artists have rapped about their ability to speak freely and make music aligned with their political and cultural views. Viper Records' Immortal Technique writes in "Freedom of Speech" (2003d): "independent in every single sense of the word, I say what I want." He raps that being indie affords him the ability to speak his mind and not be controlled by any executives who may censor his political beliefs. Other acts have similarly shared these sentiments. Sound of Color's Blu and Exile rap in "The Narrow Path" (2007c): "just dig it, or don't fuck with it, cause you can't fuck with it." Om Records' People Under the Stairs also spit in "Acid Raindrops" (2002a): "underground ground heads will fiend this musical genius." They both make the case that underground and independent hip-hop is a market in which they can engage in a wide array of sounds, styles, and lyrics. Hieroglyphics reiterates these sentiments in "Prelude" (2003b) by claiming to be "ahead of the charts." Hieroglyphics reinforces the assertion that being free from record label control allows many performers to be creatively free and offers a chance to be successful without compromising their political and economic beliefs.

Indies are also in a unique position to make the grievance that they need to create social change against the cultural practices of marginalization and objectification by the majors. Immortal Technique elaborates on his song "The Message and the Money" (2003c): "I would like to send a message to all the underground MC's…the time has come to realize you networked in a market, and stop being a fucking commodity." He argues that this rebellion must be spurred on by the notion that indie artists are seen as a commodity rather than musicians creating music both for themselves and for fans. As such, he writes that "hardcore reality hip-hop" is shunned by companies because it is not viewed as a profitable market by record executives and managers. Other independents have reinforced Immortal Technique's sentiments. As Subterraneous' Binary Star writes on "Conquistadors" (2000e): "the system we rebel, the mainstream as well." Hieroglyphics Imperium's Hieroglyphics also rap in "Powers That Be" (2003c): "fuck popular opinion…but we did it all for independence." Furthermore, the sources of these grievances can be heterogeneous from person to person. Tech N9ne and Immortal Technique demonstrate in their lyrical content, with the former focusing on darker religious lyrics and the latter focusing on economic and political issues, that heterogeneity in their lyrics does not inhibit their

Fig. 2.2 Immortal Technique (*Credit* Twitter @ImmortalTech)

collective grievance of the music industry. As they show in an interview together, they both advocate for a rebellion against major labels upon the premise that the majors objectify them and deny their autonomy and creative control (Hard Knock TV 2013). Ultimately, indies have expressed the need for rebellion and change within the music industry, which begins with creating an independent market predicated upon freedom from major corporations and the production of alternative cultural ideals (Fig. 2.2).

INDEPENDENT HIP-HOP AS AN ALTERNATIVE CULTURE

Independent artists have advocated for the rejection of major record labels and the creation of indie companies. In concordance with the formation of indie companies, some artists of this genre argue for an alternative culture predicated on the love of hip-hop music, or creating music regardless if the musician becomes rich and successful. Others in the genre utilize claims that "real" or "authentic" hip-hop requires acknowledging and honoring its origins.

For the "Love" of the Music Regardless of Money

The bifurcation between the independent and major circuit is not new, as indie rock has exhibited the same "social differentiation" (Hibbett 2005) from mainstream rock as a form of high art. Hibbett (2005) describes the antagonism between indie and mainstream rock as highly responsive to one another and interdependent. Scholars (Maher 2005, 2007; Rose 2008) make similar arguments regarding independent hip-hop as a dialectical force that legitimizes mainstream hip-hop by pulling some of its acts from the indie scene but distancing itself from the mainstream by pulling away from overt commercialization. Harrison (2006) reiterates this point by claiming that indie artists can embrace the progressive politics of subcultural inclusion in the industry. This can include lyrics that critique the domination by major corporations in popular culture and society, as well as provide an alternative indie culture predicated on alternative ideals.

Independent label Rhymesayers, which is based in Minnesota and co-created by Atmosphere (consisting of Rapper Slug and DJ/Producer Ant), has acts that have created an identifiable brand of indie culture claiming that their music is predicated upon their "love of the music." For example, Atmosphere raps about their love for hip-hop on "Give Me" (2002b), elucidating the importance of hip-hop in their own lives. They also write of the love they have for their fans, which is embodied in the music that they create and the personal relationships they form with them (Ostrow 2010).

Fellow Rhymesayers signee Aesop Rock advocates that he has a passion for making music and is dedicated to his craft. Aesop Rock's journey was unconventional as he initially funded his own debut album in 1997 entitled *Music for Earthworms* before being signed to independent label Mush in 1999. He was later signed by indie label Definitive Jux and released *Labor Days* in 2001. After a hiatus on Definitive Jux, Aesop Rock signed with Rhymesayers. In Aesop Rock's "Labor" (2001a), he writes: "I work past the surface, and I'll work until this here little flat line closes the curtains." On the track, Aesop describes that hip-hop is his life and he loves it. He views hip-hop as a lifelong commitment to which he develops his craft. More importantly, his love for the music transcends his material success as he works to survive and will perform, both literally and figuratively, until the curtain closes.

Rhymesayer label mate Brother Ali reinforces his dedication and love for the quality of music he creates. Brother Ali, a white male rapper who was born with albinism, has been with Rhymesayers since his first release entitled *Rite of Passage* in 2000. On the track entitled "The Preacher" (2009a) off of the album *Us*, he spits: "me, I'm an artist all a y'all are acts." Brother Ali metaphorically describes his passion and commitment to hip-hop as "bleeding on the track." While other acts may be concerned with creating an image and style that appeals to the masses, Brother Ali and the Rhymesayers label advocate for quality tracks with sociopolitical lyrics, which include critiques of white privilege, political agendas of Presidential candidates, and capitalism. The Rhymesayers collective distance themselves from the majors by creating an alternative culture embodied by the moniker: "for the love of hip-hop."

Indies also claim that they make music regardless of their financial success. They exhibit lyrics that demonstrate their passion and drive for creating hip-hop music despite long, arduous roads to commercial success (Avalon 2011). They cite limited economic and cultural support in comparison with major acts, which hinder their ability to garner economic success and cultural notoriety in the music industry. Despite this, they develop an alternative culture under the premise that they make hip-hop music as a means of making a living regardless of financial success and fame.

For instance, rap duo People Under the Stairs have written of their struggles to obtain financial stability and success through rapping. People Under the Stairs, consisting of members Thes One and Double K, have bounced around different indie companies until being signed to Om Records in 1999 to a four-album deal, and later to other small labels such as Basement Records, Gold Dust Media, and Thes One's own label PieceLock 70. In their track "Keepin' It Live" (2002b), they spit: "what you mean I ain't making no money off this hip-hop shit?" As seen by their movement through various labels, People Under the Stairs have maintained a strong desire to pursue their musical interests despite initially facing low profit margins. Underlying their music is the claim that they can achieve success through alternative avenues rather than adopting the culture and ideologies of the majors.

Similarly, Swollen Members has obtained mainstream success despite being labeled an alternative rap group. Under smaller companies Battle Axe and Suburban Noize, they have released nine studio albums as of 2014. Members Madchild and Prevail initially created their own label, Battle Axe Records, to release their debut album *Balance* and was met with critical acclaim, moderate record sales, and an eventual appearance on NBA Live's 2002 soundtrack. On "Long Way Down" (2002), a track on *Monsters in the Closet*, they reiterate that choosing to do hip-hop music requires that you love the music. They write from their own experiences when they created their own label to release their own brand of music, which required releasing four albums under a limited budget before being signed to a larger independent company entitled Suburban Noize. Their new indie label was founded under the idea that alternative suburban rap culture could be developed without the external pressures of large corporations.

Macklemore and Ryan Lewis are the most visible case of mainstream success by an independent rap duo (Greenburg 2013b). In 2012, they released the album entitled *The Heist* and achieved platinum status. In the song "Make the Money" (2012b), Macklemore writes: "if I'd done it for the money, I'd have been a fucking lawyer." The song focuses on their desire to change the hip-hop game rather than purely giving into the money and fame. On the chorus, they write that they have remained faithful to the indie circuit and stayed true to their intentions as artists despite the possibility of going broke (Smith 2012). They both understand the limited opportunities in hip-hop as only a few achieve financial success. Artists who have remained independent throughout their careers have reinforced the cultural moniker that they do hip-hop for the love of the music and in turn argue that financial and material success are secondary.

"Keeping It Real"

A second emergent theme is one of "keeping it real," or staying true to hip-hop and its roots, which can be traced back to the South Bronx in the 1970s. Hip-hop's origins have been represented in its pillars consisting of rapping, DJing, breakdancing, and graffiti. Its content was also focused primarily on the economic hardships of low-income minority communities in New York, which included problems of rampant gentrification, social hardships such as racial discrimination against

African-Americans and Latinos, and the prison industrial complex. In response to these hardships, hip-hop offered a wide array of social representation ranging from the creation of enclaves dedicated to hip-hop's subculture to social critiques aligned with the Civil Rights Movement, the Black Panthers, and the Young Lords (Alridge 2005; Au 2005; Chang 2005; Forman 2000; Morgan and Bennett 2011; Pough 2004; Stapleton 1998). Independent musicians of this genre have made the claim that the culture has moved away from these origins due to commodification and cooptation (Pough 2004; Rose 2008). This has led to a revival of keeping it real (Hodgman 2013) wherein artists stay true to the original message and essence of hip-hop culture and maintain a high quality product concordant with hip-hop's concept of authenticity.

Indies have expressed a desire to maintain the original message and essence of hip-hop culture. Concordant with their previous arguments of "doing it for the love," Rhymesayers' signees such as Aesop Rock and Atmosphere directly reference old school hip-hop community members who embody what the culture is supposed to be for them. Atmosphere writes in "Blamegame" (2002c) to "put your hand up if you remember the Juice Crew, they don't make em' like they used to." The Juice Crew was a collective in the 1980s founded by Marley Marl and Mr. Magic and included future stars such as Big Daddy Kane and Biz Markie. Atmosphere references the Juice Crew's ingenuity in the early hip-hop era before being dismantled by privatization and corporatization. Aesop Rock spits in "Coma" (2001b): "he was maverick enough but still scraped up, Taki 183 innovation for the kids." These lyrics reference graffiti artist Taki 183. In New York, his simple tag, "Taki 183," spawned many imitators who began mimicking his style throughout the boroughs. Tagging spread so quickly that it even received widespread media attention from the *New York Times* in 1971 (Kennedy 2011). Both Aesop Rock and Atmosphere reference the roots of hip-hop to emphasize the importance of maintaining its message of resistance to white mainstream culture. Yet Hodgman (2013) points out that white performers generally downplay the importance of race in their music and instead highlight class-based values and remaining "true to the game" in their construction of authenticity.

Underlying Atmosphere's argument of a respect for the game is the utilization of the term authentic. Brother Ali, a fellow member of the Rhymesayers label, writes on "Crown Jewel" (2009b) that "there's a certain type of glow that emanates, off the authentic that a fake could never imitate." Binary Star, a rap duo composed of One Be Lo and Senim Silla on Subterraneous Records, similarly writes on "Fellowship" (2000f) that ultimately "if you're hungry for some real hip hop, we came to feed you." For these artists, authenticity resembles the claim that they produce real hip-hop for their fans concordant with the urban, working-class landscapes of its origins (Ogbar 2007: 39). Asante (2008) reiterates these sentiments by claiming that authentic acts portray African-Americans and other disenfranchised racial groups as diverse social actors capable of innovation and culture, rather than monoliths of violence and misogyny.

Finally, the concept of authenticity is maintained by putting out a quality product that engages in an honest and open dialogue with listeners about their thoughts and life experiences to demonstrate that hip-hop has not been censored and diluted by mainstream artists and major record labels (Asante 2008). Rap duo Binary Star writes in "Reality Check" (2000g) to "never sell (his) soul is (his) philosophy" and that "honestly, (his) number one policy is quality." Rapsody, a female rapper signed under 9th Wonder's It's A Wonderful World Music Group (IWWMG), similarly raps in "Believe Me" (2012c) that IWWMG puts out quality music despite making significantly less money than major acts. She cites 9th Wonder's achieved critical acclaim for quality music production and frequent music collaborations with successful hip-hop acts (BET 2015).

The term authenticity represents a claim that artists have kept the culture alive by keeping it real despite the corporatization of the business. Previous literature (Rose 2008) questions if hip-hop has died due to over-saturation in the market by mainstream companies and acts. As Rhymesayer's Aesop Rock argues in "Save Yourself" (2001c): "promise me you gon' (...) recognize, what you holdin ain't really broken?" Blue Scholars adds in "Southside Survival" (2005) that contrary to the popular saying that hip-hop is dead, they argue that it is not broken but that it continues to thrive. It has just moved to the indie scene where many acts believe they have remained true to its history, paid respects to its origins, and maintained a high level of quality similar to its predecessors. Ultimately, conceptions of authenticity in indie hip-hop are socially constructed by artists (and fans) though signifiers (McLeod 1999) such as doing it for the love of the music and keeping it real (Hodgman 2013).

Conclusion

This chapter explicates the cultural claims independent hip-hop artists in the post-golden era make regarding class relations within the music industry and within broader class relations in the USA. First, indie musicians' lyrics present messages of resistance against the majors. In particular, they criticize: (1) mainstream artists, (2) large radio stations, and (3) major record labels. Second, their messages reject large corporations in mainstream culture in favor of smaller companies and niche subcultures. Finally, results indicate that indie culture is often predicated upon alternative cultural ideals of music production such as doing it for the love of the music and honoring hip-hop's origins. My findings uncover messages of a distinct subculture predicated upon the rejection of mainstream society and the formation of an underground movement.

References

Aesop Rock. 2001a. "Labor." *Labor Days*. Definitive Jux.
Aesop Rock. 2001b. "Coma." *Labor Days*. Definitive Jux.
Aesop Rock. 2001c. "Save Yourself." *Labor Days*. Definitive Jux.
Akom, Antwi. 2009. "Critical Hip Hop Pedagogy as a Form of Liberatory Praxis." *Equity & Excellence in Education* 42 (1): 52–66.
Alridge, Derrick. 2005. "From Civil Rights to Hip Hop: Toward a Nexus of Ideas." *The Journal of African American History* 90 (3): 226–252.
Asante, Molefi Kete. 2008. *It's Bigger Than Hip Hop: The Rise of the Post-Hip-Hop Generation*. New York: St. Martin's Press.
Atmosphere. 2002a. "One of a Kind." *God Loves Ugly*. Rhymesayers/Fat Beats.
Atmosphere. 2002b. "Give Me." *God Loves Ugly*. Rhymesayers/Fat Beats.
Atmosphere. 2002c. "Blamegame." *God Loves Ugly*. Rhymesayers/Fat Beats.
Au, Wayne. 2005. "Fresh Out of School: Rap Music's Discursive Battle with Education." *The Journal of Negro Education* 74 (3): 210–220.
Avalon, Moses. 2011. "What Are the Vegas Odds of Success on Today's Major Label Record Deals?" Retrieved April 15, 2016. www.mosesavalon.com/what-are-the-vegas-odds-of-success-on-todays-major-label-record-deal/.
Ball, Jared. 2009. "FreeMix Radio: The Original Mixtape Radio Show: A Case Study in Mixtape 'Radio' and Emancipatory Journalism." *Journal of Black Studies* 39 (4): 614–634.
Berger, David, and Richard Peterson. 1975. "Cycles in Symbol Production: The Case of Popular Music." *American Sociological Review* 40: 158–173.
BET. 2015. "10 Things You Should Know About Rapsody." Retrieved April 15, 2016. http://www.bet.com/music/photos/2015/03/10-things-you-should-know-about-rapsody.html.

Binary Star. 2000a. "Masters of the Universe." *Masters of the Universe*. Subterraneous Records.
Binary Star. 2000b. "Honest Expression." *Masters of the Universe*. Subterraneous Records.
Binary Star. 2000c. "Binary Shuffle." *Masters of the Universe*. Subterraneous Records.
Binary Star. 2000d. "Indy 500." *Masters of the Universe*. Subterraneous Records.
Binary Star. 2000e. "Conquistadors." *Masters of the Universe*. Subterraneous Records.
Binary Star. 2000f. "Fellowship." *Masters of the Universe*. Subterraneous Records.
Binary Star. 2000g. "Reality Check." *Masters of the Universe*. Subterraneous Records.
Blackalicious. 2002. "Purest Love." *Blazing Arrow*. MCA Records.
Blu and Exile. 2007a. "Simply Amazin'." *Below the Heavens*. Sound in Color.
Blu and Exile. 2007b. "Soul Amazing." *Below the Heavens*. Sound in Color.
Blu and Exile. 2007c. "The Narrow Path." *Below the Heavens*. Sound in Color.
Blue Scholars. 2005. "Southside Survival." *The Long March*. Massline.
Brother Ali. 2009a. "The Preacher." *Us*. Rhymesayers Group.
Brother Ali. 2009b. "Crown Jewel." *Us*. Rhymesayers Group.
Bush, John. 2003. "Hieroglyphics: Full Circle AllMusic Review." Retrieved April 15, 2016. www.allmusic.com/album/full-circle-mw0000326859/awards.
Chang, Jeff. 2005. *Can't Stop Won't Stop: A History of Hip-Hop Generation*. New York: St. Martin's Press.
Dimitriadis, Greg. 2009. *Performing Identity/Performing Culture: Hip Hop as Text, Pedagogy, and Lived Practice*. New York: Peter Lang.
Drake, David. 2015. "If It Ain't About the Money: Does Hip-Hop Still Need Major Labels?" Retrieved April 15, 2016. www.complex.com/music/2015/01/hip-hop-major-labels-2015.
Ducker, Eric. 2014. "A Rational Conversation: The 20-Year-Old Album That's MF Doom's Missing Link." Retrieved April 15, 2016. www.npr.org/sections/therecord/2014/11/06/361216399/a-rational-conversation-the-20-year-old-album-thats-mf-dooms-missing-link.
Dyson, Michael Eric. 2010. *Know What I Mean: Reflections on Hip-Hop*. New York: Basic Civitas.
Ferris, Kerry. 2007. "The Sociology of Celebrity." *Sociological Compass* 1 (1): 371–384.
Forman, Murray. 2000. "Represent: Race, Place, and Space in Rap Music." *Popular Music* 19 (1): 65–90.
Greenburg, Zach O' Malley. 2013a. "Tech N9ne: Hip-Hop's Secret Mogul." Retrieved April 15, 2016. www.forbes.com/sites/zackomalleygreenburg/2013/09/24/tech-n9ne-hip-hops-secret-mogul/.

Greenburg, Zach O' Malley. 2013b. "Macklemore: The Biggest Grammy-Nominated, Platinum-Selling Paradox in Music." Retrieved April 15, 2016. http://www.forbes.com/sites/zackomalleygreenburg/2013/12/16/macklemore-the-biggest-grammy-nominated-platinum-selling-paradox-in-music/#32b7305aabe4.

Hard Knock TV. 2013. "Immortal Technique and Tech N9ne Talk Independent Movement, Technology, Black + Brown." Retrieved April 15, 2016. www.youtube.com/watch?v=xzR4yDUUgO8.

Harkness, Geoff. 2012. "True School: Situational Authenticity in Chicago's Hip-Hop Underground." *Cultural Sociology* 6 (3): 283–298.

Harrison, Anthony Kwame. 2006. "Cheaper Than a CD, Plus We Really Mean It: Bay Area Underground Hip Hop Tapes as Subcultural Artefacts." *Popular Music* 25: 283–301.

Hesmondhalgh, David. 1999. "Indie: The Institutional Politics and Aesthetics of a Popular Music Genre." *Cultural Studies* 13 (1): 34–61.

Hess, Mickey. 2005. "Metal Faces, Rap Masks: Identity and Resistance in Hip-Hop's Persona Artist." *Popular Music and Society* 28 (3): 297–311.

Hibbett, Ryan. 2005. "What Is Indie Rock?" *Popular Music and Society* 28 (1): 55–77.

Hieroglyphics. 2003a. "Let It Roll." *Full Circle*. Hieroglyphics Imperium Recordings.

Hieroglyphics. 2003b. "Prelude." *Full Circle*. Hieroglyphics Imperium Recordings.

Hieroglyphics. 2003c. "Powers That Be." *Full Circle*. Hieroglyphics Imperium Recordings.

Hill, Marc Lamont. 2009. *Beats, Rhymes, and Classroom Life: Hip-Hop Pedagogy and the Politics of Identity*. New York: Teachers College Press.

Hodgman, Matthew. 2013. "Class, Race, Credibility, and Authenticity Within the Hip-Hop Music Genre." *Journal of Sociological Research* 4 (2): 402–413.

Immortal Technique. 2003a. "One Remix." *Revolutionary Vol. 2*. Viper Records.

Immortal Technique. 2003b. "Industrial Revolution." *Revolutionary Vol. 2*. Viper Records.

Immortal Technique. 2003c. "The Message and the Money." *Revolutionary Vol. 2*. Viper Records.

Immortal Technique. 2003d. "Freedom of Speech." *Revolutionary Vol. 2*. Viper Records.

Johnson, Christopher. 2008. "Danceable Capitalism: Hip-Hop's Link to Corporate Space." *The Journal of Pan African Studies* 2 (4): 80–92.

Jones, Steve. 2002. "Music That Moves: Popular Music, Distribution and Network Technologies." *Cultural Studies* 16 (2): 213–232.

Kennedy, Randy. 2011. "Celebrating Forefather of Graffiti." Retrieved April 15, 2016. www.nytimes.com/2011/07/23/arts/design/early-graffiti-artist-taki-183-still-lives.html?_r=0.

KRS-ONE. 2007. "Nothing New." *Hip-Hop Lives*. Koch Records.
Leard, Diane, and Brett Lashua. 2006. "Popular Media, Critical Pedagogy, and Inner City Youth." *Canadian Journal of Education* 29 (1): 244–264.
Lindvall, Helienne. 2010. "Behind the Music: When Artists Are Held Hostage by Labels." Retrieved January 1, 2018. https://www.theguardian.com/music/musicblog/2010/apr/15/artists-held-hostage-labels.
Macklemore and Ryan Lewis. 2012a. "Jimmy Iovine." *The Heist*. Macklemore LLC-ADA.
Macklemore and Ryan Lewis. 2012b. "Make the Money." *The Heist*. Macklemore LLC-ADA.
Maher, George Ciccariello. 2005. "Brechtian Hip-Hop: Didactics and Self-Production in Post-Gangsta Political Mixtapes." *Journal of Black Studies* 26 (1): 129–160.
Maher, George Ciccariello. 2007. "A Critique of DuBoisian Reason: Kanye West and the Fruitfulness of Double Consciousness." *Journal of Black Studies* 39 (3): 371–401.
McLeod, Kembrew. 1999. "Authenticity Within Hip-Hop and Other Cultures Threatened with Assimilation." *Journal of Communication* 49 (4): 134–150.
MF DOOM. 2009. "Gazillion Ear." *Born Like This*. Lex.
Michaels, Sean. 2010. "Outkast's Record Label Blocks Big Boi and Andre 3000 Collaboration." Retrieved January 1, 2018. https://www.theguardian.com/music/2010/jun/09/outkast-big-boi-andre-3000.
Mills, Brad. 2000. "Binary Star: Masters of the Universe, AllMusic Review." Retrieved April 15, 2016. www.allmusic.com/album/masters-of-the-universe-mw0000106803.
Moore, Ryan. 2007. "Friends Don't Let Friends Listen to Corporate Rock: Punk as a Field of Production." *Journal of Contemporary Ethnography* 36 (4): 438–474.
Morgan, Marcyliena, and Dionne Bennett. 2011. "Hip-Hop & the Global Imprint of a Black Cultural Form." *Dædalus: The Journal of the American Academy of Arts & Sciences* 140 (2): 176–196.
Myer, Letrez, and Christine Kleck. 2007. "From Independent to Corporate: A Political Economic Analysis of Rap Billboard Toppers." *Popular Music and Society* 30 (2): 137–148.
The NE Hip-Hop. 2013. "Immortal Technique on Being Independent." Retrieved April 15, 2016. www.youtube.com/watch?v=gRrlBwOBRJA.
Newman, Michael. 2005. "Rap as Literacy: A Genre Analysis of Hip-Hop Cyphers." *Text* 25 (3): 399–436.
Ogbar, Jeffrey. 2007. *Hip-Hop Revolution: The Culture and Politics of Rap*. Lawrence: University Press of Kansas.

Ostrow, Jonathan. 2010. "Indie vs. Major: Which Record Label Contract Is Right for You?" Retrieved April 15, 2016. www.musicthinktank.com/mtt-open/indie-vs-major-which-record-label-contract-is-right-for-you.html.

People Under the Stairs. 2002a. "Acid Raindrops." *OST*. Om Records.

People Under the Stairs. 2002b. "Keepin' It Live." *OST*. Om Records.

Perry, Imani. 2004. *Prophets of the Hood: Politics and Poetics in Hip Hop*. Durham, NC: Duke University Press.

Platon, Adelle. 2017. "Chance the Rapper Talks Fatherhood, Dealing with Anxiety, Record Labels & Possibly Selling His Next Album." Retrieved January 1, 2018. https://www.billboard.com/biz/articles/7720954/chance-the-rapper-talks-fatherhood-dealing-with-anxiety-record-labels-possibly.

Potter, Russell. 1995. *Spectacular Vernaculars: Hip-Hop and the Politics of Postmodernism*. Albany: State University of New York Press.

Pough, Gwendolyn. 2004. *Check It While I Wreck It: Black Womanhood, Hip-Hop Culture, and the Public Sphere*. New Hampshire: Northeastern University Press.

Rapsody. 2012a. "Kind of Love." *The Idea of Beautiful*. Jamla.

Rapsody. 2012b. "The Cards." *The Idea of Beautiful*. Jamla.

Rapsody. 2012c. "Believe Me." *The Idea of Beautiful*. Jamla.

Rose, Tricia. 2008. *The Hip Hop Wars: What We Talk About When We Talk About Hip Hop—And Why It Matters*. New York: Basic Civitas.

Smith, Clyde. 2012. "The Heist: Macklemore & Ryan Lewis Take DIY Route to iTunes #1." Retrieved April 15, 2016. http://www.hypebot.com/hypebot/2012/10/the-heist-macklemore-ryan-lewis-take-diy-route-to-itunes-1.html.

Stapleton, Katina. 1998. "From the Margins to Mainstream: The Political Power of Hip-Hop." *Media, Culture & Society* 20: 219–234.

Steiner, B. J. 2014. "Rap Albums That Got Shelved into Oblivion." Retrieved January 1, 2018. http://www.complex.com/music/2014/11/rap-albums-that-never-came-out/.

Swollen Members. 2002. "Long Way Down." *Monsters in the Closet*. Battle Axe.

Taylor, Carl, and Virgil Taylor. 2007. "Hip-Hop Is Now: An Evolving Youth Culture." *Reclaiming Children and Youth* 15 (4): 210–213.

Tech N9ne. 2008a. "Like Yeah." *Killer*. Strange Music.

Tucker, Nichole. 2015. "Tech N9ne Tells the Breakfast Club He 'Will Never Go Mainstream.' Here's Why." Retrieved April 15, 2016. www.inquisitr.com/1991886/tech-n9ne-says-real-music-is-supposed-to-spread-and-shine-but-he-will-never-go-mainsream-heres-why/.

Vito, Christopher. 2015. "Who Said Hip-Hop Was Dead?: The Politics of Hip-Hop Culture in Immortal Technique's Lyrics." *International Journal of Cultural Studies* 18 (4): 395–411.

Watkins, S. Craig. 2005. *Hip Hop Matters: Politics, Pop Culture, and the Struggle for the Soul of a Movement*. Boston, MA: Beacon Press.

Wells-Wilbon, Rhonda, Nigel Jackson, and Jerome Schiele. 2010. "Lessons from the Maafa: Rethinking the Legacy of Slain Hip-Hop Icon Tupac Amaru Shakur." *Journal of Black Studies* 40 (4): 504–526.

Zafar, Aylin. 2013. "What It's Like When a Label Won't Release Your Album." Retrieved January 1, 2018. https://www.buzzfeed.com/azafar/what-happens-when-your-favorite-artist-is-legally-unable-to?utm_term=.ux0Ew82pe#.guldxWo63.

Open Access This chapter is distributed under the terms of the Creative Commons Attribution 4.0 International License (http://creativecommons.org/licenses/by/4.0/), which permits use, duplication, adaptation, distribution and reproduction in any medium or format, as long as you give appropriate credit to the original author(s) and the source, a link is provided to the Creative Commons license and any changes made are indicated.The images or other third party material in this chapter are included in the work's Creative Commons license, unless indicated otherwise in the credit line; if such material is not included in the work's Creative Commons license and the respective action is not permitted by statutory regulation, users will need to obtain permission from the license holder to duplicate, adapt or reproduce the material.

CHAPTER 3

Just Say No to 360s: Hip-Hop's Claim of Economic Exploitation

Abstract This chapter focuses on how independent hip-hop artists in the post-golden era resist economic exploitation from mainstream culture and major corporations. Indie musicians make the grievance that major labels benefit at the expense of performers and hence are highly exploitative. Their unfair treatment is predominantly reflected in the contracts acts sign with major labels. This has repercussions for artists in numerous facets of the music industry: (1) advances/forwards, (2) control of copyrights, (3) artistic direction and relations with A&R, (4) touring, merchandising, and advertising deals, and (5) radio stations, media, and press. Finally, some hip-hop artists make the claim that creating and maintaining independent record labels helps mitigate economic exploitation, controls record label oversight, and serves for the betterment of the hip-hop community.

Keywords Economic exploitation · Corporatization · 360 degree contracts · Advances and forwards · Artist and relations (A&R)

Forbes magazine reported that Strange Music's Tech N9ne made an estimated 7.5 million dollars in 2012, which was more than mainstream artists 50 Cent, Mac Miller, and Rick Ross (Greenburg 2013). They wrote that Tech N9ne attributes a large part of his success to building a strong fan base without the help of a major record label. His business model, which includes a deal with Isolation Network's independent distribution company Fontana, ultimately produces high-profit margins with relatively low cost; as noted in "Crybaby" (2008). Tech N9ne's success has traditionally been seen as an exception to the case, as indie labels have traditionally owned only 10–15% of the market share (Day 2011). Yet recent studies have shown that this number is steadily increasing as independents now make up as much as 30% of the market share (Moore 2013).

In addition to asserting cultural differences from major record labels (see Chapter 2), independent hip-hop artists of this genre from 2000 to 2013 also resist economic exploitation from them in various ways. Indie musicians claim that the majors profit at the expense of performers and hence are highly exploitative, which is reflected in the contracts acts sign with large corporations. This exploitation has repercussions for artists in numerous facets of the music industry: (1) advances/forwards, (2) corporate control of copyrights, (3) control of the artistic direction and relations with the Artist and Repertoire Department (A&R), (4) touring, merchandising, and advertising deals, and (5) radio stations, media, and press. Finally, some musicians argue that creating and maintaining independent record labels helps mitigate economic exploitation, controls record label oversight, and better serves the hip-hop community.

THE "TAKEOVER" PART I: INDEPENDENT ARTISTS CLAIM EXPLOITATION BY THE MAJORS

Independent hip-hop artists in the post-golden era bring attention to the persistent problem of economic exploitation by major record labels. They point to the corporatization of hip-hop culture as highly exploitative. Also, they claim that record contracts, which include artist development deals and 360 degree contracts (also known as multiple rights deals), generally favor large corporations and take advantage of the musician.

The Beginnings: Major Labels Corporatize Hip-Hop and Its Music

From 1979 to its pinnacle golden era in the mid-1990s, hip-hop experienced a meteoric rise to popularity. Johnson (2008) believes that the golden era was filled with lyrical mastery, innovation in beat production, diversity in style and content, and a push toward popular media. Within this shift, large corporations were able to corporatize hip-hop music into a commodity sold in the mainstream market. The culture then saw a shift toward homogenization in musical content and cultural influences as it became predominantly consumed by whites in American culture (Myer and Kleck 2007; Rose 2008).

Subsequently, hip-hop saw a decline in one hit wonders as companies invested in musicians and albums that conformed to a standardized model of music production to ensure their investments were secure and profits were maximized (Myer and Kleck 2007). Much of their risk was mitigated by buying out smaller labels that already created a profitable business model. For example, Bad Boy Records, which housed powerhouse signees such as the Notorious B.I.G., Ma$e, Puff Daddy, and the LOX, was bought out by Sony BMG once they obtained enough capital and parity to contend for record sales with larger corporations. Sony BMG was eventually able to increase their profit margins by financially backing a credible brand name such as Bad Boy. With this corporatization, musicians began to lose control of their copyright ownership as record contracts transferred the ownership of rights to sell and promote music from the artist to the label (Rose 2008). In the post-golden era, hip-hop saw its music being concentrated in the hands of the few, mostly elite white men, that held positions of power in the entertainment industry (Chang 2005; George 2005; Myer and Kleck 2007).

Indies also complain that the majors act as venture capitalists that provide them with up-front capital in exchange for the opportunity to exploit their music and culture for monetary gain. They assert that corporations do not put their interests first, but rather are concerned with profit, growth, stability, and brand name recognition. Macklemore LLC's Macklemore and Ryan Lewis write of their experiences with companies attempting to corporatize their music. In "Jimmy Iovine" (2012a), they recall that on the verge of signing a contract, they "felt a cold hand grab on the back of my neck." Their song depicts the importance of Jimmy Iovine, co-founder of Interscope Records, in bringing hip-hop to the mainstream. Iovine has been credited with signing Tupac Shakur and financially backingDeath Row Records, signing multiplatinum acts such as Dr. Dre and Eminem, and co-launching the successful headphone brand "Beats by Dre" (Fricke 2012). They write that those higher up on the corporate ladder, such as Jimmy Iovine, lure musicians onto their label with the promise of success without revealing their desire to exploit their music to maximize profits. They believe that companies dupe acts into believing they are concerned for their well-being when in reality Macklemore and Ryan Lewis describe it as a cold and unscrupulous place ripe with failure for many who get signed.

Musicians who do align themselves with large corporations find it difficult to obtain a profit due to exploitation from the label. Jamla Records' Rapsody writes in "Believe Me" (2012a) that the industry is an organizational structure with the few powerful elite maintaining control of the industry, while many artists at the bottom struggle to gain their attention. She believes that this structure hurts musicians as they sell their music to corporations who are not concerned with their success but rather with the bottom dollar. Subterraneous' duo Binary Star rap in "Indy 500" (2000a) that "if you ever finish first a platinum trophy is risen, your prize money? ...your staff of two dozen got dibs in." They contend that corporations, which have a traditional organizational format and large bureaucratic structure, require that management and staff receive a cut of the profit before the performers get paid. Ironically, those in power are put in a position to make financial gains despite not creating the music themselves. This leads many acts to claim that the music industry is highly detrimental for them.

Major Label Contracts: A Site of Economic Exploitation

While there is much debate as to the status of artists as independent contractor or employee (Goldstein 2013), the onus is nonetheless put on the signee to fulfill their contractual agreements in exchange for a payment set by the employer. Thus, this section will discuss two prominent contracts record companies offer: Artist Development contracts and 360 degree contracts. Indies have viewed these deals as highly exploitative for the signee, as the contracts take advantage of musicians by utilizing their music for the purpose of maintaining long-term profits for the company.

Artist Development Contracts

An estimated 43,000 demos are sent to the three major record labels a year. Based on those demos, an estimated 500 record deals are offered per year. Of those 500 record deals, an estimated 100 albums are actually released from these new artists (Avalon 2011). In order to minimize risk and costs, "Artist Development" deals are often offered from music publishers and labels in place of standard record deals. Traditional artist development deals occur when an unsigned act creates a contractual agreement with a music publisher to license songs for them. The main job of the music publisher is to help them get signed to a label in exchange for a percentage of their future profits.

Similarly, major record companies also offer artist development deals to musicians directly in hopes that they can get in the green from future profits. They often lure acts into these contracts with the promise of financial backing from the company, for example, to fund equipment purchases (Brabec and Brabec 2007). In addition, they are promised that the label will take control of management and publishing to aid them in their career. The long-term goal of artist development deals for labels is to develop the act (Stahl and Meier 2012), and if they become successful to have first rights to eventually sign a long-term deal with said act.

Viper Records' Immortal Technique argues that these AD deals are not beneficial. Instead, they act as a short-term contract with little benefit to the signee. He raps in "Obnoxious" (2003d), "I take a piss on a development deal from Sony, or Def Jam, cause you like all of the rest, man." He raps that AD contracts are highly exploitative on numerous fronts. These deals usually require an investment up front from the signee. For example, half of the fee for creating a demo is usually paid up front while other half is contingent upon completion. Also, they may be forced to record their demo with in-house producers at the label's studio. Upon completion, the company usually holds option clauses, or the ability to negotiate for a full contract, discontinue relations, or match any offer from another label.

These types of deals put the onus on signees to create a product concordant with the company's values. Conversely, the company spends very little capital in comparison to their potential long-term reward. If the musician becomes successful, they are able to recoup their profits and potentially keep them on their label. If the artist is not successful, the record company is noncommittal and incurs little risk and cost.

360 Degree Contracts
Large record companies have traditionally made earnings from selling physical copies of music in the form of compact discs. After hip-hop's boom in the late 1990s, the music industry took a sharp turn toward the

digital age in the early 2000s (Karubian 2009). The digital age exponentially increased the salience of digital downloads and direct distribution models via online Web sites. First, the creation of online programs such as Napster and Kazaa created illegal P2P (person to person) music file sharing which promoted easier access to digital content. Also, easy access to Torrent Web sites such as Torrentz and The Pirate Bay have allowed for illegal music downloading online. Second, Apple's iTunes also provided access to legal digital downloads. Third, streaming music formats such as Pandora and Spotify allowed users to pay a monthly fee to access a large library of music. Finally, direct distribution models were utilized by artists to directly sell their music via online Web sites. Companies such as TuneCore (Byrd 2014) and CD Baby eliminated the need for a record label by selling music online direct to consumer. Many corporations faced lost profits due to the decline in CD sales and the proliferation of online distribution (Ostrove 2014). By 2014, the RIAA reported that music sales declined approximately 65% since its high point in 1999 (Resnikoff 2014). Yet, companies have currently adapted to the changes in the industry by reasserting control over online sales.

An immediate response to the destabilization of the music industry by the spur of the digital era was the formation of 360 degree contracts, also known as multiple rights contracts. These contracts allow record companies to extract profits from various aspects of the signees' revenue stream to account for the downturn in record sales in the digital era, which was generally not part of traditional recording deals. These aspects can include any facet of their career, hence the term 360 degrees, such as merchandising, touring, and commercial endorsements. They first appeared in an early form in 2002 with Robbie Williams' deal with EMI (Marshall 2013; Stahl and Meier 2012). Other acts such as the Pussycat Dolls, Paramore, Madonna, and Lady Gaga have subsequently signed 360 degree deals (Arts Law Centre of Australia 2008). As Day (2011) indicates, these contracts have become standard practice in the music industry. By 2010, over half of Warner Music Group's acts were signed to 360 deals (Ostrove 2014).

Indies claim that 360 degree contracts have been highly detrimental to artists' careers. They argue that these contracts are highly exploitative and limit the economic profits one can make. Subterraneous' rap duo Binary Star writes in "New Hip-Hop" (2000b) that "labels need to chill with they Clark Gable deals." Clark

Gable, an American actor signed to MGM, was once dubbed the "King of Hollywood" after his performance in *Gone with the Wind* (Lifetime 2016). Binary Star refers to the idea that companies profit from actors', such as Clark Gable, popularity and success. Within hip-hop, this has become more salient as record companies obtain their profit by extracting profits from every aspect of the musicians' careers.

Traditionally artists and labels shared equitable arrangements that benefitted both parties. For example, the label would agree to inherit the costs of the artist (which could include personal expenses, recording costs, promotion and marketing, video production, and promotional touring) in exchange for a percentage of their copyrights (rights to ownership of their music) in perpetuity. Once the musician repays the label for these expenses, both parties would share in future net profits. With most of the profits being earned from record sales, signees would willingly agree to allow companies to obtain a large percentage, for example, 85–90%, of net profits while they would take what was left, for example, 10–15% (Day 2010; Marshall 2013). They would willingly engage in these circumstances because they did not make a majority of their profits from record sales. Most of their revenue streams came from netting a large percentage of cash from touring, merchandise, and advertising deals.

With the rise of 360 degree deals, indies argue that these contracts further exploit the musician and ultimately make them disposable if they do not create profits for the corporation. Rhymesayers Atmosphere raps in "One of a Kind" (2002): "I still say fuck a major label till it limps, put your deal up our table and we'll show you who's the pimp." Sound in Color's Blu and Exile write in "I am" (2007b) that turning over all rights to the record label makes artists "the next generation of slaves." Referencing De La Soul's "I Am I Be," Blu and Exile question how they can make profits, or "papes," for the label while still being unable to pay their rent. Like Atmosphere, they understand that record companies are not concerned with their well-being and will go at lengths to maximize their profits.

In order to adapt to the changes in the market large corporations altered music contracts to dip into alternative streams of revenue to account for lost profits in royalties through record sales. These 360 degree contracts hand over to the company corporate control of all aspects of the signee. This includes profits not only from royalties of record sales, but touring, merchandise, advertising and endorsement deals. Indies have responded by arguing that these deals are highly exploitative and objectifying as the labels now control every aspect of their career. They thus have the burden to be successful in all facets of the music industry just to make scant profits compared to their labels.

THE "TAKEOVER" PART II: HOW MAJOR RECORD LABELS REACHED EVERY CORNER OF THE INDUSTRY

Economic exploitation by the majors is not merely reflected in the contractual agreements between artist and label. The corporatization and changing nature of contracts permeates into all aspects of the industry. In the following sections, I will demonstrate how indies from 2000 to 2013 have made this argument in five facets: (1) advances and forwards, (2) copyright control, (3) artistic direction and relations with A&R, (4) touring, merchandise, and advertising deals, and (5) radio/media and press. I discuss each of these in turn.

Advances and Forwards

Less than 5% of artists that sign with a major label will ever make a profit (Avalon 2011). Record companies understand this risk and thus 360 degree contracts offer financial support to maximize a musician's potential for success. One way labels provide assistance to performers is through advances or forwards in the form of a loan to help them create, distribute, and promote their music. This includes providing capital for music production, packaging, distribution, music video production, marketing, and repertoire. They also pay the musician a salary up front in exchange for their services. For instance, a company may spend up to 1 million dollars on various expenses as Table 3.1 illustrates (IFPI 2016).

A popular technique for many companies is to give forwards and loans to unsigned or independent acts that have generated enough buzz in the industry and have shown a proof of concept for their music. Major labels capitalize on this by providing them with cash flow to fund their music and even pay them a substantial fee up front, leading many acts to be enticed by large lump sums of money that make them feel they have "made it."

Table 3.1 Record label expenses

Record label expenses	Dollar amount
Personal artist expenses	$200,000
Recording costs	$200,000
Promotion and marketing	$300,000
Video production	$200,000
Promotional touring	$100,000
Total	$1,000,000

While the money that is fronted to them appears to be a sign of financial and commercial success, indies remain leery of this process. Rap collective Hieroglyphics states on "Make Your Move" (2003) that signing to a label like Jive may appear beneficial from the outset as they may receive $250,000 up front (Ostrow 2010). Many times artists will use part of this advance to purchase a home, car, jewelry, or other material goods. But as Macklemore LLC's duo Macklemore and Ryan Lewis reiterate through a mocking of "Jimmy Iovine" (2012a) himself, they write: "we'll give you a hundred thousand dollars, After your album comes out, We'll need back that money that you borrowed." Similar to Hieroglyphics, Macklemore and Ryan Lewis understand that the cash received is a loan that will have to be paid back to the company before incurring further profits. In addition, receiving an advance means that they are now controlled by the label and must adhere to any provisions outlined in the contract. Any violations of such provisions allow the corporation to null and terminate the contract all together, leaving many musicians to give up all future revenue to the company until the advance is repaid.

In many cases, musicians never see a profit but instead remain in debt during their careers. For example, Rapper "A" may make 10% of 500,000 CD purchases or downloads at $9.99. The total profit from sales is 5 million dollars, with the artist earning $500,000. But because the record label fronts the musician with 1 million dollars, which includes a $200,000 advance (see Table 3.1), they first recoup those expenses before the act nets a profit. The musician is still in debt to the record company for $500,000 and would still need to sell an additional 500,000 albums just to break even (Guidry 2014).

If these costs are eventually repaid, the label still owns a majority of the profits from record sales and also owns a percentage (anywhere from 5–50%) of alternative revenue streams due to 360 degree contracts (Day

2011). Their justification is that the music industry is risky and their investments must net a certain level of return. The 360 degree contracts have detrimental effects for the artist as they now have no viable means of profit unless they become commercially successful. In the instance that they do become successful, many do not see the amount of profits concurrent with their success. QN5's hip-hop trio Cunninlyngists spit on "Since When" (2006) that "a Maybach and a plaque, is that all you get?...shhhit." Indies understand that advances are alluring to acts as they give the perception of commercial and financial success, but in reality it will take a long time before performers themselves are paid for their labor.

Control of Copyright

A percentage of profits made from the use of music, in the form of royalties, is traditionally the main source of revenue for major record labels. Royalties are payments in perpetuity made to the owners of music whenever an album is purchased; a song is downloaded or streamed; reproduced by another artist; or performed or played in a public space (Ostrove 2014). Indies express the grievance that major labels' ownership of royalties hinders their ability to see profit in a timely manner. Major corporations offer royalties to musicians, around 10 to 15 points (or percent), off of Standard Retail List Price (SRLP) (Ostrow 2010). But because of advances/forwards taken by the artist, any royalties received will take place after the advance, which can include costs for packaging expenses, free goods, and marketing, is paid off. In many instances, musicians must sell between 100,000 and 500,000 units at Standard Retail List Price (SLRP) before they can get paid any royalties in perpetuity. But even after the advance is paid off, the record company still owns a royalty on all sales made thereafter. Sound in Color's Blu and Exile rap in "Simply Amazin'" (2007a): "it's like you tryn'a take custody of my sound?" As they describe, the record company still owns a royalty on their music, which hinders their long-term profit. Many indies view this stream of revenue as unfair, as acts without a large label can potentially become profitable without a lag time in seeing their share of royalties.

Viper Records Immortal Technique also describes the process in which artists lose in the current distribution of profits from royalties. He writes in "Industrial Revolution" (2003a) that "you're better off begging for twenty points from a label." Musicians who sign to mainstream labels negotiate points off of royalties from record sales. They may receive anywhere from 10 to 15 points on major label contracts, but must also split these percentages with songwriters, managers, and producers (Bylin 2010). This could potentially leave artists with 5–7 points after paying out their partners (Keif 2006). Thus, Immortal Technique points out they truly only see a very small portion of the profits made from their own music. Conversely, companies take about 20 points in royalties, with the rest of the points going to other branches such as marketing, free goods, and distribution/packaging. In total, around 60% of the profits from royalties are allocated directly to the company with an additional 25–30% being allocated toward distribution, which is also typically owned in-house (Cosper 2016). He continues to spit on "Industrial Revolution" (2003a), "now these parasites wanna percent of my ASCAP." On the track, Immortal Technique describes his rise to fame in the industry. Once he made a name for himself, he claims that labels again try to get in on his profits. For instance, labels also dip into a percentage of ASCAP-protected royalties. ASCAP (American Society of Composers, Artists, and Publishers) acts as a not-for-profit organization that protects copyrights when music is publicly performed or played (ASCAP 2016). In addition to taking a cut of royalties for units sold, corporations also control a portion of royalties, potentially 10–30% (Day 2011), from ASCAP whenever the song is performed or used. Indies essentially make the argument that giving up control of copyright is highly skewed toward long-term profit for the corporation and not the creators of the music.

Artistic Direction and Relations with A&R

When an act signs to a label, they also hand over partial control of their name to the company. Many indies make the claim that being signed to the majors enables the company to take control of the artistic direction and behavior of the musician. As often stipulated by their contract, they must get approval from management on their brand name, persona, and music created. As Subterraneous' rap duo Binary Star raps on "Indy 500" (2000a), "no suggestions on directions, they're controlling your wheel." The label also has significant influence on how musicians behave, which ranges from touring, interviews, radio, and television promotions, and advertising deals. Viper Records' Immortal Technique echoes these sentiments in the song "Freedom of Speech" (2003c), rapping that being "signed to the majors" is contingent on "switch[ing] up his politics and chang[ing] his behavior." On the track, he argues that companies are highly invested in their private and public image. Concurrently, acts signed to large companies see this as highly constrictive as they have to negotiate and navigate their own values and beliefs. This leads independents to be reluctant to sign with the majors because of the corporate oversight they face.

A major means of corporate control occurs in the album creation process. The artistic direction is predominantly controlled by the A&R (Artist and Repertoire) branch of the company. This branch is put in charge of finding new talent that is aligned with their ideals and brand. They also work on song selection, producer choice, recording studio selection, and the setup for the recording process (Negus 2002). Further, they act as a liaison between artist and label (Knab 2010). Indies rap about their hesitancy to trust A&R for three reasons. A&R is predominantly concerned with the success of album sales. Subterraneous rap duo Binary star spits on "New Hip-Hop" (2000b) "but you ain't, so stop and listen, platinum sales is not the mission." A&R helps to create an artist's musical content and thus are highly invested in the music creation process, even if it is at the expense of the message and creativity, which puts an undue pressure on musicians to conform to the record label's practices. Sound in Color's Blu and Exile write of their experiences of depression and stress from corporate oversight in "Dancing in the Rain" (2007c): "trying hard to be an artist, but my A&R be calling me out my zone into his office…I'm stressing to grip, cause it's hard to make music when this depression exists." The corporate oversight in the music creation process can be unnerving for Blu and Exile who make music for creative reasons. It can also lead to clashes between the artist and A&R, in which A&R often have the final say.

Homogenization also becomes more frequent as A&R can filter the music production process and make changes to the final cut of the album. Viper Records' Immortal Technique writes in "The Message and the Money" (2003b): "and to all these bitchass A&Rs…that keep recycling marketing schemes and imagery." He contends that artist creativity is stifled while interacting and negotiating with the upper management. This can temper an act's ability to create new and innovative music in favor of formulaic albums and marketing schemes, which was predominantly seen in the post-golden era.

Finally, A&R gets a financial cut of the act's revenues. In addition to paying the label for royalties, A&R gets a cut of the profits made from album sales. Subterraneous' Binary Star writes on "Indy 500" (2000a) that "you got a crew of two dozen plus an A&R," which means that they have to be paid first as well. In conjunction with poorly set up contracts by companies, Binary Star believes that the corporate oversight and lack of financial benefit make major record labels an unappealing avenue for success. Indies echo Immortal Technique's sentiments that corporate control by the label, and more specifically A&R, is objectifying and exploitative akin to colonization when he spits on "Industrial Revolution" (2003a) that: "A&R's tried jerking me thinking they call shots, offered me a deal and a blanket full of smallpox."

Touring, Merchandise, and Advertising Deals

With the proliferation of 360 degree contracts, major record labels are able to extract profits from alternative revenue streams (Day 2011). It has become so profitable that concert promoters, such as Live Nation, have even offered 360 deals to acts such as Madonna and Jay-Z. They emphasize touring, merchandising, social media, and endorsement deals, while outsourcing distribution to major labels (Marshall 2013). Indies have rapped about their displeasure with having profits being taken away from three means of cash flow that were traditionally seen as profitable: touring, merchandise, and advertising deals.

Musicians originally netted a large percentage of profits from touring, regardless of whether they are headlining and rake in a majority of the profits or are just opening to build a larger fan base. But getting gigs requieres maintaining relations with managers, promoters, other artists, and fans during the touring process. One arena of exploitation musicians always had to resist is from promoters and venues. Viper Records' Immortal Technique states in "The Message and the Money" (2003b) that promoters are "charging up to $10 at the door," and the artists see none of it. His lyrics represent the exploitation many face on tour as they are left to negotiate with numerous individuals out for profit on a nightly basis. Ostrove (2014) points out that promoters, venues, management, and booking can charge around 50% of the net profits from each show. In addition, performers under 360 degree contracts are left even more vulnerable as the record label takes a cut off the top of their show tours as well. Despite record label management playing a small role in the touring process, they are still able to take around 25–30% of profits made from touring (Gordon 2013).

Acts also face cuts in profit, anywhere from 20% to as much as 50% (Marshall 2013), from merchandise sales. They originally made revenue from selling clothing and other "merch" during shows through street teams. This was further exacerbated by online Web sites and social media, which gave musicians motivation to promote their brand name and increase direct sales. But Macklemore LLC's Macklemore and Ryan Lewis on "Jimmy Iovine" (2012a) write of the situations that many major artists face, getting only a third of "merch [sold] on the road," and "money [made] out doing shows," while the manager and booking agent each get "twenty and ten," leaving the artists with "7% (of the profits) to split."

Further, many 360 degree contracts stipulate that the record label makes a profit from any outside contracts made with other corporations. Usually, this is in the form of endorsement deals such as Pepsi or Coke, wherein artists might give up to 10–25% to the record label (Day 2011; Gordon 2013). Due to the company's stake in the musician, they also are keenly aware of their ideologies and actions when they sign endorsement deals. Viper Records' Immortal Technique writes on "Freedom of Speech" (2003c): "I ain't got no motherfuckin deal with Pepsi, no corporate sponsor telling me what to do, asking me to tone it down during the interview." Immortal Technique is directly referencing Ludacris' drop from Pepsi's advertising campaign. Ludacris acted as a spokesperson for Pepsi, but faced criticism from conservative host Bill O'Reilly (Oh 2002). Mainstream acts signed to major labels lose out on a cut of their alternative revenue streams and also face oversight from corporations who attempt to control their image, and subsequently are controlled in their financial fate. In essence, artists experience further exploitation as labels have dipped into profits of touring, merchandise, and advertising.

Radio/Media Outlets and Press

The practice of payola, or the payment of bribe by companies to be included in "regular airplay," has been banned in the USA (FCC 2015). For example, in 2005 Sony BMG was convicted of illegal payola practices and subsequently paid a 10 million dollar fine (Aldorfer 2005). The underlying logic is to prevent major corporations from obtaining a monopoly of the airwaves. Ideally, this allows for heterogeneity in the music played for the public and allows autonomy for the radio stations. Unfortunately, the practice of payola has long been circumvented by the use of independent promoters of the major record labels in the music industry to act as a "middle man" with radio stations. They hire the "indies" to represent them to different radio stations and media outlets, which in turn create profit for the radio stations accepting informal "kickbacks" from the promoters who pay for promoted airtime (Caves 2000). While technically illegal, major corporations can spend anywhere from $15,000 to $100,000 to get a single played and even $250,000 to push for a Top 40 play in the USA (Green 2015; Katunich 2002). Major corporations currently still spend millions of dollars a year promoting their roster on the radio.

The practice of payola acts as a double bind for musicians. It adversely affects mainstream artists as many of them use their advances to fund payola-like practices, which can equate to tens of thousands of USD to promote their singles. These costs for promotion are first recouped through royalties by the labels, which hinders their ability to make a profit and get in the green. Alternatively, this leaves independents economically marginalized as they compete with the vast amount of resources and capital that large labels possess. While technological advances have allowed performers to promote their works online without major support, the emergence of legal online Web sites such as iTunes as an alternative to hard copy CD sales has become increasingly valuable. But iTunes requires fees to sell and stream tracks online and thus favors those who can pay for this service (as mentioned in Jamla Rapsody's "Believe Me" [2012a]). She believes indies do not get love from the radio because they cannot afford payola-like practices to reach Top 40 radio station play. She also understands that iTunes is a venue that requires capital and thus is veered toward acts who possess financial backing similar to that of payola.

In addition, indies express the grievance that radio stations are becoming increasingly interconnected through the process of conglomeration. After the passing of the Telecommunications Act of 1996 by the FCC, the market faced deregulation under the premise that it would allow for increased competition, diversity, and localism. Within two years of its passing 4000 of the 11,000 radio stations changed hands into the conglomerate Clear Channel (Prindle 2003). By 2004 Clear Channel owned much of the radio station market, which included 1200 radio stations, 135 performing venues, 716,000 billboards, and 39 television stations. This made Clear Channel, now iHeartRadio, one of the largest corporations in the media industry (Figueroa et al. 2004). Prindle (2003) states that this has also led to greater homogeneity on the radio and acted as the "holy grail" for select artists to garner mass attention. Duck Down's Blue Scholars write in "The Long March" (2005): "clean the Clear Channel out your eardrums and throat." Independents such as Blue Scholars have made the economic grievance that Clear Channel owns much of the radio station market and can control what performers get played, thus leaving independent hip-hop musicians to find alternative means of getting airplay and acquiring concert venues.

Finally, media outlets such as XXL, Vibe, The Source, and Pitchfork create cosigns, or shout-outs and promos for artists' music, to create buzz and improve record sales. They also play a large role in providing information to fans, interviewing performers, and discussing current events and topics of debate (Harrison and Arthur 2011). This gives major press companies the ability to influence musicians' careers and futures. As Sound in Color's Blu and Exile rap on "My World Is" (2007d), "and you can only imagine how much passion that I put in this, but some magazines try to rate me on how good it is." On the track, Blu and Exile allude to the notion that they put creative and economic resources into their works, but are constantly under the microscope of magazines and other media outlets. This objectifies artists as they are merely viewed as vessels who create music to be consumed by the masses rather than musicians who are creative. Also, it is even more difficult for indies to overcome negative reviews because of lack of access to payola, marketing, and advertisements. Macklemore LLC's Macklemore and Ryan Lewis share similar sentiments on "Ten Thousand Hours" (2012b), stating "that the people decide to walk with him… regardless of Pitchfork, cosigns I've jumped." In this instance, he recollects how he was overlooked by Pitchfork and by many other media outlets who have not cosigned them. Ultimately, indies claim that major radio and media outlets are highly biased toward major record label success and marginalize many independent record labels and artists.

The Resistance:
An Age Old Story Made New for Hip-Hop

Like Tech N9ne, Macklemore LLC's Macklemore and Ryan Lewis have achieved critical acclaim for their independent success in the hip-hop industry. Their debut album, *The Heist*, was released in 2012 and reached number two on the Billboard 200 and eventually reached platinum status in 2014. Their album included notable hits such as "Can't Hold Us" featuring Ray Dalton, "Same Love" featuring Mary Lambert, and "Thrift Shop" featuring Wanz. The duo eventually earned 2014 Grammys for Best New Artist, Best Rap Album, and Best Rap Performance (iTunes 2016). Macklemore and Ryan Lewis have noted that they reached success through a small to medium size business model, which is characterized by independently owned record labels that operate with less than 500 employees in the USA (Smith 2012). But this alternative means to success is not a new phenomenon. Instead, the technological advancements and concordant shifts in the marketplace have created a new avenue for independent success despite resistance from large corporations. Indie hip-hop artists find that the small to medium size model can help mitigate economic exploitation and create a viable means of financial and commercial success with less corporate oversight and minimized economic exploitation from the majors.

The Cycle of the Indies

Perkins (1996) states that underground hip-hop flourished in the Bronx and upper Manhattan in 1979. But as it gained attention from the music industry, it faced rapid corporatization, objectification, and increased inclusion in mainstream culture. Subsequently, Forman (2000) notes that the formation of self-owned record labels has been a response to the formation of bogus 360 degree contracts, management conflicts, and poor economic relations between musicians and labels. The current landscape of the hip-hop community in the post-golden era has seen the rise of artists more familiar with the production and management side of the industry acting as entrepreneurs in the rap game.

But this dialectical struggle between major and independent labels is not new. Lopes (1992) recapitulates Berger and Peterson's notion that the music industry has periods of innovation and diversity followed by periods of homogenization. For example, in the 1920s and 1930s race-based indie companies existed in blues music. Similarly, indie brands such as MoTown and Stax emerged in the post-World War II era (Forman 2000). George (2005) finds independent black music has historically been used by corporate labels to drive popular music as they allow record labels to feel the "pulse" of the public. Once this occurs, large corporations utilize sophisticated modes of production and distribution to homogenize consumer tastes for a profit until a new proven commodity emerges.

More recently, 1970s punk music in the USA, the UK, and Australia created a push back toward growing multinational corporations with a DIY (do-it-yourself) approach to the music industry. They emphasized the democratization of music by allowing more artists to own "skin" in the business. Strachan (2007) points out that this DIY ethic is still used by UK indie labels that create a niche market adopting small-scale music production and critiquing global corporate media. In the early 1990s during the golden era, hip-hop utilized a similar approach with the formation of smaller labels such as Ruthless Records, Def Jam, and Tommy Boy (Forman 2000). As Negus (2002) notes, they can create that niche by being closer to their fan base and remaining close to the street, which allows them to stay up to date on the latest sounds, trends, fashions, and dances.

Rappers in the post-golden era have cited the constant presence of the indie movement in hip-hop since its corporatization. Koch Record's KRS-ONE spits on "Nothing New" (2007): "we won't be found man on Billboard or SoundScan, seek me, and you will find." KRS-ONE points to the constant demand of his music by listeners, despite not being recognized by large record sales and downloads. He reminds his audience that the independent movement has been alive and well since hip-hop's inception and can always be found if one looks beyond mainstream music.

In addition, artists have demonstrated their desire to reverse the commodification and corporatization of music production and distribution induced by the majors. Battle Axe Records' Swollen Members rap on the track "Act On It" (2002a): "that were cut, mastered, and released under Battle Axe…it's nice to know that I've been a part of something reversal." Swollen Members reiterate that the hip-hop community is consistently changing the economic landscape of the industry. In particular, they acknowledge these changes through their financial success despite being underrepresented in the market. They emphasize going against the grain by producing records in-house and developing a loyal fan base in the pre-Internet era. Their success has culminated in fomenting a relationship between labels Battle Axe and Suburban Noize Records to increase their brand name (Baller Status 2015). Yet indies pushing back against large corporations and creating an alternative culture is not a new phenomenon, but rather a cyclical one.

The Changing Nature of the Industry

While Lopes (1992) states that the music industry faces cycles of diversity and homogeneity, he adds that innovation in popular music depends on the system of development and production used by record companies. For example, labels may incorporate an open system of development while simultaneously maintaining control of the market. In the case of hip-hop, technological changes created the rise of DIY ethics, but continued exploitation through 360 degree contracts and further corporatization have kept major labels salient. Nonetheless, indie musicians and labels have resisted the majors' control by utilizing the changes in the industry to create successful independent business models.

In the late 1990s, independent and underground acts were able to make waves in the music industry with the explosion of the online marketplace. They were now able to circumvent the need for large labels and radio stations that have corporatized the music production process, including music videos, distribution, marketing, and networking (Karubian 2009; McLeod 2005). Leyshon (2001) notes that large corporations could not compete with p2p shares, online distributions, and online networking, which could all be done independently by musicians. Forbes magazine headliner, *Major Record Labels as Dinosaurs* (Busch 2012), illustrates how the growth of online music has led to a fragmentation in consumer tastes and a revival in niche indie music.

Strange Music's Tech N9ne and Viper Records' Immortal Technique (Hard Knock TV 2013) state that they originally gained notoriety via local and regional representation, which included street teams building their brand by handing out CDs and merchandise one by one at venues, record stores, and street corners (Forman 2000). But they both understand the changes in the industry and now utilize an online presence to maintain their success. As Ostrove (2014) notes, the days of street teams handing out CDs one by one were in the distant past, as self-release models were more accessible than ever before. For instance, former indie artist Mac Miller released four free online mixtapes between 2007 and 2010. He also toured frequently, posted free music via online music sites such as SoundCloud and DatPiff, and had a large presence through online media sites such as World Star and Twitter. By the time *Blue Slide Park* was released in 2011, Mac Miller had generated enough buzz to be commercially successful while remaining on Rostrum's indie label.

Indie artists have openly shown their support for an alternative economic model resistant to major label dependency. YONAS LLC's YONAS writes on "I Could" (2011): "I remember all the people, how they said I wouldn't make it, I just wanna show you that I'm here and I'ma take it." Battle Axe's Swollen Members refer to the "wonderful underworld" on "Breathe" (2002b), who are "tryin' to keep it independent in recruitable times." Swollen Members has stated that they willingly remain in the indie circuit despite being consistently recruited by large corporations. Similarly, Hieroglyphics Imperium's Hieroglyphics write in "Make Your Move" (2003): "starting up companies and keeping the product coming…we gotta get the dough!" Like YONAS and Swollen Members, they emphasize in their lyrics the ability to start indie labels and create an even playing field where they can actually make money and be financially successful without the support of the majors.

Macklemore LLC's Macklemore and Ryan Lewis, exemplars of financial and commercial success while remaining economically independent, highlight their long road to success on "Can't Hold Us" (2012c). On this track they acknowledge their indie status and the grind that they have put in to becoming successful, from working with a four-track audio recorder while traveling on the bus across the city. As Complex notes, Macklemore and Ryan Lewis were able to build a niche fan base using local and regional promotions and utilizing social media to their advantage (Drake 2015). Their success is also shown by their financial gains. On "Ten Thousand Hours" (2012b), they rap: "shit man I'm paying rent, about damn time that I got out of my basement." For Macklemore and Ryan Lewis, they write that this feeling of making money is a burden off of their shoulders after a long road to success. More importantly, many independent musicians like Macklemore and Ryan Lewis can make up to 50%, as opposed to 10%, off of album sales. This translates into high-profit margins once they repay their record labels despite lower album sales (Guidry 2014). They also usually own a high stake in the royalty game, usually earning between 40–75% compared to mainstream artists earning between 10–15%. They can even cut out the middleman in 360 degree contracts to earn high rates of return from marketing, promotions, and direct-to-fan activity (Gottfried 2016). In essence, indies have taken advantage of the changes in the music industry's landscape and some have obtained financial and commercial success without the backing of the majors.

The Resistance: An Economic and Political Message?

The material conditions underlying music creation and production can illicit political stances by artists as they navigate their careers (Ball 2009). For instance, indie mixtapes and radio stations can spread music outside corporate oversight and free from the filters of mainstream media. Similarly, the underground hip-hop scene can remove them from corporate infrastructure through self-production and performances (Harkness 2012). This separation from large corporations can help spur more critical political stances as they are aware of their self-production and thus can speak freely on their experiences and ideologies. For example, Maher (2005) critically analyzes Dead Prez, a hip-hop duo who has treaded independent waters, as they speak on their ghettocentric and Afrocentric experiences.

Indies alter the dynamics of the music industry as major record labels need to tighten control of their artists to increase their share of the market. This potentially creates a shared awareness among artists and listeners of their ability to resist economic exploitation and take a political stance against corporate America. Subterraneous' Binary Star spits in "Indy 500" (2000a) about the importance of "trying to keep this music to ourselves," rather than "selling out this art for some money." Binary Star understands their political resistance as they create a movement toward independent culture. They state that they refuse to sell out to the mainstream despite others who are willing to give up their culture to corporate America for money and fame. Jamla's Rapsody similarly writes in "Non-Fiction" (2012b) that: "the game is for the taking, this is history in the making." She envisions hip-hop as alive and well, with the game as strong as ever, which challenges popular sentiments that hip-hop is dead. Instead, she realizes that it can still be found in the underground. What remains to be seen is if the indie record labels can create unified grievances about the music industry that translate into social consciousness and social activism. Viper Records' Immortal Technique acknowledges on "The Message and the Money" (2003b) the sentiments of many musicians that independent hip-hop is an important "contribution to the business of hip-hop" and as a result "the more the industry will be forced to change."

CONCLUSION

This chapter examines how independent hip-hop artists in my study not only critique cultural domination by corporations, but resist and critique economic exploitation as well. They argue that major record labels shape the music industry to maximize their profits at the expense of the artists. More specifically, AD deals and 360 degree deals aim to exploit all facets of musicians' revenue stream. The exploitation occurs through the following avenues: (1) advances/forwards that artists have to repay, (2) expanded corporate control of copyrights for record companies, (3) control of artistic direction and relations by the Artist and Repertoire (A&R) Department of the label, (4) loss of profits from tours, merchandising, and advertising deals, and (5) the expanded control of radio stations, media, and press by major labels. Finally, acts choose to create and maintain indie music and take advantage of the technological changes, such as the rise of online music distribution and easier access to music production equipment, in the industry. They hope to attain financial stability while rejecting corporate oversight and control by major corporations. In turn, they have created a political and economic stance against exploitation in the music industry.

REFERENCES

Aldorfer, Melanie. 2005. "10 Million Payola Settlement." Retrieved April 15, 2016. http://www.cbsnews.com/news/10m-payola-settlement/.

Arts Law Centre of Australia. 2008. "360 Degree Record Deals." Retrieved April 15, 2016. www.artslaw.com/au/articles/entry/360-degree-record-deals/.

ASCAP. 2016. "About ASCAP." Retrieved April 15, 2016. http://www.ascap.com/about.

Atmosphere. 2002. "One of a Kind." *God Loves Ugly*. Rhymesayers/Fat Beats.

Avalon, Moses. 2011. "What Are the Vegas Odds of Success on Today's Major Label Record Deals?" Retrieved April 15, 2016. www.mosesavalon.com/what-are-the-vegas-odds-of-success-on-todays-major-label-record-deal/.

Ball, Jared. 2009. "FreeMix Radio: The Original Mixtape Radio Show: A Case Study in Mixtape 'Radio' and Emancipatory Journalism." *Journal of Black Studies* 39 (4): 614–634.

Baller Status. 2015. "Madchild Recalls Joining Rock Steady Crew, Swollen Members' Success." Retrieved April 15, 2016. http://www.ballerstatus.com/2015/06/13/madchild-recalls-joining-rock-steady-crew-swollen-members-success/.

Binary Star. 2000a. "Indy 500." *Masters of the Universe*. Subterraneous Records.

Binary Star. 2000b. "New Hip-Hop." *Masters of the Universe*. Subterraneous Records.

Blu and Exile. 2007a. "Simply Amazin'." *Below the Heavens*. Sound in Color.

Blu and Exile. 2007b. "I Am." *Below the Heavens*. Sound in Color.

Blu and Exile. 2007c. "Dancing in the Rain." *Below the Heavens*. Sound in Color.
Blu and Exile. 2007d. "My World Is." *Below the Heavens*. Sound in Color.
Blue Scholars. 2005. "The Long March." *The Long March*. Massline.
Brabec, Todd, and Jeff Brabec. 2007. "Songwriter/Artist Development Deals." Retrieved April 15, 2016. www.ascap.com/Home/Music-Center/aritcles-advice/ascapcorner/corner4.aspx.
Busch, Richard. 2012. "Major Record Labels as Dinosaurs?" Retrieved April 15, 2016. www.forbes.com/sites/richardbusch/2012/03/27/major-record-labels-as-dinosaurs/.
Bylin, Kyle. 2010. "See How Much Indie Artists Make Vs. Label Artists." Retrieved April 15, 2016. www.hypebot.com/hypebot/2010/10/see-how-much-indie-artists-make-vs.label-artists.html.
Byrd, Ayana. 2014. "How TuneCore Is Making Record Labels Unnecessary." Retrieved April 15, 2016. www.fastcompany.com/3034888/innovation-agents/how-tunecore-is-making-record-labels-unncessary/.
Caves, Richard. 2000. *Creative Industries: Contracts Between Art and Commerce*. Cambridge, MA: Harvard University Press.
Chang, Jeff. 2005. *Can't Stop Won't Stop: A History of Hip-Hop Generation*. New York: St. Martin's Press.
Cosper, Alex. 2016. "How to Divide Percentages with a Record Label." Retrieved April 15, 2016. www.smallbusiness.chron.com/divide-percentages-record-label-39258.html.
Cunninlynguists. 2006. "Since When." *A Piece of Strange*. QN5/L.A. Underground.
Day, Brian. 2011. "In Defense of Copyright: Record Labels, Creativity, and the Future of Music." *Seton Hall Journal of Sports and Entertainment Law* 21 (1): 61–103.
Day, Wendy. 2010. "Warning: Hip-Hop Artists Need to Know About Today's 360 Record Deals." Retrieved April 15, 2016. www.hiphopandpolitics.com/2010/02/05/warning-hip-hop-artist-need-to-know-about-todays-360-record-deals/.
Drake, David. 2015. "If It Ain't About the Money: Does Hip-Hop Still Need Major Labels?" Retrieved April 15, 2016. www.complex.com/music/2015/01/hip-hop-major-labels-2015.
FCC. 2015. "The FCC Payola Rules." Retrieved April 15, 2016. https://www.fcc.gov/consumers/guides/fccs-payola-rules.
Figueroa, Maria, Damone Richardson, and Pam Whitefield. 2004. *The Clear Picture on Clear Channel Communications, Inc.: A Corporate Profile*, 1–78. Ithaca, NY: Cornell University, ILR School.
Forman, Murray. 2000. "Represent: Race, Place, and Space in Rap Music." *Popular Music* 19 (1): 65–90.

Fricke, David. 2012. "Jimmy Iovine: The Man with the Magic Ears." Retrieved April 15, 2016. http://www.rollingstone.com/music/news/jimmy-iovine-the-man-with-the-magic-ears-20120412.

George, Nelson. 2005. *Hip-Hop America*. New York: Viking.

Goldstein, Brian Taylor. 2013. "Independent Contractors or Employees: What's in a Name." Retrieved April 15, 2016. http://www.musicalamerica.com/mablogs/?p=10571.

Gordon, Steve. 2013. "How to Avoid Getting Completely Screwed by a 360 Deal…" Retrieved April 15, 2016. www.digitalmusicnews.com/2013/07/02/threesixty.

Gottfried, Gideon. 2016. "Everything Is Falling Apart—Luckily." Retrieved April 15, 2016. www.imusiciandigital.com/en/blog/fragmentation-of-the-music-industry/.

Green, Talib Kweli. 2015. "Why I Left the Major Label System: And a Little Bit of What I've Learned in the Music Biz." Retrieved April 15, 2016. https://medium.com/cuepoint/why-i-left-the-major-label-system-a0ecfa06ae91#.60fmop8ap.

Greenburg, Zach O' Malley. 2013. "Tech N9ne: Hip-Hop's Secret Mogul." Retrieved April 15, 2016. www.forbes.com/sites/zackomalleygreenburg/2013/09/24/tech-n9ne-hip-hops-secret-mogul/.

Guidry, Tony. 2014. "Do the Math: Indie vs. Major—A Rap Breakdown." Retrieved April 15, 2016. www.iamthaconnect.com/2014/11/10/do-the-math-indie-vs-major-a-rap-breakdown/.

Hard Knock TV. 2013. "Immortal Technique and Tech N9ne Talk Independent Movement, Technology, Black + Brown." Retrieved April 15, 2016. www.youtube.com/watch?v=xzR4yDUUgO8.

Harkness, Geoff. 2012. "True School: Situational Authenticity in Chicago's Hip-Hop Underground." *Cultural Sociology* 6 (3): 283–298.

Harrison, Anthony Kwame, and Craig E. Arthur. 2011. "Reading Billboard 1979–89: Exploring Rap Music's Emergence Through the Music Industry's Most Influential Trade Publication." *Popular Music and Society* 34 (3): 309–327.

Hieroglyphics. 2003. "Make Your Move." *Full Circle*. Hieroglyphics Imperium Recordings.

IFPI. 2016. "How Record Labels Invest." Retrieved April 15, 2016. www.ifpi.org/how-record-labels-invest.php.

Immortal Technique. 2003a. "Industrial Revolution." *Revolutionary Vol. 2*. Viper Records.

Immortal Technique. 2003b. "The Message and the Money." *Revolutionary Vol. 2*. Viper Records.

Immortal Technique. 2003c. "Freedom of Speech." *Revolutionary Vol. 2*. Viper Records.

Immortal Technique. 2003d. "Obnoxious." *Revolutionary Vol. 2*. Viper Records.

Johnson, Christopher. 2008. "Danceable Capitalism: Hip-Hop's Link to Corporate Space." *The Journal of Pan African Studies* 2 (4): 80–92.

Karubian, Sara. 2009. "360 Deals: An Industry Reaction to the Devaluation of Recorded Music." *Southern California Interdisciplinary Law Journal* 18: 395–462.

Katunich, Lauren. 2002. "Time to Quit Paying the Payola Piper: Why Music Industry Abuse Demands a Complete System Overhaul." *Loyola of Los Angeles Law Review* 22: 643–685.

Keif. 2006. "Record Sales: Where Does the Money Go?" Retrieved April 15, 2016. https://bandzoogle.com/blog/record-sales-where-does-the-money-go.

Knab, Christopher. 2010. "Inside Record Labels: Organizing Things." Retrieved April 15, 2016. www.musicbizacademy.com/knab/articles/insidelabels/htm.

KRS-ONE. 2007. "Nothing New." *Hip-Hop Lives*. Koch Records.

Leyshon, Andrew. 2001. "Time-Space (and Digital) Compression: Software Formats, Musical Networks, and the Reorganisation of the Music Industry." *Environment and Planning* 33: 49–77.

Lifetime. 2016. "Biography: Clark Gable Lifetime." Retrieved April 15, 2016. http://www.nytimes.com/movies/person/10097/Clark-Gable/biography.

Lopes, Paul. 1992. "Innovation and Diversity in the Popular Music Industry: 1969–1990." *American Sociological Review* 57 (1): 56–71.

Macklemore, and Ryan Lewis. 2012a. "Jimmy Iovine." *The Heist*. Macklemore LLC-ADA.

Macklemore, and Ryan Lewis. 2012b. "Ten Thousand Hours." *The Heist*. Macklemore LLC-ADA.

Macklemore, and Ryan Lewis. 2012c. "Can't Hold Us." *The Heist*. Macklemore LLC-ADA.

Maher, George Ciccariello. 2005. "Brechtian Hip-Hop: Didactics and Self-Production in Post-Gangsta Political Mix-tapes." *Journal of Black Studies* 26 (1): 129–160.

Marshall, Lee. 2013. "The 360 Deal and the 'New' Music Industry." *European Journal of Cultural Studies* 16 (1): 77–99.

McLeod, Kembrew. 2005. "MP3s Are Killing Home Taping: The Rise of Internet Distribution and Its Challenge to the Major Label Music Monopoly." *Popular Music and Society* 28 (4): 521–531.

Moore, Jacob. 2013. "How to Start an Independent Record Label." Retrieved April 15, 2016. www.pigeonsandplanes.com/2013/03/how-to-start-an-independent-record-label/s/be-careful-with-your-cash/.

Myer, Letrez, and Christine Kleck. 2007. "From Independent to Corporate: A Political Economic Analysis of Rap Billboard Toppers." *Popular Music and Society* 30 (2): 137–148.

Negus, Keith. 2002. "The Cultural Work of Intermediaries and the Enduring Distance Between Production and Consumption." *Cultural Studies* 16 (4): 501–515.

Oh, Minya. 2002. "Ludacris Barks Back at Pepsi, O'Reilly; P-Roach Antics Not an Issue for Soda Giant." Retrieved April 15, 2016. http://www.mtv.com/news/1457357/ludacris-barks-back-at-pepsi-oreilly-p-roach-antics-not-an-issue-for-soda-giant/.

Ostrove, Geoffrey. 2014. "The Political Economy of Financially Successful Independent Artists." *Class, Race and Corporate Power* 2 (1): 1–22.

Ostrow, Jonathan. 2010. "Indie vs. Major: Which Record Label Contract Is Right for You?" Retrieved April 15, 2016. www.musicthinktank.com/mtt-open/indie-vs-major-which-record-label-contract-is-right-for-you.hml.

Perkins, William. 1996. *Droppin' Science: Critical Essays on Rap Music and Hip-Hop Culture*. Philadelphia: Temple University Press.

Prindle, Gregory. 2003. "No Competition: How Radio Consolidation Has Diminished Diversity and Sacrificed Localism." *Fordham Intellectual Property, Media, and Entertainment Journal Law* 14 (1): 279–325.

Rapsody. 2012a. "Believe Me." *The Idea of Beautiful*. Jamla.

Rapsody. 2012b. "Non-Fiction." *The Idea of Beautiful*. Jamla.

Resnikoff, Paul. 2014. "Why Major Labels Are the Best Thing That Happened to Artists…" Retrieved April 15, 2016. www.digitalmusicnews.com/2014/09/19/major-labels-best-thing-happened-artists/.

Rose, Tricia. 2008. *The Hip Hop Wars: What We Talk About When We Talk About Hip Hop—And Why It Matters*. New York: Basic Civitas.

Smith, Clyde. 2012. "The Heist: Macklemore & Ryan Lewis Take DIY Route to iTunes #1." Retrieved April 15, 2016. http://www.hypebot.com/hypebot/2012/10/the-heist-macklemore-ryan-lewis-take-diy-route-to-itunes-1.html.

Stahl, Matt, and Leslie Meier. 2012. "The Firm Foundation of Organizational Flexibility: The 360 Contract in the Digitalizing Music Industry." *Canadian Journal of Communication* 37: 441–458.

Strachan, Robert. 2007. "Micro-Independent Record Labels in the UK." *European Journal of Cultural Studies* 10 (2): 245–265.

Swollen Members. 2002a. "Act on It." *Monsters in the Closet*. Battle Axe.

Swollen Members. 2002b. "Breathe." *Monsters in the Closet*. Battle Axe.

Tech N9ne. 2008. "Crybaby." *Killer*. Strange Music.

YONAS. 2011. "I Could." *The Proven Theory*. City of Dreams.

Open Access This chapter is distributed under the terms of the Creative Commons Attribution 4.0 International License (http://creativecommons.org/licenses/by/4.0/), which permits use, duplication, adaptation, distribution and reproduction in any medium or format, as long as you give appropriate credit to the original author(s) and the source, a link is provided to the Creative Commons license and any changes made are indicated.The images or other third party material in this chapter are included in the work's Creative Commons license, unless indicated otherwise in the credit line; if such material is not included in the work's Creative Commons license and the respective action is not permitted by statutory regulation, users will need to obtain permission from the license holder to duplicate, adapt or reproduce the material.

CHAPTER 4

The Death of Indie Hip-Hop?: The Blurry Lines Between the Majors and Independent Hip-Hop

Abstract This chapter utilizes forty-six interviews with self-identified independent hip-hop listeners to navigate the changing meanings of indie hip-hop in the post-golden era. The author elaborates on listener's definitions of independent and mainstream hip-hop and analyzes their interpretations of race, class, gender, sexual orientation, and oppositional consciousness. Listeners suggest that indie hip-hop often focuses on race and class but often ignores issues of gender and sexuality. Female and queer listeners are more conscious of this omission than male and straight listeners, despite a current push toward female and LGBTQ representation in hip-hop's mainstream. Also, there remains a blurry line between independents and majors that many artists navigate as they attempt to retain economic and creative freedom while still attempting to become financially successful. Technological shifts and advances, such as marketing and distribution channels, have further exacerbated the blurry lines of hip-hop.

Keywords Authenticity · Race and class · Gender and sexuality · Technological advancements in hip-hop · Independent hip-hop movement

A-Trak, a renowned DJ, producer, artist, and founder of the record label Fool's Gold, stated on Medium's Cuepoint that hip-hop's "left field seeped out of the margins and into the mainstream" (A-Trak 2014).

© The Author(s) 2019
C. Vito, *The Values of Independent Hip-Hop in the Post-Golden Era*,
https://doi.org/10.1007/978-3-030-02481-9_4

He claimed that the way we are listening to music has changed over the past 15 years, and it is becoming clear that hip-hop's major and independent musicians are becoming more intertwined than ever. David, an independent hip-hop listener, echoes A-Trak's sentiments: "ironically the same indie emcees I used to listen to are now active in the mainstream market…(and) the emcees I've heard attack mainstream artists are now trying to be signed."

Unlike previous chapters (Chapters 2 and 3) that focused on artists' lyrics, this chapter examines how listeners interpret and navigate the changing landscape and increasingly blurry differences between major and independent hip-hop following the culture's push toward independence from 2000 to 2013, particularly in relation to race, class, gender, and sexual politics. My analysis draws on forty-six in-person and online interviews with self-identified independent hip-hop listeners of which two are also indie musicians themselves. The respondents range from the age of 18 to 35 living in Southern California and represent a heterogeneous snowball sample with regard to gender, sexual orientation, race/ethnicity, income, self-defined social class, educational attainment, and political affiliation (see Chapter 1 and Appendix C). The age demographic represents the population that was highly influenced by hip-hop in the post-golden era and analyzes their interpretations of hip-hop and hip-hop music in that time period.

My analysis below emphasizes three main themes. Interviewees indicate that the traditional definitions of major and independent remain intact. They corroborate indie hip-hop's claims that record label affiliation remains salient to the bifurcation between mainstream and indie culture. Listeners help create a notion of authenticity for musicians through their interpretations of artists' messages regarding race, class, gender, and sexual orientation. In particular, they state that mainstream musicians' messages often do not reflect their social locations and experiences. Rather, male indies of color present lyrics that reflect the struggles of the listeners in regard to race and class; yet claims of authenticity remain vexed as respondents believe that much of independent hip-hop often ignores issues of gender and sexuality despite the increased diversity of artists and listeners. Thus, female and LGBTQA (alliance) respondents highlight artists concordant with their social identities, which helps destabilize the conceptions of authenticity as technology allows for a wider array of the population to produce and consume music.

Also, the results show that the line between the majors and independents has become increasingly blurred following hip-hop's push for independence in the early 2000s. Hip-hop culture is not viewed as binary oppositions, but rather as fluid and constantly changing as performers attempt to retain economic and creative freedom while still attempting to become financially successful. For instance, listeners recognize that large corporations frequently pull from the indie market and musicians are often pushed into the majors by financial motives. This has led to many indie acts and labels to navigate between the two markets in different ways as they try to further their careers.

Finally, respondents discuss waves of commodification and resistance in the "indie" movement. They state that a period of resistance followed the mass commodification of hip-hop in the early 2000s. Currently, major advances in technology have allowed artists to become commercially successful without the aid of large corporations. Even so, interviews reveal that they still remain intensely intertwined with major companies in old and new ways to utilize their marketing and distribution channels. Ultimately, independent hip-hop listeners express the complexity of the music industry and hip-hop culture.

Perceived Distinctions Between the Majors and Independent Hip-Hop

Interviews indicate that record label status remains a key characteristic in hip-hop culture today. While label status remains salient, artists' access to economic and cultural resources remains a key issue. My results also find that listeners frequently believe major acts remain homogeneous in their lyrics and thus, their authenticity is consistently questioned by fans concerned about commercialization. They argue that indies are alternatively allowed more creative freedom but require validation of authenticity from listeners that usually come from meaningful social, political, and cultural messages that relate to the respondents' social locations of race, class, and gender. As discussed more fully below, both males and females emphasize the progressive nature of race and class themes found within independent hip-hop. A number of female and LGBTQA respondents suggest that, although there are notable exceptions, problems of the objectification of women and heteronormativity are common within indie hip-hop and tend to be produced by straight working-class men of color, which challenges traditional post-golden era narratives of authenticity.

Record Label Matters?

Forman (2000) argues that the formation of indie labels has historically been as a response to the economic competition with major labels and thus forms a large part of artists' identity. Nearly 75% (thirty-four) of respondents similarly state that one of the most important distinctions between acts is still their record label status. David states that "mainstream artists are financially backed by large record companies." On the other hand, indies "produce everything without the financial backing of a major record label." Instead, they are signed by smaller labels or sometimes not signed at all. Felipe argues that in many instances they are "left to fund their own music, tours, and projects." Kathy emphasizes that they are usually relegated to the underground or peripheries of hip-hop culture. Their access to resources remains limited and their public exposure is generally centered on a particular genre, fan base, or geographical location.

Both musicians interviewed note the vast economic disparity between the two industries. Anthony Colon, founder and CEO of AGC Productions, writes "the big deal and the locals are two different worlds." He recapitulates David's sentiments, stating that they remain relatively local and small scale as they are pushing to make a name for themselves in the underground market. Carlos, an unsigned rapper from San Diego who goes by the name Mac Dirrty, adds that "I'm independent cause I pay for all my own shit in music. I pay for the studio time [and] rip the beats…I even [have] homies making beats for me now." He notes that "the majors can afford to buy big name producers such as Dr. Dre for a million dollars…I have my roommates rip me beats for a couple hundred dollars and I'm only making .005 cents a stream." Like Anthony, he details the large gap in the economic disparity between the mainstream and independents. Carlos recalls having to navigate between working his full-time job to make ends meet and making music in his spare time, which he believes is a very different experience than musicians who are economically supported by large corporations for a majority of their careers. For both listeners and rappers themselves, record label status remains salient (Fig. 4.1).

Fig. 4.1 Carlos (Stagename: Mac Dirrty) (*Credit* Carlos Sanchez)

What's Behind the Label?

A second dominant theme regarding the distinction between major and indie hip-hop today is the importance of creative musical freedom, which about 75% (thirty-five) of respondents mentioned in their interviews. Hibbett (2005) points out that simply looking at major record label status is a "benign" definition. In the case of indie rock, it is marked by the awareness of a new aesthetic in which punks created a movement based on the audiences' desire for social differentiation. In the 1970s, they created this desire by pushing a "do-it-yourself" ethic focused on messages less regulated than mainstream radio (Strachan 2007). David states that:

> Often major record companies [today] will make [an] artist portray a certain image for marketing, which can go against the artists' beliefs. Independent artists usually have no influence in regards to a marketing image, and they're free to be who they want to be.

David highlights that limitations on creative freedom can hinder the musicians' ability to freely make music. In addition, Kathy differentiates major and independent hip-hop by stating that musicians in the mainstream have less control because companies view them primarily as an "avenue for sales." She alternatively mentions that indies primarily operate in the underground and are not as highly swayed by the influence of large corporations.

Both rappers Anthony and Carlos emphasize the importance of maintaining creative and economic control of their own music. As Moore (2007) argues, the act of producing music and media that is relatively autonomous from corporate industry motivates smaller acts to create an alternative field of cultural production that is not reliant upon big businesses. While Anthony and Carlos remain relatively local and underground, they understand the benefits of keeping middlemen out and controlling the day-to-day operations of their music and their label. As Anthony vehemently states, "I cut out every middle man during this project! I did not need a promoter or talent scout. My company supports only one artist, which is me."

What Is "Real" Hip-Hop?

The question of authenticity remains a recurring topic among 50% (twenty-three) of the interviewees. They argue that authenticity, or the negotiated validation by both artists and listeners, is important in determining if the performers' persona is "genuine or accurate in its depiction." Respondents highlight that major label acts are limited in their messages and their authenticity is frequently challenged, while independent musicians have more creative freedom but need to obtain their authenticity from fans.

About 70% (thirty-one) of listeners believe that the majors are highly constrained in their creative freedom. The immersion of large corporations in hip-hop has decreased lyrical and musical diversity due to the pressure to be financially successful (Fox 2004; Myer and Kleck 2007). Liz writes: "mainstream is music that is heard repeatedly on the radio. It's music that the public wants to hear." Carlos, an unsigned musician himself, calls this type of music "bubble gum [and] sing-along rap" where the "lyrics are shallow and the beats are poppy." Interviewees such as Samantha and Jackie add that hip-hop generally follows formulaic trends. For Jackie, these trends are repeated messages of "sex, money, drugs, and violence" that appeal to the broader audience. The idea of sex is prominent in a male-oriented perspective that treats women as "sexual objects," in which Samantha states she "did not even notice growing up." They both note that the obsession with money, drugs, and violence becomes the stereotypical image for rappers as it preys on "the desires of urban Americans who want to be successful themselves."

About 40% (twenty) of respondents believe that social and political messages addressing problems in contemporary American society only appear during times of social distress. Liz states that generally large label musicians do not "speak much on social or political issues." Andrew supports her statement by arguing:

> The main messages on the [radio] being shared are controlled by whatever the industry wants you to hear. The industry regulates what is to be heard or not. These are the reasons we don't hear music on police brutality or racial superiority on the radio. Mainstream hip-hop is regulating people only to what is on the radio as if that is the only music being made.

Andrew's responses indicate that messages addressing the issues of urban communities are generally ignored, with much of the music producing messages concordant with the dominant culture and status quo. Sebastian adds that the majors generally do not reflect on social issues unless it is during a period of social crises. He believes that they do not try to rap about controversial issues, but notes that political and social messages may appear if they reflect the popular sentiments of American society at a particular time. He cites the song "FDT (Fuck Donald Trump)" by YG and Nipsey Hussle as a song that represents mainstream political issues during the 2016 presidential elections. He concludes that companies would only approve these messages if it were financially beneficial for them in the long run; otherwise, they are often dropped from publicized album releases. Sierra recaps these sentiments by stating that major acts are a reflection of "what the people specifically may 'want' to hear at a certain time and what sells rather than substance."

65% (thirty) of interviews indicate that corporate control puts into question the legitimacy of a rapper's persona and musical content. Hesmondhalgh (1999) points out that hip-hop faces similar problems to rock n' roll with the notion of "sell outs, or the pressures towards professionalization and partnership." This is particularly problematic for acts that garnered attention in the underground and were later signed by the majors to address issues of dispersion and diffusion (Jones 2002). For example, Christina thinks "the industry is a bit censored because there are only so many things you can put out in popular music…because obviously you give up something, especially if you were political before." Shawn reiterates Christina's sentiments, claiming that many rappers are questioned for selling out, which for him means changing their image and music to appease labels and appeal to a wider array of audiences. He writes, "a big part of hip-hop is the message the music sends, and that's what a lot of listeners are in it for. So I've had people tell me they don't like mainstream because the artists are 'sell outs'."

Even indies themselves corroborate the notion of selling out. Anthony, founder and CEO of AGC Productions, speaks of his fear of large corporations when he says, "yeah, I've turned down opportunities because I was afraid of people taking my ideas or trying to change me." He continues to speak of his love for the music and being afraid that his message and style would be altered by companies seeking to capitalize on his brand name and ideas. This is reinforced during his album release party when he reminds his friends that he hosts his own shows on his own terms without sponsors. More importantly for him, he argues that "[I] don't have to kiss anyone's ass…that's why this whole project is independent, all the way down bro."

In addition, roughly 50% (twenty-four) of interviews mention that musicians who choose to remain independent generally have a different "vibe" to their music. The vibe tends to focus on socially conscious messages that attempt to distance itself from mass commercialization (Rose 2008). As performers Aesop Rock and Rob Sonic state, "as long as we can do what we want to do…then [independent] is the move" (The NE Hip-Hop 2015). In this alternative underground space, there is more room to critically challenge the conventional norms of mainstream hip-hop culture (Morgan and Bennett 2011; Harrison 2006). Listeners claim that indies focus on lyrical and musical innovation not constrained by corporate executives. Crystal writes, "[indie artists'] creativity is on another level. They are not withheld so much and you feel that passion in their lyrics. You can tell that they put in the effort and are trying to reach from within to get a message out [to the public]." Janine adds that they can freely delve deeper into issues because they are not constrained by a slew of production and management teams making decisions for them. More importantly, Pathik notes that these messages and issues are visibly important to them because they willingly choose to rap about them.

Alyssa, a full-time student and part-time server at a restaurant, writes of her first experiences with Immortal Technique's music. She recalls the first time she heard the track "Dance with the Devil":

> I was 15 and after school every day I would hang out with my boyfriend. We would drink at this park in my apartment complex. It was raining so we were sitting in an obstacle course near the slides under a blanket and he showed me this song. I was...amazed. I had never heard hip-hip that actually had a message besides 'fuck bitches, get money.' Even though that particular song wasn't something I can relate to it was something that people don't like to talk about, but a lot of underground artists rap about... the issues that people ignore or don't care about enough. That's when I first really got into hip-hop.

While she points out that the song was not something she experienced herself, she finds that the meaningful images it portrayed were immediately felt. Alyssa expresses that these creative and political messages would be much harder to find with major acts that are heavily constrained in their freedom of speech.

50% (twenty-three) of interviews indicate that much of indie culture hinges on the perceived authenticity of musicians. While the notion of authenticity is constantly negotiated between performers and listeners (Harkness 2012), many fans believe authenticity to be real and measurable. Respondents similarly state that major acts have to appeal to the masses and thus are less focused on socially and politically conscious messages and musical innovation, but rather on sales and profit. Conversely, independents have greater ability to make music freely because they are appealing to smaller, niche markets. But these messages need to be positively received by the hip-hop community in order for them to build a fan base. Listeners need to validate their music in order for them to be perceived as authentic.

One such means of validation is to reconnect with hip-hop's roots. Matt writes that:

> I began listening to older hip-hop and not just the mainstream hip-hop singles on the radio. It was a form of music that was different and it featured a lot of storytelling and personal narrative(s) that reflected everyday experiences that were more relevant to the general population than just money, women, and cars. It talked about education, working-class issues, racism, politics, and the influence of money.

He adds that much of the culture today has been far removed from its origins in the streets of New York where issues of racism and classism were discussed. Samantha shares that independents are much more similar to the roots of how hip-hop used to be. She believes that you can feel the emotions and that it comes from a different place, predominantly before hip-hop was commodified and globalized by whites. Interviewee Liz believes that this is particularly important because the current generation is less informed on social and political issues and becoming more entrenched with individualism. My interviews ultimately show that fans believe authenticity still needs to be gained through the artists' messages. As Sasha writes, "independent hip-hop is more meaningful, personal, and [more about the] history attached to peoples' lives."

What's Race, Class, and Gender Got to Do with It?

Respondents frequently find a more intimate understanding of social locations with indie artists that operate outside of the mainstream market. In particular, they mention the importance of lyrics connecting with their life experiences concordant with their social locations of race, class, and gender. But interviewees state that while musicians frequently address issues of race and class critically, they often mirror broader hip-hop culture in regards to the objectification of women and heteronormativity.

First, nearly 60% (twenty-six) of listeners, overwhelmingly the working-class interviewees of color, feel independents portray similar everyday life struggles as themselves. Folami (2007) states that hip-hop provides a commentary on social life, particularly given the invisibility and marginality of poor racial minorities in American society. Interviewees similarly mention that majors depict an image of being economically successful, which creates a disjuncture with many listeners barely getting by in America. Pathik, a working-class Indian, recalls the first time he heard Strange Records' Tech N9ne:

> It was my senior year in high school and I was really feeling down in the dumps. I was being called a dumb-fool if I believed I could become something in my life. Two of my neighbors flunked out of college, while another dropped out because he was in too much debt. Inside I was super-happy to have been accepted to college, and it was always my dream. I wanted to go out into the world, get a college degree, and become

something so that my parents wouldn't have to work anymore. That's when I first listened to the song "Mental Giant" by Tech N9ne. He wrote: 'Even though I'm 5 foot 8 inches and 195 pounds I'm looking down on your niggaz, so tall I can't even hear any of the sound you deliver.'

He claims that these types of songs better address class issues in the USA than the messages delivered in the mainstream because the rappers face similar struggles as their working-class listeners. Pathik emphasizes the song "Mental Giant" to represent the hardships he has endured just making it to college. He notes that he can relate his experiences with Tech N9ne's because of the struggle that he endured to create a successful career in the hip-hop game.

Issues of race remain particularly important for black and Latino interviewees. Scholars (Forman 2010; Gosa 2010) argue that Obama's recent administration has spurred multiple performers and fans to address issues of race and class in a post-Civil Rights America (Forman 2010). While respondents construct their racial and ethnic identity differently, many connect their racial and ethnic background to hip-hop through a similar struggle against a legacy of imperialism and their personal experiences of racism. Sebastian highlights music by Viper Records' Immortal Technique, particularly the song entitled "Poverty of Philosophy":

> Immortal Technique speaks about the inequality there is in the world between the rich and the poor and the history that made this evident. [But] he speaks about how the European nations during colonial imperialism used the 'new world' as a way to only export resources and did not really care about the effects on the indigenous people. He speaks about how classism is as an important issue to deal with as racism and that people at the bottom should stick together and not go against each other in order to help everyone [to] rise together and move forward.

Alternatively, white and Asian interviewees did not highlight their racial and ethnic identity and the importance of the opposition to white supremacy within independent hip-hop as frequently as black and Latino listeners. Asians in particular focus on the lack of representation in the culture's community, but emphasize their class struggle to recognize their shared marginalized position in society. Nonetheless, respondents assert that compared to the majors, independent rappers better address their personal social locations regarding race and class.

Further, interviews highlight the importance of race and class inequality in the music industry itself. Myer and Kleck (2007) argue that white males in the three major record labels are overrepresented in managerial and ownership positions. For instance, Angelica describes the hip-hop industry as controlled by "white men." She claims that those in positions of power at record companies control the industry and seek to turn it into a profitable business. As she states,

> What started out as an outlet to rebel against mistreatment [and] a voice to fight back, has now turned and focused on the number of albums sold and tour dates. Hip-hop is directly and almost always linked with blacks. The difference between whites and blacks in the industry is the way they are portrayed in the media. Blacks are talked down upon, disregarded, and exploited…or they are seen as aggressive and angry. Whites are always talked about so respectfully, gracefully and praised for every little good thing they do.

These sentiments mirror other respondents, as they argue that white elites often control the messages presented in the music that black rappers create. While many minorities, particularly black entrepreneurs such as Dr. Dre, Jay-Z, Master P, Puff Daddy, Queen Latifah, and Russell Simmons, have been able to make a dent in white domination and the appropriation of hip-hop culture (Basu and Werbner 2001; Sköld and Rehn 2007), there remains problems of racial inequality within the music industry. Moreover, black musicians often reproduce white ideology despite the detrimental effects it may have on their own community. As a result, interviewees believe that various messages presented by major acts do not represent their social experiences but instead represent broad generalizations and stereotypes about low-income urban communities of color.

Second, listeners believe independent musicians in the post-golden era remained sexist, heteronormative, and homophobic in their lyrics and personas despite their progressive views on race and class relations. This is due to indie hip-hop still being composed predominantly of straight working-class men of color who most commonly make claims of authenticity within hip-hop culture. Oware (2014) makes a similar argument, stating that messages of violence and misogyny are still present in the underground despite claims of being rebellious and socially conscious. Of the twenty-two female and LGBTQA interviewees, nearly 70% (fifteen) mention female and LGBTQA indie artists that are more attentive to issues of gender and sexuality in their responses. They contend that hip-hop still has the potential to reproduce unequal gender relations, particularly for young black girls navigating their sexuality (Alim et al. 2010; Asante 2008; Gupta-Carlson 2010; Pough 2004). Amanda states, "Even though I listen to it and enjoy it, I still recognize that a lot of hip-hop reinforces sexism and is beyond disrespectful toward women." Samantha adds that often these representations of women are "as sex symbols, as submissive, as a commodity" viewed through a heteronormative male lens that emphasizes hegemonic masculinity (Alim et al. 2010; Hunter 2011). More importantly for Angelica, they are "not just any women, [but] usually black and Latina women." For female respondents in particular, they argue that indie culture is still an industry predominated and controlled by heterosexual men who parrot misogynistic, violent, and materialist lyrics of their mainstream counterparts.

They did report instances of socially conscious indie rappers being more attentive to the issues of gender and sexuality, which shifts the boundaries of authenticity to address increased representation by women and LBTQA members. Kathy writes that Macklemore LLC's Macklemore and Ryan Lewis have numerous songs on race, class, and gender inequality. The song "Same Love" openly addresses issues of sexuality and advocates for gay marriage. She notes that "even though I'm straight, I hated how LGBT groups were being judged and hated just because they liked the same sex rather than the opposite sex… they're still human beings." Following the legacy of many socially conscious rappers, Sierra argues that artists and listeners can "take this norm of dehumanizing women in hip-hop music out of society…and [we can] implement a more accepting mindset."

Similarly, LGBTQ rappers have been able to create niche spaces in hip-hop's underground. As Christina states, "LGBTQ rappers are setting a new trend in the hip-hop community of defying traditional stereotypes about rappers." Mykki Blanco, an independent transgender rapper on New York-based label UNO, has obtained buzz in the hip-hop world. While his songs are outwardly vulgar, his lyrics bring attention to issues of the LGBTQ community and he gives rappers a cultural space to navigate their sexual identity (Stern 2016). For example, Mykki Blanco has publicly addressed the problem of HIV and the stigmas attached with coming out. Mykki Blanco states (Reynolds 2015):

> I've been HIV-Positive since 2011, my entire career. Fuck stigma and hiding in the dark, this is my real life. I'm healthy... I've toured the world 3 times but I've been living in the dark, it's time to actually be as punk as I say I am...No more living a lie. HAPPY PRIDE.

Other acts have also gained traction in the LGBTQ hip-hop community. After *Pitchfork*'s cosign (Raymer 2013), Mishka Records' queer rapper Cakes da Killa has obtained more mainstream success as part of the LGBTQ hip-hop genre with his album *The Eulogy*. While Queen Pen was originally seen as the first lesbian rapper in 1997, a new genre of lesbian artists such as "Kelow, Elektrik, Envy, MC Angel, RoxXxan, Yo Majesty, and God-des & She" is gaining popular support (Schwartzberg 2014). Rainbow Noise has also cultivated a movement under the premise that labels need to highlight LGBTQ talent in the hip-hop community (Carter 2014).

By reflecting on the intersections of race, class, and gender within their lyrics, independent musicians can more freely express their life experiences and ideas with audiences that understand, relate, or sympathize with marginalized social locations to promote oppositional consciousness (Harkness 2012; Jeffries 2011; Mansbridge and Morris 2001). Yet, while respondents note that indie culture is more inclined to include messages critical of the relations of dominations with regard to race, class, and gender than major musicians, they acknowledge exceptions. They often include the caveat that large label acts can present meaningful messages, while indie rappers may not be politically or socially conscious at all. Felipe notes that indie hip-hop "doesn't have to have a 'meaningful message' because I've heard underground artists rap about girls and money." He goes on to state that many indies merely reflect the ideologies of mainstream hip-hop culture and broader American culture as a whole. Like other informants, he suggests that the distinction between major and indie is not black and white but blurry.

The Blurry Lines Between the Mainstream and Indies

While interviews suggest that the division between major and indie status remains salient, responses often allude to the fact that many acts today navigate a "mixed space" by which performers attempt to retain economic and creative freedom while still attempting to become financially successful. Listeners do not view major and indie hip-hop as mutually exclusive or opposing types of music. Instead, the distinctions between them are fluid and constantly changing, particularly in two ways. They note that independent acts are frequently pulled and pushed toward large record labels. Respondents state that numerous rappers they listen to try to remain indie. But because of the need to survive in the hip-hop industry, they believe numerous musicians have to navigate the borders of major and indie. Also, interviewees believe that the indie movement has changed over time. They frequently note the recent period of commodification by large corporations, as well as resistance by smaller businesses utilizing advances in technology to enter the market without the support of the majors. Nonetheless, results indicate that both the mainstream and indie markets remain complexly intertwined with one another in various ways such as affiliating with major companies to utilize their marketing and distribution channels.

Mixed Space Between the Majors and Indies

The blurred lines between the majors and indies exist due to frequent pull and push factors, which is cited by roughly 25% (thirteen) of respondents. On the one hand, interviewees indicate that many acts get pulled by the majors as they become increasingly popular. Karubian (2009) argues that big labels sign fewer acts today and instead focus on signing established independent acts that have already gained visibility in the underground and are looking to break into the mainstream. Pathik reinforces this point by pointing out that nearly "every artist starts off underground regardless…like Wiz Khalifa or 50 Cent before they came up." Souphakone makes a similar observation with Wiz, stating that "when Wiz Khalifa was an independent artist…hella dope. I respected his lyrics, respected the grind, even the trademark I'm high as fuck laugh." But Souphakone continues to state that certain performers get enough buzz that they eventually become popular acts that get pulled into the majors.

Alyssa states: "I feel like Logic has changed since he has gotten bigger even though he claims he hasn't." Logic, originally signed to Visionary Music Group, proclaimed on his mixtapes that he would remain independent. But in 2013, his mixtapes were approaching one million downloads and he eventually signed to Def Jam Recordings (Paine 2013).

David similarly uses the example of Anderson Paak (formerly known as Breezy Lovejoy), "who worked with a lot of well-known emcees and producers…he's now on Aftermath." As Anderson Paak, he initially released an album entitled *Venice* on Steel Wool Entertainment. After obtaining more popularity in 2015 with an appearance on Dr. Dre's *Compton*, he eventually signed with Aftermath Entertainment, a subsidiary of Universal Music Group's Interscope Records (Peters and Martin 2016).

On the other hand, respondents point out that many musicians get pushed into large corporations due to the need for financial security and resources. Various artists may treat the indie and underground scene as a "waiting station or the minor leagues" until they achieve more popularity and sign lucrative contracts with major labels (Oware 2014). As Julian states, numerous rappers utilize the underground market to gain popularity with the intention of obtaining wealth and fame. He states, "Well I think what happens is that they get a taste of all that fame and fortune, and it begins to overwhelm them." Julian cites rapper Chief Keef as a primary example as he gained popularity in Chicago's underground and eventually signed a 6 million dollar deal with Interscope. The contract included $440,000 in advances and the creation of his own imprint called Glory Boyz Entertainment (Markman 2013). Carlos similarly speaks of Mac Miller leaving Pittsburg indie label Rostrum Records for Warner Bros. Records. Rostrum obtained success through a strong digital presence and investing heavily in touring (Ostrove 2014). But Mac Miller joined Warner Bros. Records for a 10 million dollar signing deal and the creation of his own subsidiary label REMember Music. In both cases, the artists left smaller companies in exchange for financial advances and resources. Drake (2015), a Complex.com writer, argues that many musicians who reach a high level of popularity but lack capital may also be pushed into the majors to meet demand. He cites examples of Young Thug and Bobby Shmurda as acts that likely needed to sign deals with large companies who own a vast amount of financial capital. This is likely to push them into the mainstream, despite less favorable terms on their contract due to the need for resources (Karubian 2009).

With the frequent pull and push factors, listeners state that they are frequently left to determine if acts who shift spaces are still considered "authentic." For many listeners, it is becoming harder and harder to determine what is truly independent (Andrews 2006; Hess 2012; Oware 2014). Souphakone writes that he "doesn't listen to [Wiz Khalifa] like that anymore" because his lyrics and persona changed. Pathik adds that he understands that being signed to a large corporation can change the music because they are now controlled by outside parties with different interests. Yet, listeners also argue that rappers who sign to the majors do not always change their message. Felipe and Julian add that some rap legends like Nas and Common "came up as underground hip-hop but they've also blown up so big that they have tasted the fame and money, but I think they still stay true to what they were all about when they first came up." Academics and respondents suggest that there is a gray area between major and independent that many acts navigate as a result of the constant pull and push factors within hip-hop.

In addition, about 40% (eighteen) of listeners state that numerous musicians navigate between being major and independent. Harrison (2006) argues that underground acts, whose popularity largely consists of friends, family, and other associates, attempt to extend their fan base outside their circle. Once they do, they must decide throughout their careers whether to be unsigned, sign with or create an independent company, or sign with a big mainstream corporation. For example, some acts began their careers signing with a large label but have since dropped their label to obtain successful careers as indie artists (Hess 2012; Oware 2014). Felipe states that "I see artists like Del who are better in the indie circuit." Del the Funky Homosapien had released two commercially successful albums in the early 1990s with Elektra, a subsidiary of Warner Bros. Music. In 1997, Elektra dropped him from their label a month before the release of *Future Development*. He later signed with Hieroglyphics Imperium Recordings and released the album in 2002. Del the Funky Homosapien has remained independent and voiced his discontent with Elektra. He has since released nine studio albums and signed to indie label Definitive Jux in 2007 (Bechtel 2016; Ostrove 2014).

Julian points to Killer Mike as a successful act who also did better without a big contract. Killer Mike released *Monster* in 2003 under Sony Records' Columbia. With singles such as Akshon (Yeah!) and A.D.I.D.A.S., Killer Mike reached Billboard's Hot 100. But following his release he had a fallout with Outkast and Sony Records and was not able to release *I Pledge Allegiance to the Grind* until 2006 under his self-formed label Grind Time Official (Markman 2011). He has since released three solo albums and collaborated with El-P to form Run the Jewels on Universal subsidiary Fool's Gold.

Respondents also state that many musicians navigate between major and independent status as they try to remain culturally relevant and financially profitable. For some, this means moving between the major and indie circuit as their careers progress. Julian recalls MURS' move to Strange Records and calling his album "straight fire." In 2008, MURS garnered attention as he was set to release *MURS for President* on Warner Bros. Records. He had previously been linked to the indie hip-hop scene, but stated that he "had a bigger budget to work with…[could] get any names [he] wanted…and the album was mixed better" (Ollison 2008). After his album's debut, Warner Bros. Records released MURS over a "difference in opinion" (Cooper 2009). He has since signed with Tech N9ne's Strange Records and then released *Have A Nice Life* in 2015 to positive reviews (Moore 2015).

Rappers such as Lupe Fiasco have voiced their discontent with their contracts. Alyssa mentions that "I've always considered Lupe Fiasco to be major because I heard him on the radio." In fact, Lupe Fiasco has remained on a large record company for a majority of his career despite his tensions with Warner Bros. Music's Atlantic. The release of 2011's *Lasers* was met with much controversy. Atlantic executives felt the album needed guest stars and star-potential hits, which caused Lupe to alter the production of his album (Frazier 2010). While he ultimately worked with them to release Lasers, he later voiced his distaste for the work and even offered to destroy any physical copies of the record that his fans purchased (Ahmed 2011). Alyssa notes that "of all his albums, *Lasers* was by far the worst because of the production." Lupe himself has stated that he wants off Atlantic Records due to being treated as a "third class citizen" because he did not sign a 360-degree contract with them. These contracts are preferred because they allow companies to extract profits from various aspects of the signees' revenue stream to account for the downturn in record sales in the digital era, which was generally not part of traditional recording deals. These aspects can include any aspect of their career and hence the term 360 degrees, such as merchandising, touring, and commercial endorsements (Marshall 2013; Stahl and Meier 2012). More recently, Lupe departed from Atlantic and signed with Nashville-based entertainment company Thirty Tigers.

Independent labels themselves also face the same dilemma as they attempt to earn profits, obtain success, and expand. Interviewees Felix and Julian recall how small companies such as Death Row and Bad Boy were bought out or merged with big labels in the 1990s (Knab 2004).

As Warner Bros. Music's owner Len Blavatnik, Universal CEO Lucian Grainge, and Sony's Music Chief Doug Morris state (Greenburg 2015), "the majors have figured out that it's smarter to bully their way into companies seeking to take their lunch." Respondents also cite the process of musicians having to sign with the majors when their indie labels are bought out. As David states, "Ironically the same indie emcees I used to listen to are now active in the mainstream market. Mos Def [is] not only well known in mainstream music and movies... [but now is] signed." Arianna adds that Mos Def still has "inspiring and thoughtful message[s], but navigate[s] between major and indie throughout the years." In Mos Def's case, he was originally signed with Rawkus Records. They gained notoriety as a premier underground hip-hop label in the 1990s. But in the early 2000s Rawkus Records folded and was bought out by Interscope (Greene 2015). Since the merger, Mos Def has verbally sparred with the company until he fulfilled his last contractual album *True Magic* in 2006 (Baker 2014). He then signed to independent label Downtown's roster and released *The Ecstatic* in 2009. Ultimately, these cases illustrate the mixed space between major and indie by which many musicians navigate throughout their careers.

The Changing Nature of Hip-Hop's Indie Movement

Nearly 50% (twenty-two) of respondents describe how independent hip-hop has evolved and changed in numerous ways over the years. Older interviewees point to the prominence of indie rappers in the early 2000s. Like punk rock (Hesmondalgh 1999), independent hip-hop has seen periods of commodification and resistance. But as Lopes (1992) points out, these periods are specific to the industry. During its roots in the 1970s, New York hip-hop focused on performances in the streets and was concerned with social and political issues such as poverty and racism. As the culture became more popular in the late 1980s and early 1990s, the golden era saw the mass commodification of numerous acts by large corporations hoping to gain financial success. Following the decline of the golden era in the late 1990s and early 2000s came a period of underground and indie hip-hop resisting major label corporatization. For example, David writes that "ten years ago I used to pay attention to see who's either mainstream or independent. There is a lot of pride with music from an independent artist because everything was created from the artist." Jayson similarly states that "in the 2000s I did listen to a lot of underground acts because it was pushed hard back in the day." Both respondents indicate that the late 1990s and early 2000s were periods marked by the rise of an indie movement. Older interviewees recall that independents utilized an "anti-mainstream" approach that appropriated street culture and the rejection of corporate America in music. Jayson cites acts such as "Living Legends, Grouch and Eligh, Slug, Murs, and Immortal Technique back in the day at Rock the Bells and other Hip-Hop Festivals" as highly influential to the movement.

In response to the rise of a revitalized indie movement in the early 2000s, major labels attempted to remain relevant by creating 360-degree contracts. These contracts extract profits from various aspects of the signee's revenue stream such as merchandising, touring, and commercial endorsements (Marshall 2013; Stahl and Meier 2012), and utilize the new modes of musical production to offset declining record sales (Leyshon et al. 2005) (see Chapter 3). Fox (2004) also argues that large companies attempted to control online music through the creation of copyright-protected files and lawsuits against the providers of free music. As Christina writes, "popular discourse is tightly controlled by labels and corporations like iTunes." She argues that companies re-secured the modes of musical production by restricting illegal downloads and investing heavily in online models such as iTunes, Spotify, Pandora, and Shazam. In 2014, Warner Music Group bought 5% of a then bankrupt SoundCloud, while Universal owned rights to Beats by Dre and obtained 13% of Apple stock. Greenburg (2015) adds that the major labels—Warner, Universal, and Sony—owned 10–20% of the entertainment startups in the digital space in 2015. As a result, listeners contend that the indie culture of the early 2000s declined. Jayson further elaborates: "I did listen to a lot of underground because I hate the radio…but it's just different now." David clarifies by stating that "back then a lot of independent artists would attack mainstream artists for selling out, being fake and manufactured by the record label. Because of [changes to] the industry, I feel that things are different now." He argues that after re-commodification by large corporations the indie movement declined and forced many rappers to become mainstream.

Yet, slightly over 50% (twenty-four) of respondents of all ages argue that current indie culture has been able to better obtain commercial success utilizing advances in technology, such as online distribution and social media outlets, without the support of large corporations (Karubian

2009). Jones (2002) asserts that the rise of the phonograph and radio in the first quarter of the twentieth century changed the landscape of music. Up until the 1970s, the recording industry was able to monopolize access to recording studios and other means of distribution. By the early 1990s, the music industry shifted again due to the prevalence of the Internet's music distribution capabilities. Despite major labels' attempts to control the Internet, independent acts have been able to secure the means of musical production and thus the marketplace has shifted to a more democratic organizational system (McLeod 2005). As Andrews (2006) argues, "the internet and file-sharing systems have allowed for more accessibility and better distribution for smaller labels and imprints." Musicians Aesop Rock and Rob Sonic concur, stating that "technology open [ed] up different doors and avenues [for hip-hop culture]" (The NE Hip-Hop 2015). Rapper Brother Ali adds that these avenues were not even fathomable in the late 1990s (Hip Hop Since 1987 TV 2013).

Interviewees such as Carlos share similar sentiments about technological advancements. He recalls recording music on blank tapes off the radio: "I would wait for songs I liked and I would run to record them when they were about to start." He notes that major radio stations controlled the music he heard growing up, but interviewee Jessica N. remembers the rise of iPods and MP3 formats in making music consumption easier to access for both producer and consumer. David adds that the rise of "YouTube has given [artists] the ability to put music out there much easier." Nielson's study (Burgess 2012) shows that "64% of teenagers now listen to music through YouTube than through any other source." More recently Jessica F., a 21-year-old college student, points to SoundCloud as a primary medium of music consumption among the people she knows. SoundCloud acts face a low barrier to entry, with an understanding that becoming viral is highly dependent upon direct fan contact. As a result, the recent movement of "SoundCloud rap" has become more popular among performers and fans today (Caramanica 2017).

Social media web sites have spurred on the popularity of acts without the expensive traditional means of promotion such as Street Teams and fliers. Christina notes that "independent hip-hop had an opportunity with Myspace and other internet mediums." Rapper Talib Kweli (Greene 2015) shares similar views, writing that "Myspace is what got me online [in] a real way." Other Web sites such as Facebook, Instagram, Snapchat, and Twitter have given musicians a platform to release and promote their music. In particular, these mediums allow numerous acts to enter the eyes and ears of listeners easier and faster. As Jayson argues, "the internet plays a big role now...you can get fame easier if you put yourself out there. People talk about you and share your music through the world wide web...and you're sitting in the comforts of your own home and not going out there to promote." David states that this ultimately allows many more musicians to gain mainstream popularity.

Respondents frequently referred to rappers such as Tech N9ne and Macklemore and Ryan Lewis, who have demonstrated how small homegrown labels can promote successful acts through the use of technology and social media. More recently, unsigned performer Chance the Rapper has released music on free platforms such as Datpiff and SoundCloud, focusing on a strong relationship with listeners using social media to achieve monumental success. Interviewee and unsigned act Carlos states that "I see artists like Tech N9ne as pioneers who changed the game." Tech N9ne, a hip-hop veteran, has chosen to remain on Strange Records since the 1990s. He attributes his success to building a strong brand name characterized by strong shows with a solid fan base (Nguyen 2015a). This is aided by a strong online presence focused on "stay[ing] within an arms-length of his fans" (Biondo 2012). Strange Music's Twitter and Facebook pages remain active and full of cosigns from other celebrities who endorse their brand. Andrew, a 21-year-old college student, additionally points to Macklemore and Ryan Lewis as trendsetters in hip-hop today. Macklemore LLC's Macklemore and Ryan Lewis have become successful through similar promotional techniques to Tech N9ne. Smith (2012) cites Macklemore's success to savvy social media marketing, a socially conscious message, a DIY stance, and a unique personal image. Like Tech N9ne, a streamlined and personal relationship with fans decreases the need of A&R from major labels (Drake 2015). Andrew also cites more recent rappers such as Migos and Fetty Wap, who have joined independent label 300 Entertainment. Under Lyor Cohen and Todd Moscowitz's vision, 300 Entertainment gives local stars an opportunity to become successful through a strong focus on analytics (Nguyen 2015b). Utilizing data, Quality Control Music's "Coach" and "Pee" were given an innovative deal with 300 Entertainment for distribution and marketing. Their successful model includes hiring their own radio and promotion staff, personally publishing and managing venues, and hiring in-demand producers and engineers (Peisner 2015). As such, Strange Records, Macklemore LLC, and 300 Entertainment all push for a strong online presence with an attuned ear to the digital age (Drake 2015). Ultimately, the new wave of indie hip-hop utilizes the technological advancements made by major corporations to resist corporatization and produce music outside of the traditional modes of distribution.

Further, the most recent wave of independent artists and labels has remained highly intertwined with major record companies as they continue to coexist in the music industry. Suhr's (2011) finds that recent shifts in the music industry show major and independent labels converging despite their consistently changing relations of tension and compatibility. For instance, many acts signed to indie labels maximize sales through the process of affiliating with large corporations (Knab 2004). They reduce the risk of bankruptcy with independent distributors by instead using a major label distribution system, which usually has the backing of a parent company such as Warner Bros. or Universal. Large corporations see the value in distribution because they still obtain a significant portion of the profits despite not owning the company (Marshall 2013).

Interviewees Julian and Felix recall several popular labels adopting this model in the 1990s. In 1998, Cash Money Records signed a widely publicized blockbuster 30 million dollar distribution deal with Universal (XXL Staff 2008). Although this received considerable attention from fans, many alleged indie labels of the era such as Def Jam, Roc-A-Fella, Bad Boy, and No Limit were also subsidiaries of large corporations. While the idea of affiliating is not new, it has become more frequent with self-proclaimed "indie-DIY" artists today, thus again challenging the significance of the term indie.

Jayson similarly remembers more recently that even Rhymesayers Entertainment, along with one of its flagship acts Brother Ali, signed a distribution deal with Alternative Distribution Alliance (ADA), Warner Bros. Music Groups' independent distributor, to expand their company. Matt similarly states that "I don't really like Macklemore and Ryan Lewis because I question their music." He elaborates that "Sometimes I feel their message but other times they put out pop shit." Matt's concerns were shared by others in the hip-hop community as Macklemore and Ryan Lewis fell under attack by National Public Radio (NPR) and Rap Radar for falsely calling themselves independent (Smith 2013). As Figure 4 illustrates, Macklemore and Ryan Lewis were also distributed and promoted by ADA (Fig. 4.2).

In a 2012 interview, Macklemore stated that he was not opposed to major corporations but merely acting in his own best career interests

(Bootleg Kev 2012). While there has been resistance to distribution deals, for example by small British labels (Gottfried 2014), indie companies have become less "indie" because of their need for capital from major corporations to keep up with demand.

Publicity and promotion also play a large part of the music industry in the digital age. Smaller labels often need to hire professional teams to market and license their songs to compete (Andrews 2006). Both of the two independent artists interviewed acknowledged the importance of successful marketing, which is easier to obtain with the help the financial resources of large companies. One method they find useful is online streaming playlist placement with corporations such as Spotify or YouTube. While this does not necessarily increase profits as the average artist only gets paid .006 to .008 cents per stream on Spotify (Sehgal 2018), it provides high exposure for lesser-known acts that possess the capital to pay for it. Thus, many artists such as Carlos and Anthony are left to choose between sharing scant profits from streams with corporations or doing it themselves but facing the possibility of little to no airplay.

Some established indie labels such as Rhymesayers have signed promotion deals. In 2007, they signed with Warner Music Group and its co-founder Brent "Siddiq" Sayers stated that, after the deal, they had access to all the services of companies under Warner's ILB umbrella (Scholtes 2007). Macklemore and Ryan Lewis signed a similar promotion deal with ADA (Smith 2012), who provided assistance in their airplay and promotion for a flat monthly fee. In 2016, Chance the Rapper paired with Apple Music to exclusively release his album *Coloring Book* for two

Fig. 4.2 Macklemore and Ryan Lewis' distribution model

weeks and became the first "streaming only" album to chart on Billboard 200. While remaining unsigned, Chance has been alternatively sponsored by other large businesses such as Apple, Bud Light, and CitiBank to become commercially successful (Austen 2016; Best et al. 2017; Phillips 2017). Other major corporations such as Live Nation (Live Nation 2013) and potentially Spotify (Resnikoff 2017) are attempting to create their own record labels to circumvent the control of the traditional three major labels. In essence, many independent acts rely on various large corporations to become commercially successful despite promoting DIY ethics.

As a result, slightly more than 20% (ten) of listeners argue that it has become more evident that rappers work with large corporations when it is in their mutual best interest (Suhr 2011). As Pathik writes, "independent artists now *need* the help of major companies to be commercially successful in our society today." Nathan S (2015) writes of the rise of nicknamed "mindie" rappers, or indie rappers who are secretly aided by big companies. He lists Kevin Gates, Skizzy Mars, and most notably Logic as examples. Funk Volume's CEO Damien Ritter (Nathan 2015) argues that these acts are promoted as indie even though they already have relations with large marketing and promotion companies to aid their success. Once they "organically" and "independently" reach financial and commercial success, they leave their "indie" status to join the label affiliated with those marketing and promotion companies. In essence, numerous musicians negotiate terms for mutually beneficial outcomes by turning indie music into a fetishized commodity to generate profits (Ostrove 2014).

Ultimately, my study indicates that listeners view major and independent hip-hop as fluid and constantly changing, which leads to a mixed space rather than binary oppositions. My findings show that there is a pull and push dynamic. Listeners believe that many musicians frequently navigate the mixed space as they try to maintain economic and creative freedom while attempting to stay culturally relevant and financially profitable. Also, interviewees state that the term indie has changed over time. They argue that hip-hop's indie movement of the early 2000s focused on anti-corporate sentiments. Following 360-degree contracts and the reassertion of technology by the majors, current independent musicians focus on online distribution and social media to circumvent their control. Yet major label and independent artists remain highly intertwined and dependent upon one another in complex ways, which makes the term "indie" a constantly evolving term for listeners today.

Conclusion

Interviews indicate that the distinction between majors and independents are still meaningful in hip-hop's culture. As Immortal Technique famously said on "Industrial Revolution" (2003a) about his rise as a rapper: "stuck in the underground, a general that rose to the limit, without distribution managers, a deal, or a gimmick." Immortal Technique's rise to fame is indicative of numerous musicians who willingly choose to remain indie. Listeners claim that access to economic and cultural resources remains a key issue in the hip-hop community. Additionally, they raise issues of authenticity, citing that indie rappers are better able to create music aligned with listeners' social locations and experiences of race and class, and in some instances gender and sexuality. The results show that many female and LGBTQA listeners believe that a large majority of musicians remain sexist, heteronormative, and homophobic in their lyrics despite having progressive views of race and class in the USA. Yet for respondents like Sierra, hip-hop still has the potential to address pertinent social issues relevant to her social life, such as "racial discrimination, gender inequality, poverty, and LGBTQ rights."

Nonetheless, the concept of "indie" has frequently been questioned by listeners. As Immortal Technique raps on 2003s "Crossing the Boundary" (2003b), "you're only minor 'til your major." At times, listeners and the broader hip-hop community have even declared the "death" of indie hip-hop. Interviewees suggest that the categories indie and major are not binary because so many artists operate in a mixed space with blurred lines wherein independent and major companies remain highly intertwined. For example, listeners mention that indie musicians are frequently pulled and pushed into the mainstream as they attempt to be financially successful.

The definition of "indie" has changed over time as it faces waves of commodification and resistance. This has become more evident with the rapid advances in technology, namely the utilization of the Internet to distribute music and promote social media. This most recent change has created new problems for hip-hop culture, as it searches to find itself among a dispersed group of artists and listeners (Karubian 2009). Listeners are well aware that the majors and indies coexist and are codependent upon one another in the music industry. As Andrews (2006) states, "independent culture can survive…though the definition might remain ever-changing."

REFERENCES

A-Trak. 2014. "Why 2014 Was One of the Best Years for Rap: The Left Field Seeped Out of the Margins and into the Mainstream." Retrieved April 15, 2016. www.medium.com/cuepoint/why-2014-was-one-of-the-best-years-for-rap-4-ecab5b0ecf#.kj6dx5wp.

Ahmed, Insanul. 2011. "Interview: Lupe Fiasco Hates His Own Album." Retrieved April 15, 2016. http://www.complex.com/music/2011/02/interview-lupe-fiasco-hates-lasers.

Alim, Samy, Jooyoung Lee, and Lauren Mason Carris. 2010. "'Short Fried-Rice-Eating Chinese MCs' and 'Good-Hair-Havin Uncle Tom Niggas': Performing Race and Ethnicity in Freestyle Rap Battles." *Journal of Linguistic Anthropology* 20 (1): 116–133.

Andrews, Catherine. 2006. "If It's Cool, Creative and Different, It's Indie." Retrieved April 15, 2016. http://www.cnn.com/2006/SHOWBIZ/Music/09/19/indie.overview/.

Asante, Molefi Kete. 2008. *It's Bigger Than Hip Hop: The Rise of the Post-Hip-Hop Generation.* New York: St. Martin's Press.

Austen, Ben. 2016. "The New Pioneers: Chance the Rapper Is One of the Hottest Acts in Music, Has a Top 10 Album and His Own Festival—All Without a Label or Physical Release." Retrieved January 1, 2018. https://www.billboard.com/articles/news/magazine-feature/7468570/chance-the-rapper-coloring-book-labels-grammys.

Baker, Soren. 2014. "50 Cent Leaves Interscope: How Nas, Busta Rhymes, Ghostface Killah & Mos Def Fared After Leaving Their Longtime Label Homes." Retrieved April 15, 2016. http://hiphopdx.com/news/id.27806/title.50-cent-leaves-interscope-how-nas-busta-rhymes-ghostface-killah-mos-def-fared-after-leaving-their-longtime-label-homes.

Basu, Dipannita, and Pnina Werbner. 2001. "Bootstrap Capitalism and the Culture Industries: A Critique of Invidious Comparisons in the Study of Ethnic Entrepreneurship." *Ethnic and Racial Studies* 24 (2): 236–262.

Bechtel, Craig. 2016. "Knowledge Drop: The Evolution of Del the Funky Homosapien." Retrieved April 15, 2016. http://music.newcity.com/2016/05/05/knowledge-drop-the-evolution-of-del-the-funky-homosapien/.

Best, Cassidy, Katie Braile, Emily Falvey, Samantha Ross, Julia Rotunno, and David Schreiber. 2017. "A 'Chance' of Success: The Influence of Subcultural Capital on the Commercial Success of Chance The Rapper." *Journal of the Music & Entertainment Industry Educators Association* 17 (1): 31–58.

Biondo, Michael. 2012. "Strange Music's Social Media Marketing May Have a Hand in Their Success." Retrieved April 15, 2016. http://www.mainstreethost.com/blog/strange-musics-social-media-marketing-may-have-a-hand-in-their-success/.

Bootleg Kev. 2012. "Macklemore Talks L.A. Reid Trying to Sign Him & Atmosphere Comparisons w/ Bootleg Kev." Retrieved April 15, 2016. https://www.youtube.com/watch?v=ojD1OSymbbk.

Burgess, Omar. 2012. "Today's Mathematics: How Hip-Hop Measures Commercial Success." Retrieved April 15, 2016. http://hiphopdx.com/editorials/id.2023/title.todays-mathematics-how-hip-hop-measures-commercialsuccess.

Caramanica, Jon. 2017. "The Rowdy World of Rap's New Underground: The Lo-Fi Rap That Thrives on SoundCloud Teems with Unruly Energy. Can It Survive the Mainstream?" Retrieved January 1, 2018. https://www.nytimes.com/2017/06/22/arts/music/soundcloud-rap-lil-pump-smokepurrp-xxx-tentacion.html.

Carter, Sophia. 2014. "Rainbow Noise Entertainment—Turning Music Upside Down." Retrieved April 15, 2016. http://vadamagazine.com/entertainment/music/rainbow-noise-entertainment.

Cooper, Roman. 2009. "MURS Leaves Warner Bros., Talks New Projects." Retrieved April 15, 2016. http://hiphopdx.com/news/id.9829/title.murs-leaves-warner-bros-talks-new-projects.

Drake, David. 2015. "If It Ain't About the Money: Does Hip-Hop Still Need Major Labels?" Retrieved April 15, 2016. www.complex.com/music/2015/01/hip-hop-major-labels-2015.

Folami, Akilah. 2007. "From Habermas to Get Rich or Die Tryin: Hip-Hop, the Telecommunications Act of 1996, and the Black Public Sphere." *Michigan Journal of Race and Law* 12: 235–304.

Forman, Murray. 2000. "Represent: Race, Place, and Space in Rap Music." *Popular Music* 19 (1): 65–90.

Forman, Murray. 2010. "Conscious Hip-Hop, Change, and the Obama Era." *American Studies Journal* 54: 1–20.

Fox, Mark. 2004. "E-commerce Business Models for the Music Industry." *Popular Music and Society* 27 (2): 201–220.

Frazier, Walter. 2010. "Lupe Fiasco Drops Label Beef to Focus on 'Lasers'." Retrieved April 15, 2016. http://www.billboard.com/articles/news/948646/lupe-fiasco-drops-label-beef-to-focus-on-lasers.

Gosa, Travis. 2010. "Not Another Remix: How Obama Became the First Hip-Hop President." *Journal of Popular Music Studies* 22 (4): 289–415.

Gottfried, Gideon. 2014. "Fragmentation of the Music Industry: Everything Is Falling Apart—Luckily." Retrieved April 15, 2016. www.imusicandigital.com/en/blog/fragmentation-of-the-music-industry.

Greenburg, Zach O' Malley. 2015. "Revenge of the Record Labels: How the Majors Renewed Their Grip On Music." Retrieved April 15, 2016. http://www.forbes.com/sites/zackomalleygreenburg/2015/04/15/revenge-of-the-record-labels-how-the-majors-renewed-their-grip-on-music/.

Greene, Talib Kweli. 2015. "Why I Left the Major Label System: And a Little Bit of What I've Learned in the Music Biz." Retrieved April 15, 2016. https://medium.com/cuepoint/why-i-left-the-major-label-system-a0ecfa06ae91#.60fmop8ap.

Gupta-Carlson, Himanee. 2010. "Planet B-Girl: Community Building and Feminism in Hip-Hop." *New Political Science* 32 (4): 515–529.

Harkness, Geoff. 2012. "True School: Situational Authenticity in Chicago's Hip-Hop Underground." *Cultural Sociology* 6 (3): 283–298.

Harrison, Anthony Kwame. 2006. "Cheaper Than a CD, Plus We Really Mean It: Bay Area Underground Hip Hop Tapes as Subcultural Artefacts." *Popular Music* 25: 283–301.

Hesmondhalgh, David. 1999. "Indie: The Institutional Politics and Aesthetics of a Popular Music Genre." *Cultural Studies* 13 (1): 34–61.

Hess, Mickey, 2012. "The Rap Career." In *That's the Joint: The Hip Hop Studies Reader*, edited by Murray Forman and Marc Anthony Neal, 634–654. New York: Routledge.

Hibbett, Ryan. 2005. "What Is Indie Rock?" *Popular Music and Society* 28 (1): 55–77.

Hip Hop Since 1987 TV. 2013. "Brother Ali Talks Being Independent, 90s Business Model Being Popular Today & more." Retrieved April 15, 2016. https://www.youtube.com/watch?v=eYK0lc_gwTw.

Hunter, Margaret. 2011. "Shake It, Baby, Shake It: Consumption and the New Gender Relation in Hip-Hop." *Sociological Perspectives* 54 (1): 15–26.

Immortal Technique. 2003a. "Industrial Revolution." *Revolutionary Vol. 2*. Viper Records.

Immortal Technique. 2003b. "Obnoxious." *Revolutionary Vol. 2*. Viper Records.

Jeffries, Michael. 2011. *Thug Life: Race, Gender, and the Meaning of Hip-Hop*. Chicago: University of Chicago Press.

Jones, Steve. 2002. "Music That Moves: Popular Music, Distribution and Network Technologies." *Cultural Studies* 16 (2): 213–232.

Karubian, Sara. 2009. "360 Deals: An Industry Reaction to the Devaluation of Recorded Music." *Southern California Interdisciplinary Law Journal* 18: 395–462.

Knab, Christopher. 2004. "How and Why Major Labels and Independent Labels Work Together." Retrieved April 15, 2016. http://www.musicbizacademy.com/knab/articles/majorindie.htm.

Leyshon, Andrew, Peter Webb, Shaun French, Nigel Thrift, and Louise Crew. 2005. "On the Reproduction of the Musical Economy After the Internet." *Media, Culture and Society* 27 (2): 177–209.

Live Nation. 2013. "Live Nation's Artist Nation Introduces G-Major Lead by Veteran Artist Manager Virginia Davis." Retrieved January 1, 2018. http://investors.livenationentertainment.com/news-center/

news-center-details/2013/Live-Nations-Artist-Nation-Introduces-G-Major-Lead-By-Veteran-Artist-Manager-Virginia-Davis/default.aspx.

Lopes, Paul. 1992. "Innovation and Diversity in the Popular Music Industry: 1969–1990." *American Sociological Review* 57 (1): 56–71.

Mansbridge, Jane, and Aldon Morris. 2001. *Oppositional Consciousness: The Subjective Roots of Social Protest*. Chicago: University of Chicago Press.

Markman, Rob. 2011. "Killer Mike Talks Reconciling with Big Boi." Retrieved April 15, 2016. http://www.mtv.com/news/1662818/killer-mike-big-boi/.

Markman, Rob. 2013. "Chief Keef's Interscope Deal Revealed to Be Worth $6 Million." Retrieved April 15, 2016. http://www.mtv.com/news/1700678/chief-keef-recording-contract/.

Marshall, Lee. 2013. "The 360 Deal and the 'New' Music Industry." *European Journal of Cultural Studies* 16 (1): 77–99.

McLeod, Kembrew. 2005. "MP3s are Killing Home Taping: The Rise of Internet Distribution and Its Challenge to the Major Label Music Monopoly." *Popular Music and Society* 28 (4): 521–531.

Moore, Marcus. 2015. "MURS: Have a Nice Life." Retrieved April 15, 2016. http://pitchfork.com/reviews/albums/20622-have-a-nice-life/.

Moore, Ryan. 2007. "Friends Don't Let Friends Listen to Corporate Rock: Punk as a Field of Production." *Journal of Contemporary Ethnography* 36 (4): 438–474.

Morgan, Marcyliena, and Dionne Bennett. 2011. "Hip-Hop & the Global Imprint of a Black Cultural Form." *Dædalus: the Journal of the American Academy of Arts & Sciences* 140 (2): 176–196.

Myer, Letrez, and Christine Kleck. 2007. "From Independent to Corporate: A Political Economic Analysis of Rap Billboard Toppers." *Popular Music and Society* 30 (2): 137–148.

Nathan S. 2015. "Your Favorite Indie Rapper is Secretly Signed to a Major Label." Retrieved April 15, 2016. http://djbooth.net/news/entry/indie-rapper-secretly-signed-major-label.

Nguyen, Hao. 2015a. "How Tech N9ne Became the Top Independent Hip-Hop Artist in the Game Today." Retrieved April 15, 2016. http://www.stopthebreaks.com/independent-case-studies/how-tech-n9ne-became-top-independent-hip-hop-artist-game-today/.

Nguyen, Hao. 2015b. "Independent Hip-Hop Record Label Profile: 300 Entertainment." Retrieved April 15, 2016. http://www.stopthebreaks.com/independent-case-studies/independent-hip-hop-record-label-profile-300-entertainment/.

Ollison, Rashod. 2008. "MURS Goes Mainstream." Retrieved April 15, 2016. http://articles.baltimoresun.com/2008-10-30/entertainment/0810280109_1_murs-for-president-rapper-major-label.

Ostrove, Geoffrey. 2014. "The Political Economy of Financially Successful Independent Artists." *Class, Race and Corporate Power* 2 (1): 1–22.

Oware, Matthew. 2014. "(Un)Conscious (Popular) Underground: Restricted Cultural Production and Underground Rap Music." *Poetics* 42: 60–81.

Paine, Jake. 2013. "Logic Signs to Def Jam Records, NO I.D. to Executive Produce Album." Retrieved April 15, 2016. http://hiphopdx.com/news/id.23588/title.logic-signs-to-def-jam-records-no-i-d-to-executive-produce-debut-album/.

Peisner, David. 2015. "Why the Rap Veterans Behind Atlanta Indie Label Quality Control Music Are the Smartest Guys in Hip-Hop." Retrieved April 15, 2016. http://www.billboard.com/articles/news/6443743/quality-control-smartest-guys-in-hip-hop.

Peters, Mitchell, and Chris Martins. 2016. "Watch Dr. Dre Welcome Anderson. Paak to Aftermath Roster." Retrieved April 15, 2016. http://www.billboard.com/articles/columns/hip-hop/6859424/dr-dre-anderson-paak-compton-malibu-aftermath-entertainment.

Phillips, Amy. 2017. "Chance the Rapper Explains How He's Still Independent, Despite Apple Music Deal." Retrieved January 1, 2018. https://pitchfork.com/news/71701-chance-the-rapper-explains-how-hes-still-independent-despite-apple-music-deal/.

Pough, Gwendolyn. 2004. *Check It While I Wreck It: Black Womanhood, Hip-Hop Culture, and the Public Sphere.* Boston, NH: Northeastern University Press.

Raymer, Miles. 2013. "Cakes Da Killa: The Eulogy." Retrieved April 15, 2016. http://pitchfork.com/reviews/albums/17684-the-eulogy/.

Resnikoff, Paul. 2017. "How to Get Signed by Spotify Records." Retrieved January 1, 2018. https://www.digitalmusicnews.com/2017/03/20/get-signed-spotify-records/.

Reynolds, Daniel. 2015. "The Exclusive Interview with Mykki Blanco You've Been Waiting For." Retrieved April 15, 2016. http://www.hivplusmag.com/people/2015/10/08/mykkis-mad-genius.

Rose, Tricia. 2008. *The Hip Hop Wars: What We Talk About When We Talk About Hip Hop—And Why It Matters.* New York: Basic Civitas.

Scholtes, Peter. 2007. "Rhymesayers Sign Deal with Warner." Retrieved April 15, 2016. http://www.citypages.com/music/rhymesayers-sign-deal-with-warners-6620729.

Schwartzberg, Lauren. 2014. "Lesbian Hip-Hop Hits Primetime." Retrieved April 15, 2016. https://www.vice.com/en_us/article/out-comes-the-lesbian-rap-ballad-456.

Sehgal, Kabir. 2018. "Spotify and Apple Music Should Become Record Labels so Musicians Can Make a Fair Living." Retrieved January 1, 2018. https://www.cnbc.com/2018/01/26/how-spotify-apple-music-can-pay-musicians-more-commentary.html.

Sköld, David, and Alf Rehn. 2007. "Makin' It, by Keeping It Real Street Talk, Rap Music, and the Forgotten Entrepreneurship from 'the Hood.'" *Group & Organization Management* 32 (1): 50–78.

Smith, Clyde. 2012. "The Heist: Macklemore & Ryan Lewis Take DIY Route to iTunes #1." Retrieved April 15, 2016. http://www.hypebot.com/hypebot/2012/10/the-heist-macklemore-ryan-lewis-take-diy-route-to-itunes-1.html.

Smith, Clyde. 2013. "The Major 'Exposure' of Macklemore and the Myth of the Indie Artist." Retrieved April 15, 2016. http://www.hypebot.com/hypebot/2013/02/the-exposure-of-macklemore-and-the-myth-of-the-indie-artist.html.

Stahl, Matt, and Leslie Meier. 2012. "The Firm Foundation of Organizational Flexibility: The 360 Contract in the Digitalizing Music Industry." *Canadian Journal of Communication* 37: 441–458.

Stern, Bradley. 2016. "Mykki Blanco Is Right: Gay Media Has an Inclusivity Problem." Retrieved April 15, 2016. http://popcrush.com/mykki-blanco-gay-media-inclusivity-problem/.

Strachan, Robert. 2007. "Micro-Independent Record Labels in the UK." *European Journal of Cultural Studies* 10 (2): 245–265.

Suhr, Hiesun. 2011. "Understanding the Hegemonic Struggle Between Mainstream Vs. Independent Forces: The Music Industry and Musicians in the Age of Social Media." *International Journal of Technology, Knowledge and Society* 7 (6): 123–136.

The NE Hip-Hop. 2015. "Aesop Rock & Rob Sonic Talk Soundset, Indy Hip-Hop Today, Upcoming Solo Projects & More!" Retrieved April 15, 2016. https://www.youtube.com/watch?v=Z8Pf2eBDR-8.

XXL Staff. 2008. "The #6 Biggest Moment: Cash Money Signs with Universal." Retrieved April 15, 2016. http://www.xxlmag.com/xxl-magazine/2008/02/the-6-biggest-moment-cash-money-signs-with-universal/.

Open Access This chapter is distributed under the terms of the Creative Commons Attribution 4.0 International License (http://creativecommons.org/licenses/by/4.0/), which permits use, duplication, adaptation, distribution and reproduction in any medium or format, as long as you give appropriate credit to the original author(s) and the source, a link is provided to the Creative Commons license and any changes made are indicated.The images or other third party material in this chapter are included in the work's Creative Commons license, unless indicated otherwise in the credit line; if such material is not included in the work's Creative Commons license and the respective action is not permitted by statutory regulation, users will need to obtain permission from the license holder to duplicate, adapt or reproduce the material.

CHAPTER 5

Conclusions and Implications

Abstract This chapter discusses how previous chapters fill gaps in the literature and how this has implications for academics, readers, and the hip-hop community. Future research needs to be done to understand the current state of hip-hop and its relationship to the broader community. Artists' and listeners' grievances are changing, especially as independent hip-hop artists and listeners are becoming more diverse in terms of their gender, sexuality, and racial and ethnic make up, a new generation of artists and listeners is emerging, technological and media changes are shifting the boundaries between independent and major, and the political and economic context is shifting. All of these changes are likely to have important implications for the potential of indie hip-hop to inspire oppositional consciousness among its listeners.

Keywords Cooptation and resistance · Diaspora and glocalization · Music and technology · Old school and new school hip-hop · Millennial generation · Fil-Am hip-hop

Independent hip-hop has seen a revival in response to the mass corporatization of its culture in the 1990s (Watkins 2005). Songs such as "Commencement Day" by Blue Scholars (2005) write: "instead, rock the mixtape and Walkman discrete, with the headphones threaded from the pocket through the sleeve, you received education through the music you heard." They demonstrate the resurgence of an indie culture that emphasizes messages of resistance to domination and oppression. My book addresses an age-old question: to what extent and how independent hip-hop challenges or reproduces mainstream hip-hop culture and US culture more generally. In particular, I explore and analyze the historical trajectory of indie hip-hop in the post-golden era and how it has affected the culture today. I contend that indie hip-hop remains a complex contemporary subculture. While it consistently expresses grievances related to both race and class inequality, its gender and sexual politics are contradictory (Oware 2014). Nonetheless, independent hip-hop expresses the oppositional consciousness of its artists and listeners as well as the limits of that consciousness (Harkness 2012; Kubrin 2005; Lena and Peterson 2008; Martinez 1997; Myer and Kleck 2007; Stapleton 1998).

My research combines theoretical insights from neo-Marxist, critical race, intersectional feminist, and queer theories as well as Mansbridge and Morris' (2001) concept of oppositional consciousness to critically analyze the politics of hip-hop culture. The previous chapters utilize a mixed method approach to answer these research questions using qualitative data. Chapters 2 and 3 use acontent analysis of twenty-five independent hip-hop albums from 2000 to 2013 to determine the salient themes in artists' lyrics. Chapter 4 gathers data from forty-six interviews of independent hip-hop community members who are self-defined listeners or fans that are active in the community to unpack the meanings they associate with hip-hop culture, how technology and media have created changes for the artists and listeners, and how it shapes their engagement in oppositional consciousness.

Overall, my findings highlight the vexed and contradictory nature of the politics of independent hip-hop. Chapter 2 finds that independent hip-hop in the post-golden era indeed challenges US mainstream hip-hop culture and US culture more generally. First, these acts resist the majors in three ways: (1) mainstream artists, (2) large radio stations, and (3) major record labels. Second, they reject the corporatization and commodification by major record companies and mainstream culture in favor of independently owned companies. Third, they advocate for a culture based on alternative cultural ideals, and thus socially construct and advocate for a brand of authenticity rooted in hip-hop's origins.

In addition to cultural differences, Chapter 3 focuses on how independent hip-hop of the genre resists economic exploitation from mainstream culture and large corporations in various ways.

For example, indie musicians claim that major labels profit at the expense of performers. Their exploitation is predominantly reflected in the contracts acts sign with major labels. This has repercussions for artists in numerous facets of the music industry: (1) advances/forwards, (2) control of copyrights, (3) artistic direction and relations with A&R, (4) touring, merchandising, and advertising deals, and (5) radio stations, media, and press. Finally, some hip-hop artists argue that creating and maintaining independent record labels helps mitigate economic exploitation, controls record label oversight, and better serves the hip-hop community.

Chapter 4 unpacks how listeners interpret and navigate the changing landscape and blurring lines of major and independent hip-hop culture in the post-golden era. It also analyzes their interpretations of race, class, gender, sexual orientation, and the fomentation of oppositional consciousness. Interviewees indicate that the traditional definitions of major and independent remain intact as record label affiliation remains salient to listeners. Interviews suggest that authenticity is socially constructed and reinforced through listener's interpretations of artist messages regarding race, class, gender, and sexual orientation. Many respondents, particularly women and queer listeners, claim that heterosexual working-class men of color dominate indie hip-hop, and thus issues of gender and sexuality remain at the margins. Yet, their representation has increased and led to challenges in the traditional conceptions of authenticity within hip-hop. Also, results show that there is a blurred line between the majors and independents as performers attempt to retain economic and creative freedom while still attempting to become financially successful. In essence, the culture is not viewed as binary oppositions but rather as fluid and constantly changing in the ways that they are complexly intertwined. Lastly, many respondents discuss waves of commodification and resistance in the "indie" movement. They state that a period of resistance followed the mass commodification of hip-hop in the early 2000s. Currently, major advances in technology have allowed artists to become commercially successful without the aid of large corporations. But interviews reveal that they still remain intensely intertwined with large businesses in various ways such as affiliating with major companies to utilize their marketing and distribution channels. Ultimately, the findings reported show that hip-hop is indeed highly intertwined with broader technological shifts and resistance.

This Chapter first recapitulated the key findings of my work. Currently, my research fills two large gaps in the literature. Most work tends to focus on mainstream hip-hop (Kelley 1994; Perry 2004; Rose 1994), disparate underground groups (Ball 2009; Harrison 2006; Wang 2014), or global hip-hop (Androutsopoulos and Scholz 2003; Bennett 1999; Mitchell 2003), leaving a large portion of the culture in the USA understudied. Also, a majority of hip-hop (Kelley 1994; Perry 2004; Rose 1994) focuses on the "old school" generation, leaving a plethora of research on younger artists and listeners understudied. Thus, my research: (1) aimed to better understand the politics of independent hip-hop through the lens of artists and listeners in America today, (2) added to the current scholarship by giving a voice to the new generation in the hip-hop community concerned with issues of race, class, gender, sexuality, and oppositional consciousness, and (3) understood the historical trajectory of independent hip-hop in the post-golden era and how that affects the complex and changing nature of the culture.

Future research needs to be done to understand the current state of hip-hop and its relationship to the broader community in order to anticipate future directions in society. Artists' grievances are changing, especially as indie hip-hop acts and listeners are becoming more diverse in terms of their gender, sexuality, and racial and ethnic make up, a new generation of artists and listeners is emerging, advances in technology and media are occurring, and the political and economic context is shifting. All of these changes are likely to have important implications for the potential of independent hip-hop to inspire oppositional consciousness among its listeners.

Important Implications

My work has various implications for academics, readers, and the hip-hop community. My research provides valuable insight to the academic community and readers in three ways: (1) the emphasis on the dialectical process of cooptation and resistance, (2) a reminder of hip-hop's vitality and contribution to broader society, and (3) its potential to subvert domination and oppression by fomenting oppositional consciousness and the potential for resistance. It also contributes to the hip-hop community by explicating how it has changed and evolved since its inception. This is particularly useful for the Millennial and Generation Z population in understanding hip-hop's history when facing continued problems of racism, classism, and sexism, yet possessing new means of technology such as the Internet and social media to create a discourse about these salient issues.

Research Implications

My work highlights the importance of the continued need to study independent hip-hop, which has many complex pockets of cooptation and resistance (Rose 1994; Terkourafi 2010; Vito 2015a; Watkins 2005). A nuanced understanding of the struggles between cooptation and resistance will allow scholars to understand hip-hop as a site of contestation within the social landscape in America; particularly the contradictions among artists and listeners regarding issues of race, class, gender, and sexuality. In this current generation, much of the culture is still marred with patriarchy and heteronormativity (Harkness 2012; Kubrin 2005; Lena and Peterson 2008; Martinez 1997; Myer and Kleck 2007; Stapleton 1998). Socially conscious rappers such as Kendrick Lamar and J. Cole have ascended into the spotlight. While being touted as intellectual leaders of their generation, they still struggle to not fall into the hands of capitalism, engage in misogyny, and uphold heteronormative standards. Similarly, artists such as Frank Ocean and Young Ma helped push issues of gender and sexuality into the forefront of American culture and challenge many traditionally held notions of heteronormativity in hip-hop. Yet they must still deal with the problems of assimilation into Western European capitalist ideology, espousing heteronormative ideology, and the commodification of queer culture.

My research also supports the expanding body of literature that analyzes the diaspora of hip-hop around the world. For example, indie Iraqi act Lowkey utilizes glocalization to address issues of race and class in his local community (Vito 2015b). Lowkey has since returned from a hiatus in 2011 to continue rapping about the current sociopolitical landscape in the UK. My analysis emphasizes the complex dialectical struggle between cooptation and resistance as communities use hip-hop to address pertinent local and global social issues (Delamont and Stephens 2008; Dennis 2006; Hesmondhalgh and Melville 2002; Lin 2006; Maxwell 1994; Mitchell 2000; Omoniyi 2006). I believe that scholars need to continue to look both within the USA and globally to understand how different subcultures respond to periods of cooptation and resistance. This means that these dialectical forces must be analyzed with a strong understanding of the long history of struggle for power within the hip-hop community (Vito 2015a).

Further, scholars such as Tricia Rose (2008) have previously questioned hip-hop's vitality as it moved past the golden era. While much of the mainstream has been co-opted by major record labels and corporate culture, I argue that independent hip-hop has remained relevant and significantly impacts society today as artists and listeners continue to challenge the status quo and engage in critical thought. California rapper Hopsin has amassed an established fan-base in the independent hip-hop community for his critical opinions of American society. After obtaining popular success in 2012, he has continued his "Ill-Mind" song franchise and started his own label: *Undercover Prodigy*. In 2017, he signed with 300 Entertainment. New York's Marlon Craft has gained popularity on the East Coast underground scene as an unsigned act addressing many social issues Millennials and Generation Zs face today. Similar to his predecessors like Eminem and Macklemore and Ryan Lewis, Marlon Craft addresses issues of being white in a predominantly African-American and Latino scene. I believe that the new generation of acts will continue to challenge mainstream culture in various ways despite shifting conceptions of indie culture and music. Scholars must remain attuned to three trends in the industry such as the new methods of music distribution such as online mixtapes and streaming media sites, the innovative ways of garnering buzz in the digital age, and alternative deals with corporations that keep big business at arms length from their musical content, persona, and daily operations.

While I believe that artists are finding new means of music production, distribution, and advertising that may minimize the need for record label involvement and subsequently subvert the power structure that favors large corporations, they must be aware that companies constantly attempt to forge new ways of expanding their market and regain control of these revolutionized means of production (Maher 2005; Rose 2008; Morgan and Bennett 2011). The previous generation of scholars explicated the lasting impact that CDs and P2P sharing had on the industry, but this generation is still seeing the profound effects that the Internet, social media, and even virtual reality will have for the future. I argue that scholars need to continue to study these dialectical forces to better understand the broad historical patterns that shape the current industry.

I conclude that the future of hip-hop studies remains bright. Authors such as Tricia Rose (1994, 2008), Michael Eric Dyson (2010), and Nelson George (2005) have paved the way for the new wave of hip-hop enthusiasts. This current generation of scholars must be able to analyze the complexity of the new youth movement as they find new ways of subverting mainstream America. Söderman (2013) discusses the process of academization in hip-hop studies in which it must both be defended and criticized. Emery Petchauer (2015) continues to advocate for a discourse of hip-hop music in the classroom as it remains a valuable tool for political engagement. Similarly, new literature is being formed around highly contested social issues in the USA ranging from race and class in hip-hop's urbanism (Jeffries 2014; Villegas et al. 2013), representations of race and masculinity (Belle 2014; McTaggart and O' Brien 2017; Oware 2011; Shabazz 2014), and the ascendance of hip-hop feminism (Durham et al. 2013) (Fig. 5.1).

Additionally, writers continue to analyze the impact that hip-hop has globally (Saunders 2016; Taviano 2016). Current research has demonstrated that hip-hop scholarship is still relevant even as it continues to

Fig. 5.1 DJ Kuttin Kandi (*Credit* djkuttinkandi.com)

be commercialized and connects with other genres of music, television, movies, and social media. Yet the key question remains: How will the next generation interact with other forms of media, the community, and social issues?

Implications for the Hip-Hop Community

As a fan and avid listener, I believe that in order to grow hip-hop must continue its affiliation with racial and ethnic minority groups in the USA and globally, bridge the gap between the "old school" and "new school," and stand united in opposition to all forms of oppression and domination. Hip-hop needs to increase its affiliation with minority groups in the USA and globally. For example, Fil-Ams (Filipino-Americans) continue to be marginalized in the community. Hip-hop must be inclusive of other minority groups rather than asserting that only "African-American hip-hop" is authentic and genuine. This requires an understanding of the multiple axes of oppression, which includes race, ethnicity, gender, and sexuality, to spark critical thought and encourage oppositional consciousness. California rapper Ruby Ibarra addresses these multiple axes when rapping about her experiences as a female immigrant coming from the Philippines to the USA.

I also believe that the previous generation must work with the Millennial and Generation Z population to build strong bridges between the "old school" and "new school." Some old school enthusiasts argue that the new generation has become popular music and merely reproduces dominant ideologies. I remind critics that the previous generation responded to a similar changing landscape in their era—namely—the rise of recorded music and the widespread availability of television and computers in disseminating hip-hop culture. Concordantly, the new generation has faced similar shifts in technological advancement, globalization, and unstable sociopolitical climates. While the new school has adapted to these changes, they still need to learn from the past in order to positively shape the present and future. These generations may clash in terms of their views on the true "authentic" version of hip-hop culture, but they must maintain a common ground—namely engaging in critical thinking and the opposition to oppression—to instigate social change.

Ultimately, the hip-hop community needs to stand united in its opposition to social oppression and domination. Its value lies in the ability to challenge multiple relations of domination and to support the causes of multiple types of left-leaning social movements. For example, hip-hop has played a major role in expressing the ideas, broadening the reach, and publicizing the events of various social movements such as Occupy Wall Street, Black Lives Matter, the Women's March and #MeToo, and A Day without Immigrants Movement. Yet I predict the industry is headed toward another period of commodification. With the releases of artists under the independent brand but still possess strong ties to major corporations, I contend that we will see major record labels and corporations taking back much of social media, the means of production, and technology. With this, I think that hip-hop will need to again revolutionize the means of production and come up with innovative ways to resist cooptation and corporatization if they are to continue challenging status quo.

Future Research

The field of hip-hop studies continues to expand as we explore the complex ways in which culture plays a vital role in our society. I hope to continue to contribute to this literature by interviewing and observing local independent artists in San Diego. I believe that their lyrics are a valid source of data, but interacting with them beyond their lyrics will yield valuable results. More specifically, their way of thinking, their motivations, their actions, and their interpretations of society will become clearer.

I also intend to study a local barbershop in San Diego and their connection to the hip-hop community. Knowledge, culture, and language are disseminated at these local shops and thus act as an important source of potential resistance to mainstream America. In addition, they act as a transcultural space wherein individuals of various racial and ethnic backgrounds interact with one another in an intimate setting. In San Diego, many shops have to adapt to their local demographics, which can include forming ethnically homogenous enclaves or creating sites of multicultural production. I am particularly interested in how Fil-Ams (Filipino-Americans), particularly second and third generation Fil-Ams, negotiate their identity by incorporating hip-hop and barber shop culture into their everyday experiences. I ultimately believe that analyzing the independent hip-hop community in San Diego will allow for a rich understanding of the culture's relationship to local and global social processes (Fig. 5.2).

Fig. 5.2 Goodfellas Barbershop Shave Parlor (*Credit* Christopher Vito)

References

Androutsopoulos, Jannis, and Arno Scholz. 2003. "Spaghetti Funk: Appropriations of Hip-Hop Culture and Rap Music in Europe." *Popular Music and Society* 26 (4): 463–479.

Ball, Jared. 2009. "FreeMix Radio: The Original Mixtape Radio Show: A Case Study in Mixtape 'Radio' and Emancipatory Journalism." *Journal of Black Studies* 39 (4): 614–634.

Belle, Crystal. 2014. "From Jay-Z to Dead Prez: Examining Representations of Black Masculinity in Mainstream Versus Underground Hip-Hop Music." *Journal of Black Studies* 45 (4): 287–300.

Bennett, Andy. 1999. "Rappin' on the Tyne: White Hip Hop Culture in Northeast England—An Ethnographic Study." *The Sociological Review* 47: 1–24.

Blue Scholars. 2005. "Commencement Day." *The Long March*. Massline.

Delamont, Sara, and Neil Stephens. 2008. "Up on the Roof: The Embodied Habitus of Diasporic Capoeira." *Cultural Sociology* 2 (1): 57–74.

Dennis, Chrisopher. 2006. "Afro-Columbian Hip-Hop: Globalization, Popular Music and Ethnic Identities." *Studies in Latin American Popular Culture* 25: 271–295.

Durnham, Aisha, Brittney Cooper, and Susuna Morris. 2013. "The Stage Hip-Hop Feminism Built: A New Directions Essay." *Signs* 38 (3): 721–737.

Dyson, Michael Eric. 2010. *Know What I Mean: Reflections on Hip-Hop*. New York: Basic Civitas.

George, Nelson. 2005. *Hip-Hop America*. New York: Viking.

Harkness, Geoff. 2012. "True School: Situational Authenticity in Chicago's Hip-Hop Underground." *Cultural Sociology* 6 (3): 283–298.

Harrison, Anthony Kwame. 2006. "Cheaper Than a CD, Plus We Really Mean It: Bay Area Underground Hip Hop Tapes as Subcultural Artefacts." *Popular Music* 25: 283–301.

Hesmondhalgh, David, and Caspar Melville. 2002. "Urban Breakbeat Culture—Repercussions of Hip-Hop in the United Kingdom." In *Global Noise: Rap and Hip Hop Outside the USA*, edited by Tony Mitchell, 86–110. Middletown, CT: Wesleyan University Press.

Jeffries, Michael. 2014. "Hip-Hop Urbanism Old and New." *International Journal of Urban and Regional Research* 38 (2): 706–715.

Kelley, Robin. 1994. *Race Rebels: Culture, Politics, and the Black Working Class*. New York: Free Press.

Kubrin, Charis. 2005. "Gangstas, Thugs, and Hustlas: Identity and the Code of the Street in Rap Music." *Social Problems* 52 (3): 360–378.

Lena, Jennifer, and Richard Peterson. 2008. "Classification of Culture: Types and Trajectories of Music Genres." *American Sociological Review* 73: 697–718.

Lin, Angel. 2006. "Independent Hip-Hop Artists in Hong-Kong: Cultural Capitalism, Youth Subculture Resistance, and Alternative Modes of Cultural Production." *Mobile and Popular Culture* 1: 1–18.

Maher, George Ciccariello. 2005. "Brechtian Hip-Hop: Didactics and Self-Production in Post-Gangsta Political Mixtapes." *Journal of Black Studies* 26 (1): 129–160.

Mansbridge, Jane, and Aldon Morris. 2001. *Oppositional Consciousness: The Subjective*. Chicago and London: The University of Chicago Press.

Martinez, Theresa. 1997. "Popular Culture as Oppositional Culture: Rap as Resistance." *Sociological Perspectives* 40 (2): 265–286.

Maxwell, Ian. 1994. "True to the Music: Authenticity, Articulation and Authorship in Sydney Hip Hop Culture." *Social Semiotics* 4 (1–2): 117–137.

McTaggart, Ninochka, and Eileen O' Brien. 2017. "Seeking Liberation, Facing Marginalization: Asian Americans and Pacific Islanders' Conditional Acceptance in Hip-Hop Culture." *Sociological Inquiry* 87 (4): 634–658.

Mitchell, Tony. 2000. "Doin' Damage in My Native Language: The Use of 'Resistance Vernaculars' in Hip Hop in France, Italy, and Aotearoa/New Zealand." *Popular Music and Society* 24 (3): 41–54.

Mitchell, Tony. 2003. "Australian Hip-Hop as a Subculture." *Youth Studies Australia* 22 (2): 40–47.

Morgan, Marcyliena, and Dionne Bennett. 2011. "Hip-Hop & the Global Imprint of a Black Cultural Form." *Dædalus: The Journal of the American Academy of Arts & Sciences* 140 (2): 176–196.

Myer, Letrez, and Christine Kleck. 2007. "From Independent to Corporate: A Political Economic Analysis of Rap Billboard Toppers." *Popular Music and Society* 30 (2): 137–148.

Omoniyi, Tope. 2006. "Hip-Hop Through the World Englishes Lens: A Response to Globalization." *World Englishes* 25 (2): 195–208.

Oware, Matthew. 2011. "Brotherly Love: Homosociality and Black Masculinity in Gangsta Rap Music." *Journal of African American Studies* 15: 22–39.

Oware, Matthew. 2014. "(Un)Conscious (Popular) Underground: Restricted Cultural Production and Underground Rap Music." *Poetics* 42: 60–81.

Perry, Imani. 2004. *Prophets of the Hood: Politics and Poetics in Hip Hop*. Durham, NC: Duke University Press.

Petchauer, Emery. 2015. "Starting with Style: Toward a Second Wave of Hip-Hop Education Research and Practice." *Urban Education* 50 (1): 78–105.

Rose, Tricia. 1994. *Black Noise: Rap Music and Black Culture in Contemporary America*. New York: Wesleyan University Press.

Rose, Tricia. 2008. *The Hip Hop Wars: What We Talk About When We Talk About Hip Hop—And Why It Matters*. New York: Basic Civitas.

Saunders, Tanya. 2016. "Towards a Transnational Hip-Hop Feminist Liberatory Praxis: A View from the Americas." *Social Identities* 22 (2): 178–194.

Shabazz, Rashad. 2014. "Masculinity and the Mic: Confronting the Uneven Geography of Hip-Hop." *Gender, Place, & Culture* 21 (3): 370–386.

Söderman, Johan. 2013. "The Formation of 'Hip-Hop Academicus'—How American Scholars Talk About the Academisation of Hip-Hop." *British Journal of Music Education* 30 (3): 369–381.

Stapleton, Katina. 1998. "From the Margins to Mainstream: The Political Power of Hip-Hop." *Media, Culture & Society* 20: 219–234.

Taviano, Stefania. 2016. "The Global Imaginary of Arab Hip Hop: A Case Study." *Im@go: A Journal of the Social Imaginary* 5 (7): 183–199.

Terkourafi, Marina. 2010. *Languages of Global Hip Hop*. London: Continuum.

Villegas, Mark, DJ Kuttin' Kandi, and Roderick Labrador. 2013. *Empire of Funk: Hip-Hop and Representation in Filipina/o America*. San Diego, CA: Cognella Academic Publishing.

Vito, Christopher. 2015a. "Who Said Hip-Hop Was Dead?: The Politics of Hip-Hop Culture in Immortal Technique's Lyrics." *International Journal of Cultural Studies* 18 (4): 395–411.

Vito, Christopher. 2015b. "Can We Keep Independent Hip-Hop Lowkey?: Using Content Analysis to Analyze Globalization In Lowkey's Lyrics." *Studies in Media and Communication* 3 (2): 109–116.

Wang, Oliver. 2014. *Legions of Boom: Filipino American Mobile DJ Crews in the San Francisco Bay Area*. Durham, NC: Duke University Press.

Watkins, S. Craig. 2005. *Hip Hop Matters: Politics, Pop Culture, and the Struggle for the Soul of a Movement*. Boston, MA: Beacon Press.

Open Access This chapter is distributed under the terms of the Creative Commons Attribution 4.0 International License (http://creativecommons.org/licenses/by/4.0/), which permits use, duplication, adaptation, distribution and reproduction in any medium or format, as long as you give appropriate credit to the original author(s) and the source, a link is provided to the Creative Commons license and any changes made are indicated.The images or other third party material in this chapter are included in the work's Creative Commons license, unless indicated otherwise in the credit line; if such material is not included in the work's Creative Commons license and the respective action is not permitted by statutory regulation, users will need to obtain permission from the license holder to duplicate, adapt or reproduce the material.

Appendix A

Intake Survey

1. Background Information:
   a. Name
   b. Age
   c. Gender
   d. Sexual Orientation
   e. Race/Ethnicity
   f. Contact Information (cell phone number or e-mail)
   g. How were you referred to this intake survey and interview process?
2. Interview Requirements:
   a. What is an independent hip-hop listener and fan?
   b. Are you a self-defined independent hip-hop listener and fan?
   c. Do you have familiarity with at least 10 of the 25 independent hip-hop artists in this study?
   d. Have you been to at least 5 hip-hop-related events, which range anywhere but not limited to concerts, talks by artists and the hip-hop community, or parties involving hip-hop events, in the past 3 years?
3. Consent:

   I, _____, hereby consent to providing information on this intake survey to be used by the Principle Investigator to determine if I am a suitable

candidate for this study.   X_____
Date:_____

Appendix B

Interview Sample Population Demographics

ID#	Age	Education	Income	Employment status	Social class	Gender	Sexual orientation	Race/Ethnicity	Political orientation
1	21	In College	10,000	Part time	Working	Male	Heterosexual	Black (African American)	Liberal
2	20	In College	None	Unemployed	Middle	Male	Homosexual	Black (African American)	Liberal
3	20	In College	15,000	Part time	Working	Female	Heterosexual	Black (African American)	Liberal
4	19	In College	12,000	Part time	Middle	Male	Heterosexual	Black (African American)	Moderate
5	22	Bachelors	36,000	Full time	Working	Male	Heterosexual	Black (African American)	Moderate
6	28	In College	33,000	Full time	Working	Female	Heterosexual	Latino (Mexican)	Moderate
7	20	In College	10,000	Part time	Working	Male	Heterosexual	Latino (Mexican)	Liberal
8	23	In College	5000	Part time	Working	Male	Heterosexual	Latino (Mexican)	Liberal
9	22	High School	26,000	Full time	Working	Male	Heterosexual	Latino (Mexican)	Moderate
10	27	AA	30,000	Full time	Working	Male	Heterosexual	Asian (Filipino)	Moderate
11	22	Bachelors	30,000	Full time	Upper	Male	Heterosexual	Latino (Mexican)	Moderate
12	33	Bachelors	100,000	Full time	Working	Male	Heterosexual	Asian (Korean)	Moderate
13	30	High School	40,000	Full time	Upper	Male	Heterosexual	Latino (Mexican)	Moderate
14	28	Masters	90,000	Full time	Upper	Female	Bi-Sexual	Mixed (Chinese, White)	Liberal
15	24	Masters	40,000	Full time	Middle	Female	Heterosexual	Asian (Filipino)	Liberal
16	22	AA	13,000	Part time	Working	Male	Heterosexual	Latino (Mexican)	Moderate
17	22	In College	None	Unemployed	Upper	Female	Heterosexual	Latino (Mexican)	Moderate
18	25	Bachelors	25,000	Part time	Working	Female	Heterosexual	Latino (Mexican)	Moderate
19	20	In College	12,000	Part time	Working	Female	Heterosexual	Latino (Mexican)	Liberal
20	28	Bachelors	45,000	Full time	Working	Female	Heterosexual	Mixed (Black, Korean)	Moderate
21	20	In College	10,000	Part time	Working	Female	Bi-Sexual	Asian (Vietnamese)	Liberal
22	20	In College	None	Unemployed	Upper	Female	Heterosexual	Asian (Taiwanese)	Moderate
23	23	Bachelors	30,000	Full time	Working	Female	Bi-Sexual	White	Moderate
24	27	Bachelors	50,000	Full time	Working	Male	Heterosexual	Latino (Mexican)	Liberal
25	24	Bachelors	32,000	Full time	Working	Female	Heterosexual	Latino (Mexican)	Conservative

(continued)

(continued)

ID#	Age	Education	Income	Employment status	Social class	Gender	Sexual orientation	Race/Ethnicity	Political orientation
26	28	AA	50,000	Full time	Working	Male	Heterosexual	Asian (Filipino)	Liberal
27	33	Masters	45,000	Full time	Working	Female	Heterosexual	Latino (Mexican)	Liberal
28	21	Bachelors	None	Unemployed	Working	Male	Heterosexual	Latino (Mexican)	Liberal
29	21	In College	None	Unemployed	Middle	Female	Heterosexual	Black (Nigerian)	Liberal
30	21	In College	16,000	Part time	Working	Female	Heterosexual	Latino (Puerto Rican)	Moderate
31	30	High School	50,000	Full time	Working	Male	Heterosexual	Latino (Mexican)	Moderate
32	23	Masters	50,000	Full time	Working	Male	Heterosexual	Asian (Thai)	Liberal
33	20	In College	20,000	Part time	Working	Female	Heterosexual	Latino (Mexican)	Moderate
34	28	Bachelors	35,000	Full time	Working	Female	Heterosexual	Asian (Filipino)	Moderate
35	20	In College	None	Unemployed	Working	Gender Fluid	Homosexual	Black (African American)	Liberal
36	23	In College	15,000	Part time	Working	Male	Heterosexual	Latino (Mexican)	Liberal
37	21	In College	16,000	Part time	Working	Male	Heterosexual	Latino (Mexican)	Liberal
38	29	High School	100,000	Full time	Middle	Female	Heterosexual	Latino (Mexican)	Conservative
39	30	Masters	33,000	Full time	Working	Male	Bi-Sexual	White	Liberal
40	28	Bachelors	45,000	Full time	Working	Male	Heterosexual	Latino (Mexican)	Moderate
41	30	High School	40,000	Full time	Working	Male	Heterosexual	Asian (Filipino)	Moderate
42	21	Bachelors	15,000	Part time	Working	Male	Heterosexual	Asian (Indian)	Moderate
43	21	Bachelors	20,000	Part time	Middle	Male	Heterosexual	Black (African American)	Conservative
44	23	Bachelors	40,000	Full time	Working	Male	Heterosexual	Asian (Laotian)	Moderate
45	31	Bachelors	40,000	Part time	Upper	Female	Heterosexual	Asian (Filipino)	Conservative
46	23	Bachelors	45,000	Full time	Middle	Female	Heterosexual	Asian (Vietnamese, Cambodian, Laotian)	Liberal

Appendix C

Interview Guide

I. Demographics

    a. Name:
    b. Age:
    c. Educational Attainment:
    d. Student or/and Employment Status:
    e. Current Occupation:
    f. Income:
    g. Parents' Occupations and Educational Attainment:
    h. Gender:
    i. Sexual Orientation:
    j. Race/Ethnicity:
    k. Place of Birth and Current City of Residence:
    l. Immigration Status:

II. Independent Hip-Hop

    a. How did you begin listening to hip-hop music?
    b. How did you begin listening to independent hip-hop music?
    c. What is the reason you began listening and currently listen to independent hip-hop music?
    d. How do you define an independent hip-hop listener/fan? How are you an independent hip-hop listener/fan?

e. What types of emotions, moods, or states of mind do you feel when listening to hip-hop music? How does it differ by genre?
   f. How does independent hip-hop differentiate itself from other forms of music and entertainment?
   g. What experiences do you remember that were important in your life regarding independent hip-hop?
   h. What do you get out of listening to independent hip-hop music?
III. The Messages of Independent Hip-Hop Music
   a. What favorite artists have you previously listened to or are currently listening to?
   b. Why did/do you listen to these particular artists?
   c. For some of the artists or songs you enjoy the most, what general messages do you get from them?
   d. Why are these messages important to you? How do you connect them to your general life?
IV. The Politics of Independent Hip-Hop Music
   a. What is mainstream hip-hop music? What are their main (political and social) messages? What do you believe is occurring regarding mainstream hip-hop music?
   b. What is independent hip-hop music? What is the difference between mainstream and independent hip-hop? What are their main messages? What are the subsequent responses by independent hip-hop artists to the mainstreaming of hip-hop?
   c. Are there messages of resistance to the corporatization or mainstreaming of hip-hip culture? If so, elaborate on them and how they might differ.
   d. Do you believe that this can translate into social activism or social change regarding the trajectory of hip-hop culture? If so, elaborate on how.
V. Social Positions and Intersections of Race, Class, Gender, and Sexuality
   a. What issues of race have appeared in the lyrics of the independent hip-hop artists you have listened to?
   b. What meaningful messages do you obtain from independent hip-hop regarding race, racism, race relations, or race inequality?

c. What issues of class have appeared in the lyrics of the independent hip-hop artists you have listened to?
d. What meaningful messages do you obtain from independent hip-hop regarding class and class relations/inequality?
e. What issues of gender have appeared in the lyrics of the independent hip-hop artists you have listened to?
f. What meaningful messages do you obtain from independent hip-hop regarding men and women (gender)?
g. What issues of sexuality have appeared in the lyrics of the independent hip-hop artists you have listened to?
h. What meaningful messages do you obtain from independent hip-hop regarding sexuality?
i. What does authenticity mean to you?
   i. What is "selling out" and how does one do it?
   ii. How do you feel about the spread of hip-hop into other ethnic groups, subcultures, and nations?
j. Are there any particular instances in which you changed the way you think about race, class, gender, or sexuality from listening to music?
k. Are there any contradictions in the messages you receive from independent hip-hop? If so, what are they?

VI. Oppositional Consciousness and Social Activism
   a. Do you believe that independent hip-hop encourages artists and listeners to engage in critical thinking? If so, how? Can you cite specific examples in your life?
      i. Conversely, do you believe that hip-hop has created critical thinking for you? Or do you believe that you were already a critical thinker who has further engaged in it because of hip-hop?
   b. Do you believe that independent hip-hop can change people's views on social life? If so, can you cite examples from your own experiences or people you know?
   c. Do you believe that independent hip-hop encourages critical consciousness (or actively challenging/questioning) regarding people's social position? For example, does hip-hop allow racial minorities to gain collective consciousness? If so, how? Can you cite specific examples in your life?

d. Do you believe that independent hip-hop can be transformed into oppositional consciousness (consciousness rejecting status quo) and subsequent means of displaying it, such as social activism (acts of resistance at any level ranging from the micro to the macro)? If so, how? Can you cite specific examples in your life?

   i. What are your experiences with social activism or participation in social movements in general? How has hip-hop reinforced or challenged your activity in social activism and social movements?

e. Ultimately, do you believe hip-hop challenges or reinforces US mainstream culture? In what ways?

References

A-Trak. 2014. "Why 2014 Was One of the Best Years for Rap: The Left Field Seeped Out of the Margins and into the Mainstream." Retrieved April 15, 2016. www.medium.com/cuepoint/why-2014-was-one-of-the-best-years-for-rap-4-ecab5b0ecf#.kj6dx5wp.

Adams, Teri, and Douglas Fuller. 2006. "The Words Have Changed but the Ideology Remains the Same: Misogynistic Lyrics in Rap Music." *Journal of Black Studies* 36 (6): 938–957.

Adorno, Theodor, and Max Horkheimer. 1969. *The Dialectic of Enlightenment*. New York: Continuum.

Aesop Rock. 2001a. "Labor." *Labor Days*. Definitive Jux.

Aesop Rock. 2001b. "Coma. *Labor Days*. Definitive Jux.

Aesop Rock. 2001c. "Save Yourself." *Labor Days*. Definitive Jux.

Ahmed, Insanul. 2011. "Interview: Lupe Fiasco Hates His Own Album." Retrieved April 15, 2016. http://www.complex.com/music/2011/02/interview-lupe-fiasco-hates-lasers.

Akom, Antwi. 2009. "Critical Hip Hop Pedagogy as a Form of Liberatory Praxis." *Equity & Excellence in Education* 42 (1): 52–66.

Aldorfer, Melanie. 2005. "10 Million Payola Settlement." Retrieved April 15, 2016. http://www.cbsnews.com/news/10m-payola-settlement/.

Alim, Samy. 2007. "Critical Hip-Hop Language Pedagogies: Combat, Consciousness and the Cultural Politics of Communication." *Journal of Language, Identity & Education* 6 (2): 161–176.

Alim, Samy, Jooyoung Lee, and Lauren Mason Carris. 2010. "'Short Fried-Rice-Eating Chinese MCs' and 'Good-Hair-Havin Uncle Tom Niggas': Performing Race and Ethnicity in Freestyle Rap Battles." *Journal of Linguistic Anthropology* 20 (1): 116–133.

Alridge, Derrick. 2005. "From Civil Rights to Hip Hop: Toward a Nexus of Ideas." *The Journal of African American History* 90 (3): 226–252.

Andrews, Catherine. 2006. "If It's Cool, Creative and Different, It's Indie." Retrieved April 15, 2016. http://www.cnn.com/2006/SHOWBIZ/Music/09/19/indie.overview/.

Androutsopoulos, Jannis, and Arno Scholz. 2003. "Spaghetti Funk: Appropriations of Hip-Hop Culture and Rap Music in Europe." *Popular Music and Society* 26 (4): 463–479.

Arts Law Centre of Australia. 2008. "360 Degree Record Deals." Retrieved April 15, 2016. www.artslaw.com/au/articles/entry/360-degree-record-deals/.

Asante, Molefi Kete. 2008. *It's Bigger Than Hip Hop: The Rise of the Post-Hip-Hop Generation.* New York: St. Martin's Press.

ASCAP. 2016. "About ASCAP." Retrieved April 15, 2016. http://www.ascap.com/about.

Atmosphere. 2002a. "God Loves Ugly." *God Loves Ugly.* Rhymesayers/Fat Beats.

Atmosphere. 2002b. "One of a Kind." *God Loves Ugly.* Rhymesayers/Fat Beats.

Atmosphere. 2002c. "Give Me." *God Loves Ugly.* Rhymesayers/Fat Beats.

Atmosphere. 2002d. "Blamegame." *God Loves Ugly.* Rhymesayers/Fat Beats.

Au, Wayne. 2005. "Fresh Out of School: Rap Music's Discursive Battle with Education." *The Journal of Negro Education* 74 (3): 210–220.

Austen, Ben. 2016. "The New Pioneers: Chance the Rapper Is One of the Hottest Acts in Music, Has a Top 10 Album and His Own Festival—All Without a Label or Physical Release." Retrieved January 1, 2018. https://www.billboard.com/articles/news/magazine-feature/7468570/chance-the-rapper-coloring-book-labels-grammys.

Avalon, Moses. 2011. "What Are the Vegas Odds of Success on Today's Major Label Record Deals?" Retrieved April 15, 2016. www.mosesavalon.com/what-are-the-vegas-odds-of-success-on-todays-major-label-record-deal/.

Baker, Geoffrey. 2005. "Hip Hop Revolucion! Nationalizing Rap in Cuba." *Ethnomusicology* 49 (3): 368–402.

Baker, Soren. 2014. "50 Cent Leaves Interscope: How Nas, Busta Rhymes, Ghostface Killah & Mos Def Fared After Leaving Their Longtime Label Homes." Retrieved April 15, 2016. http://hiphopdx.com/news/id.27806/title.50-cent-leaves-interscope-how-nas-busta-rhymes-ghostface-killah-mos-def-fared-after-leaving-their-longtime-label-homes.

Balaji, Murali. 2010. "Vixen Resistin': Redefining Black Womanhood in Hip-Hop Music Videos." *Journal of Black Studies* 41(1): 5–20.

Ball, Jared. 2009. "FreeMix Radio: The Original Mixtape Radio Show: A Case Study in Mixtape 'Radio' and Emancipatory Journalism." *Journal of Black Studies* 39 (4): 614–634.

Baller Status. 2015. "Madchild Recalls Joining Rock Steady Crew, Swollen Members' Success." Retrieved April 15, 2016. http://www.ballerstatus.com/2015/06/13/madchild-recalls-joining-rock-steady-crew-swollen-members-success/.

Basu, Dipannita, and Pnina Werbner. 2001. "Bootstrap Capitalism and the Culture Industries: A Critique of Invidious Comparisons in the Study of Ethnic Entrepreneurship." *Ethnic and Racial Studies* 24 (2): 236–262.

Bechtel, Craig. 2016. "Knowledge Drop: The Evolution of Del the Funky Homosapien." Retrieved April 15, 2016. http://music.newcity.com/2016/05/05/knowledge-drop-the-evolution-of-del-the-funky-homosapien/.

Belle, Crystal. 2014. "From Jay-Z to Dead Prez: Examining Representations of Black Masculinity in Mainstream Versus Underground Hip-Hop Music." *Journal of Black Studies* 45 (4): 287–300.

Bennett, Andy. 1999a. "Hip Hop Am Main: The Localization of Rap Music and Hip Hop Culture." *Media, Culture & Society* 21 (1): 77–91.

Bennett, Andy. 1999b. "Rappin' on the Tyne: White Hip Hop Culture in Northeast England—An Ethnographic Study." *The Sociological Review* 47: 1–24.

Berger, David, and Richard Peterson. 1975. "Cycles in Symbol Production: The Case of Popular Music." *American Sociological Review* 40: 158–173.

Best, Cassidy, Katie Braile, Emily Falvey, Samantha Ross, Julia Rotunno, and David Schreiber. 2017. "A 'Chance' of Success: The Influence of Subcultural Capital on the Commercial Success of Chance the Rapper." *Journal of the Music & Entertainment Industry Educators Association* 17 (1): 31–58.

BET. 2015. "10 Things You Should Know About Rapsody." Retrieved April 15, 2016. http://www.bet.com/music/photos/2015/03/10-things-you-should-know-about-rapsody.html.

Binary Star. 2000a. "Masters of the Universe." *Masters of the Universe*. Subterraneous Records.

Binary Star. 2000b. "Honest Expression." *Masters of the Universe*. Subterraneous Records.

Binary Star. 2000c. "Binary Shuffle." *Masters of the Universe*. Subterraneous Records.

Binary Star. 2000d. "Indy 500." *Masters of the Universe*. Subterraneous Records.

Binary Star. 2000e. "Conquistadors." *Masters of the Universe*. Subterraneous Records.

Binary Star. 2000f. "Fellowship." *Masters of the Universe*. Subterraneous Records.

Binary Star. 2000g. "Reality Check." *Masters of the Universe*. Subterraneous Records.

Binary Star. 2000h. "New Hip-Hop." *Masters of the Universe*. Subterraneous Records.

Biondo, Michael. 2012. "Strange Music's Social Media Marketing May Have a Hand in Their Success." Retrieved April 15, 2016. http://www.mainstreethost.com/blog/strange-musics-social-media-marketing-may-have-a-hand-in-their-success/.

Blackalicious. 2002. "Purest Love." *Blazing Arrow*. MCA Records.

Blair, Elizabeth. 1993. "Commercialization of the Rap Music Youth Subculture." In *That's the Joint! The Hip-Hop Studies Reader*, edited by Murray Forman and Marc Anthony Neal, 493–504. New York: Routledge.
Blu and Exile. 2007a. "Simply Amazin'." *Below the Heavens*. Sound in Color.
Blu and Exile. 2007b. "Soul Amazing." *Below the Heavens*. Sound in Color.
Blu and Exile. 2007c. "The Narrow Path." *Below the Heavens*. Sound in Color.
Blu and Exile. 2007d. "I Am." *Below the Heavens*. Sound in Color.
Blu and Exile. 2007e. "Dancing in the Rain." *Below the Heavens*. Sound in Color.
Blu and Exile. 2007f. "My World Is." *Below the Heavens*. Sound in Color.
Blue Scholars. 2005a. "Southside Survival." *The Long March*. Massline.
Blue Scholars. 2005b. "The Long March." *The Long March*. Massline.
Blue Scholars. 2005c. "Commencement Day." *The Long March*. Massline.
Bootleg Kev. 2012. "Macklemore Talks L.A. Reid Trying to Sign Him & Atmosphere Comparisons w/ Bootleg Kev." Retrieved April 15, 2016. https://www.youtube.com/watch?v=ojD1OSymbbk.
Brabec, Todd, and Jeff Brabec. 2007. "Songwriter/Artist Development Deals." Retrieved April 15, 2016. www.ascap.com/Home/Music-Center/aritcles-advice/ascapcorner/corner4.aspx.
Brother Ali. 2009a. "The Preacher." *Us*. Rhymesayers Group.
Brother Ali. 2009b. "Crown Jewel." *Us*. Rhymesayers Group.
Burgess, Omar. 2012. "Today's Mathematics: How Hip-Hop Measures Commercial Success." Retrieved April 15, 2016. http://hiphopdx.com/editorials/id.2023/title.todays-mathematics-how-hip-hop-measures-commercial-success.
Busch, Richard. 2012. "Major Record Labels as Dinosaurs?" Retrieved April 15, 2016. www.forbes.com/sites/richardbusch/2012/03/27/major-record-labels-as-dinosaurs/.
Bush, John. 2003. "Hieroglyphics: Full Circle AllMusic Review." Retrieved April 15, 2016. www.allmusic.com/album/full-circle-mw0000326859/awards.
Bylin, Kyle. 2010. "See How Much Indie Artists Make Vs. Label Artists." Retrieved April 15, 2016. www.hypebot.com/hypebot/2010/10/see-how-much-indie-artists-make-vs.label-artists.html.
Byrd, Ayana. 2014. "How TuneCore Is Making Record Labels Unnecessary." Retrieved April 15, 2016. www.fastcompany.com/3034888/innovation-agents/how-tunecore-is-making-record-labels-unncessary/.
Caramanica, Jon. 2017. "The Rowdy World of Rap's New Underground: The Lo-Fi Rap That Thrives on SoundCloud Teems with Unruly Energy. Can It Survive the Mainstream?" Retrieved January 1, 2018. https://www.nytimes.com/2017/06/22/arts/music/soundcloud-rap-lil-pump-smokepurrp-xxxtentacion.html.
Carter, Sophia. 2014. "Rainbow Noise Entertainment—Turning Music Upside Down." Retrieved April 15, 2016. http://vadamagazine.com/entertainment/music/rainbow-noise-entertainment.

Caves, Richard. 2000. *Creative Industries: Contracts Between Art and Commerce.* Cambridge, MA: Harvard University Press.
Chang, Jeff. 2005. *Can't Stop Won't Stop: A History of Hip-Hop Generation.* New York: St. Martin's Press.
Charmaz, Kathy. 1983. "The Grounded Theory Method: An Explication and Interpretation." In *Contemporary Field Research: A Collection of Readings*, edited by Robert Emerson, 109–126. Boston: Waveland.
Charmaz, Kathy, and Liska Belgrave. 2012. "Qualitative Interviewing and Grounded Theory Analysis." In *The SAGE Handbook of Interview Research: The Complexity of the Craft*, edited by Jaber Gubrium, James Holstein, Amir Marvasti, and Karyn McKinney, 2nd ed., 347–366. Thousand Oaks, CA: Sage.
Clark, Msia Kibona. 2013. "The Struggle for Hip Hop Authenticity and Against Commercialization in Tanzania." *The Journal of Pan African Studies* 6 (3): 5–21.
Clay, Andreana. 2006. "All I Need Is One Mic: Mobilizing Youth for Social Change in the Post Civil Rights Era." *Social Justice* 33 (2): 105–121.
Cohen, Cathy. 1997. "Punks, Bulldaggers, and Queens: The Radical Potential of Queer Politics?" *GLQ: A Journal of Lesbian and Gay Studies* 3 (4): 437–465.
Collins, Patricia Hill. 2005. *Black Sexual Politics: African Americans, Gender, and the New Racism.* New York: Routledge.
Connell, Raewyn. 1995. *Masculinities.* Berkeley: University of California Press.
Connell, Raewyn, and James Messerschmidt. 2005. "Hegemonic Masculinity: Rethinking the Concept." *Gender & Society* 19 (6): 829–859.
Cooper, Roman. 2009. "MURS Leaves Warner Bros., Talks New Projects." Retrieved April 15, 2016. http://hiphopdx.com/news/id.9829/title.murs-leaves-warner-bros-talks-new-projects.
Cosper, Alex. 2016. "How to Divide Percentages with a Record Label." Retrieved April 15, 2016. www.smallbusiness.chron.com/divide-percentages-record-label-39258.html.
Crenshaw, Kimberle. 1991. "Beyond Racism and Misogyny: Black Feminism and 2 Live Crew." *Boston Review: A Political and Literary Forum* 16 (6): 30–33.
Cunninlynguists. 2006. "Since When." *A Piece of Strange*. QN5/L.A. Underground.
Davey D. 1984. "What Is Hip Hop?" Retrieved January 1, 2018. http://www.daveyd.com/whatishipdav.html.
Day, Brian. 2011. "In Defense of Copyright: Record Labels, Creativity, and the Future of Music." *Seton Hall Journal of Sports and Entertainment Law* 21 (1): 61–103.
Day, Wendy. 2010. "Warning: Hip-Hop Artists Need to Know About Today's 360 Record Deals." Retrieved April 15, 2016. www.hiphopandpolitics.com/2010/02/05/warning-hip-hop-artist-need-to-know-about-todays-360-record-deals/.
Decker, Jeffrey Louis. 1993. "The State of Rap: Time and Place in Hip Hop Nationalism." *Social Text* 34: 53–84.

Dedman, Todd. 2011. "Agency in UK Hip-Hop and Grime Youth Subcultures—Peripherals and Purists." *Journal of Youth Studies* 14 (5): 507–522.

Delamont, Sara, and Neil Stephens. 2008. "Up on the Roof: The Embodied Habitus of Diasporic Capoeira." *Cultural Sociology* 2 (1): 57–74.

Dennis, Chrisopher. 2006. "Afro-Columbian Hip-Hop: Globalization, Popular Music and Ethnic Identities." *Studies in Latin American Popular Culture* 25: 271–295.

DeVault, Marjorie. 1999. *Liberating Method: Feminism and Social Research*. Philadelphia: Temple University Press.

Dimaggio, Paul. 2010. *Art in the Lives of Immigrant Communities in the United States*. New Brunswick, NJ: Rutgers University Press.

Dimitriadis, Greg. 2009. *Performing Identity/Performing Culture: Hip Hop as Text, Pedagogy, and Lived Practice*. New York: Peter Lang.

Drake, David. 2015. "If It Ain't About the Money: Does Hip-Hop Still Need Major Labels?" Retrieved April 15, 2016. www.complex.com/music/2015/01/hip-hop-major-labels-2015.

Ducker, Eric. 2014. "A Rational Conversation: The 20-Year-Old Album That's MF Doom's Missing Link." Retrieved April 15, 2016. www.npr.org/sections/therecord/2014/11/06/361216399/a-rational-conversation-the-20-year-old-album-thats-mf-dooms-missing-link.

Durnham, Aisha, Brittney Cooper, and Susuna Morris. 2013. "The Stage Hip-Hop Feminism Built: A New Directions Essay." *Signs* 38 (3): 721–737.

Dwyer, Sonya, and Jennifer Buckle. 2009. "The Space Between: On Being an Insider-Outsider in Qualitative Research." *International Journal of Qualitative Methods* 8: 54–63.

Dyson, Michael Eric. 2010. *Know What I Mean: Reflections on Hip-Hop*. New York: Basic Civitas.

Emerson, Rana. 2002. "Where My Girls At?: Negotiating Black Womanhood in Music Videos." *Gender and Society* 16 (1): 115–135.

FCC. 2015. "The FCC Payola Rules." Retrieved April 15, 2016. https://www.fcc.gov/consumers/guides/fccs-payola-rules.

Ferguson, Roderick. 2004. *Aberrations in Black: Toward a Queer of Color Critique*. Minneapolis: University of Minnesota Press.

Ferris, Kerry. 2007. "The Sociology of Celebrity." *Sociological Compass* 1 (1): 371–384.

Figueroa, Maria, Damone Richardson, and Pam Whitefield. 2004. *The Clear Picture on Clear Channel Communications, Inc.: A Corporate Profile*, 1–78. Ithaca, NY: Cornell University, ILR School.

Folami, Akilah. 2007. "From Habermas to Get Rich or Die Tryin: Hip-Hop, the Telecommunications Act of 1996, and the Black Public Sphere." *Michigan Journal of Race and Law* 12: 235–304.

Forman, Murray. 2000. "Represent: Race, Place, and Space in Rap Music." *Popular Music* 19 (1): 65–90.

Forman, Murray. 2010. "Conscious Hip-Hop, Change, and the Obama Era." *American Studies Journal* 54: 1–20.
Forman, Murray, and Marc Anthony Neal. 2004. *That's The Joint! The Hip-Hop Studies Reader*. New York: Routledge.
Fox, Mark. 2004. "E-commerce Business Models for the Music Industry." *Popular Music and Society* 27 (2): 201–220.
Fraley, Todd. 2009. "I Got a Natural Skill...Hip-Hop, Authenticity, and Whiteness." *Howard Journal of Communication* 20 (1): 37–54.
Frazier, Walter. 2010. "Lupe Fiasco Drops Label Beef to Focus on 'Lasers'." Retrieved April 15, 2016. http://www.billboard.com/articles/news/948646/lupe-fiasco-drops-label-beef-to-focus-on-lasers.
Freire, Paulo. 1970. *Pedagogy of the Oppressed*. New York: The Continuum International Publishing Group.
Fricke, David. 2012. "Jimmy Iovine: The Man with the Magic Ears." Retrieved April 15, 2016. http://www.rollingstone.com/music/news/jimmy-iovine-the-man-with-the-magic-ears-20120412.
George, Nelson. 2005. *Hip-Hop America*. New York: Viking.
Goldstein, Brian Taylor. 2013. "Independent Contractors or Employees: What's in a Name." Retrieved April 15, 2016. http://www.musicalamerica.com/mablogs/?p=10571.
Gordon, Steve. 2013. "How to Avoid Getting Completely Screwed by a 360 Deal..." Retrieved April 15, 2016. www.digitalmusicnews.com/2013/07/02/threesixty.
Gosa, Travis. 2010. "Not Another Remix: How Obama Became the First Hip-Hop President." *Journal of Popular Music Studies* 22 (4): 289–415.
Gosa, Travis. 2011. "Counterknowledge, Racial Paranoia, and the Cultic Milieu: Decoding Hip-Hop Conspiracy Theory." *Poetics* 39: 187–204.
Gottfried, Gideon. 2014. "Fragmentation of the Music Industry: Everything Is Falling Apart—Luckily." Retrieved April 15, 2016. www.imusiciandigital.com/en/blog/fragmentation-of-the-music-industry.
Gottfried, Gideon. 2016. "Everything Is Falling Apart—Luckily." Retrieved April 15, 2016. www.imusiciandigital.com/en/blog/fragmentation-of-the-music-industry/.
Gramsci, Antonio. 1971. *Selections from the Prison Notebooks*. New York: International Publishers.
Green, Talib Kweli. 2015. "Why I Left the Major Label System: And a Little Bit of What I've Learned in the Music Biz." Retrieved April 15, 2016. https://medium.com/cuepoint/why-i-left-the-major-label-system-a0ecfa06ae91#.60fmop8ap.
Greenburg, Zach O' Malley. 2013a. "Tech N9ne: Hip-Hop's Secret Mogul." Retrieved April 15, 2016. www.forbes.com/sites/zackomalleygreenburg/2013/09/24/tech-n9ne-hip-hops-secret-mogul/.

Greenburg, Zach O' Malley. 2013b. "Macklemore: The Biggest Grammy-Nominated, Platinum-Selling Paradox in Music." Retrieved April 15, 2016. http://www.forbes.com/sites/zackomalleygreenburg/2013/12/16/macklemore-the-biggest-grammy-nominated-platinum-selling-paradox-in-music/#32b7305aabe4.

Greenburg, Zach O' Malley. 2015. "Revenge of the Record Labels: How the Majors Renewed Their Grip on Music." Retrieved April 15, 2016. http://www.forbes.com/sites/zackomalleygreenburg/2015/04/15/revenge-of-the-record-labels-how-the-majors-renewed-their-grip-on-music/.

Griswold, Wendy. 1987. "A Methodological Framework for the Sociology of Culture." *Sociological Methodology* 17: 1–35.

Guidry, Tony. 2014. "Do the Math: Indie vs. Major—A Rap Breakdown." Retrieved April 15, 2016. www.iamthaconnect.com/2014/11/10/do-the-math-indie-vs-major-a-rap-breakdown/.

Gupta-Carlson, Himanee. 2010. "Planet B-Girl: Community Building and Feminism in Hip-Hop." *New Political Science* 32 (4): 515–529.

Hammonds, Evelynn. 1994. "Black (W)holes and the Geometry of Black Female Sexuality." *Differences* 6 (2): 126–145.

Hard Knock TV. 2013. "Immortal Technique and Tech N9ne Talk Independent Movement, Technology, Black + Brown." Retrieved April 15, 2016. www.youtube.com/watch?v=xzR4yDUUgO8.

Harkness, Geoff. 2012. "True School: Situational Authenticity in Chicago's Hip-Hop Underground." *Cultural Sociology* 6 (3): 283–298.

Harkness, Geoff. 2014. *Chicago Hustle & Flow: Gangs, Gangsta Rap, and Social Class*. Minneapolis: University of Minnesota Press.

Harrison, Anthony Kwame. 2006. "Cheaper Than a CD, Plus We Really Mean It: Bay Area Underground Hip Hop Tapes as Subcultural Artefacts." *Popular Music* 25: 283–301.

Harrison, Anthony Kwame. 2009. *Hip Hop Underground: The Integrity and Ethics of Racial Identification*. Philadelphia: Temple University Press.

Harrison, Anthony Kwame, and Craig E. Arthur. 2011. "Reading Billboard 1979–89: Exploring Rap Music's Emergence Through the Music Industry's Most Influential Trade Publication." *Popular Music and Society* 34 (3): 309–327.

Hernandez, Jillian. 2014. "Carnal Teachings: Raunch Aesthetics as Queer Feminist Pedagogies in Yo! Majesty's Hip-Hop Practice." *Women and Performance: A Journal of Feminist Theory* 24 (1): 88–106.

Hesmondhalgh, David. 1999. "Indie: The Institutional Politics and Aesthetics of a Popular Music Genre." *Cultural Studies* 13 (1): 34–61.

Hesmondhalgh, David, and Caspar Melville. 2002. "Urban Breakbeat Culture—Repercussions of Hip-Hop in the United Kingdom." In *Global Noise: Rap and Hip Hop Outside the USA*, edited by Tony Mitchell, 86–110. Middletown, CT: Wesleyan University Press.

Hess, Mickey. 2005. "Metal Faces, Rap Masks: Identity and Resistance in Hip-Hop's Persona Artist." *Popular Music and Society* 28 (3): 297–311.

Hess, Mickey, 2012. "The Rap Career." In *That's the Joint: The Hip Hop Studies Reader*, edited by Murray Forman and Marc Anthony Neal, 634–654. New York: Routledge Press.

Hibbett, Ryan. 2005. "What Is Indie Rock?" *Popular Music and Society* 28 (1): 55–77.

Hieroglyphics. 2003a. "Let It Roll." *Full Circle*. Hieroglyphics Imperium Recordings.

Hieroglyphics. 2003b. "Prelude." *Full Circle*. Hieroglyphics Imperium Recordings.

Hieroglyphics. 2003c. "Powers That Be." *Full Circle*. Hieroglyphics Imperium Recordings.

Hieroglyphics. 2003d. "Make Your Move." *Full Circle*. Hieroglyphics Imperium Recordings.

Hill, Marc Lamont. 2009. *Beats, Rhymes, and Classroom Life: Hip-Hop Pedagogy and the Politics of Identity*. New York: Teachers College Press.

Hip Hop Since 1987 TV. 2013. "Brother Ali Talks Being Independent, 90s Business Model Being Popular Today & More." Retrieved April 15, 2016. https://www.youtube.com/watch?v=eYK0lc_gwTw.

Hodgman, Matthew. 2013. "Class, Race, Credibility, and Authenticity Within the Hip-Hop Music Genre." *Journal of Sociological Research* 4 (2): 402–413.

Hunter, Margaret. 2011. "Shake It, Baby, Shake It: Consumption and the New Gender Relation in Hip-Hop." *Sociological Perspectives* 54 (1): 15–26.

IFPI. 2016. "How Record Labels Invest." Retrieved April 15, 2016. www.ifpi.org/how-record-labels-invest.php.

Immortal Technique. 2003a. "One Remix." *Revolutionary Vol. 2*. Viper Records.

Immortal Technique. 2003b. "Industrial Revolution." *Revolutionary Vol. 2*. Viper Records.

Immortal Technique. 2003c. "The Message and the Money." *Revolutionary Vol. 2*. Viper Records.

Immortal Technique. 2003d. "Freedom of Speech." *Revolutionary Vol. 2*. Viper Records.

Immortal Technique. 2003e. "Obnoxious." *Revolutionary Vol. 2*. Viper Records.

iTunes. 2016. "Macklemore and Ryan Lewis." Retrieved April 15, 2016. https://itunes.apple.com/us/artist/macklemore-ryan-lewis/id543948286#fullText.

Iwamoto, Derek. 2003. "Tupac Shakur: Understanding the Identity Formation of Hyper-Masculinity of a Popular Hip-Hop Artist." *Black Scholar* 33 (2): 226–252.

Jeffries, Michael. 2011. *Thug Life: Race, Gender, and the Meaning of Hip-Hop*. Chicago: University of Chicago Press.

Jeffries, Michael. 2014. "Hip-Hop Urbanism Old and New." *International Journal of Urban and Regional Research* 38 (2): 706–715.

Jenkins, Toby. 2011. "A Beautiful Mind: Black Male Intellectual Identity and Hip-Hop Culture." *Journal of Black Studies* 42 (8): 1231–1251.

Johnson, Christopher. 2008. "Danceable Capitalism: Hip-Hop's Link to Corporate Space." *The Journal of Pan African Studies* 2 (4): 80–92.

Jones, Steve. 2002. "Music That Moves: Popular Music, Distribution and Network Technologies." *Cultural Studies* 16 (2): 213–232.

Karubian, Sara. 2009. "360 Deals: An Industry Reaction to the Devaluation of Recorded Music." *Southern California Interdisciplinary Law Journal* 18: 395–462.

Katunich, Lauren. 2002. "Time to Quit Paying the Payola Piper: Why Music Industry Abuse Demands A Complete System Overhaul." *Loyola of Los Angeles Law Review* 22 (3): 643–685.

Keif. 2006. "Record Sales: Where Does the Money Go?" Retrieved April 15, 2016. https://bandzoogle.com/blog/record-sales-where-does-the-money-go.

Kelley, Robin. 1994. *Race Rebels: Culture, Politics, and the Black Working Class*. New York: Free Press.

Kennedy, Randy. 2011. "Celebrating Forefather of Graffiti." Retrieved April 15, 2016. www.nytimes.com/2011/07/23/arts/design/early-graffiti-artist-taki-183-still-lives.html?_r=0.

Kerstetter, Katie. 2012. "Insider, Outsider, or Somewhere in Between: The Impact of Researchers' Identities on the Community Based Research Process." *Journal of Rural Social Sciences* 27 (2): 99–117.

Kitwana, Bakari. 2002. *The Hip-Hop Generation: Young Blacks and the Crisis in African-American Culture*. New York: Basic Civitas.

Klatch, Rebecca. 1999. *A Generation Divided: The New Left, the New Right, and the 1960s*. Berkeley: University of California Press.

Knab, Christopher. 2004. "How and Why Major Labels and Independent Labels Work Together." Retrieved April 15, 2016. http://www.musicbizacademy.com/knab/articles/majorindie.htm.

Knab, Christopher. 2010. "Inside Record Labels: Organizing Things." Retrieved April 15, 2016. www.musicbizacademy.com/knab/articles/insidelabels/htm.

KRS-ONE. 2007. "Nothing New." *Hip-Hop Lives*. Koch Records.

Kubrin, Charis. 2005. "Gangstas, Thugs, and Hustlas: Identity and the Code of the Street in Rap Music." *Social Problems* 52 (3): 360–378.

Leard, Diane, and Brett Lashua. 2006. "Popular Media, Critical Pedagogy, and Inner City Youth." *Canadian Journal of Education* 29 (1): 244–264.

Lena, Jennifer. 2006. "Social Context and Musical Content of Rap Music, 1979–1995." *Social Forces* 85 (1): 479–496.

Lena, Jennifer. 2013. "Authenticity and Independence in Rap Music and Other Genre Communities." In *Explorations in Music Sociology: Examining the Role of Music in Social Life*, edited by S. Horsfall, J. M. Meij, and M. Probstfield, 232–240. Boulder, CO: Paradigm Publishing.

Lena, Jennifer, and Richard Peterson. 2008. "Classification of Culture: Types and Trajectories of Music Genres." *American Sociological Review* 73: 697–718.

Leyshon, Andrew. 2001. "Time-Space (and Digital) Compression: Software Formats, Musical Networks, and the Reorganisation of the Music Industry." *Environment and Planning* 33: 49–77.

Leyshon, Andrew, Peter Webb, Shaun French, Nigel Thrift, and Louise Crew. 2005. "On the Reproduction of the Musical Economy After the Internet." *Media, Culture & Society* 27 (2): 177–209.

Lifetime. 2016. "Biography: Clark Gable Lifetime." Retrieved April 15, 2016. http://www.nytimes.com/movies/person/10097/Clark-Gable/biography.

Lin, Angel. 2006. "Independent Hip-Hop Artists in Hong-Kong: Cultural Capitalism, Youth Subculture Resistance, and Alternative Modes of Cultural Production." *Mobile and Popular Culture* 1: 1–18.

Lindvall, Helienne. 2010. "Behind the Music: When Artists Are Held Hostage by Labels." Retrieved January 1, 2018. https://www.theguardian.com/music/musicblog/2010/apr/15/artists-held-hostage-labels.

Lio, Shoon, Scott Melzer, and Ellen Reese. 2008. "Constructing Threat and Appropriating 'Civil Rights': Rhetorical Strategies of Gun Rights and English Only Leaders." *Symbolic Interaction* 31 (1): 5–31.

Live Nation. 2013. "Live Nation's Artist Nation Introduces G-Major Lead by Veteran Artist Manager Virginia Davis." Retrieved January 1, 2018. http://investors.livenationentertainment.com/news-center/news-center-details/2013/Live-Nations-Artist-Nation-Introduces-G-Major-Lead-By-Veteran-Artist-Manager-Virginia-Davis/default.aspx.

Lopes, Paul. 1992. "Innovation and Diversity in the Popular Music Industry: 1969–1990." *American Sociological Review* 57 (1): 56–71.

Low, Bronwen. 2010. "The Tale of the Talent Night Rap: Hip-Hop Culture in Schools and the Challenge of Interpretation." *Urban Education* 45 (2): 194–220.

Macklemore and Ryan Lewis. 2012a. "Jimmy Iovine." *The Heist*. Macklemore LLC-ADA.

Macklemore and Ryan Lewis. 2012b. "Make the Money." *The Heist*. Macklemore LLC-ADA.

Macklemore and Ryan Lewis. 2012c. "Ten Thousand Hours." *The Heist*. Macklemore LLC-ADA.

Macklemore and Ryan Lewis. 2012d. "Can't Hold Us." *The Heist*. Macklemore LLC-ADA.

Maher, George Ciccariello. 2005. "Brechtian Hip-Hop: Didactics and Self-Production in Post-Gangsta Political Mixtapes." *Journal of Black Studies* 26 (1): 129–160.

Maher, George Ciccariello. 2007. "A Critique of DuBoisian Reason: Kanye West and the Fruitfulness of Double Consciousness." *Journal of Black Studies* 39 (3): 371–401.

Mansbridge, Jane, and Aldon Morris. 2001. *Oppositional Consciousness: The Subjective Roots of Social Protest.* Chicago: University of Chicago Press.

Markman, Rob. 2011. "Killer Mike Talks Reconciling with Big Boi." Retrieved April 15, 2016. http://www.mtv.com/news/1662818/killer-mike-big-boi/.

Markman, Rob. 2013. "Chief Keef's Interscope Deal Revealed to Be Worth $6 Million." Retrieved April 15, 2016. http://www.mtv.com/news/1700678/chief-keef-recording-contract/.

Marshall, Lee. 2013. "The 360 Deal and the 'New' Music Industry." *European Journal of Cultural Studies* 16 (1): 77–99.

Martinez, Theresa. 1997. "Popular Culture as Oppositional Culture: Rap as Resistance." *Sociological Perspectives* 40 (2): 265–286.

Maxwell, Ian. 1994. "True to the Music: Authenticity, Articulation and Authorship in Sydney Hip Hop Culture." *Social Semiotics* 4 (1–2): 117–137.

McCall, Nathan. 1994. *Makes Me Wanna Holler: A Young Black Man in America.* New York: Vintage Books.

McLeod, Kembrew. 1999. "Authenticity Within Hip-Hop and Other Cultures Threatened with Assimilation." *Journal of Communication* 49 (4): 134–150.

McLeod, Kembrew. 2005. "MP3s are Killing Home Taping: The Rise of Internet Distribution and its Challenge to the Major Label Music Monopoly." *Popular Music and Society* 28 (4): 521–531.

McTaggart, Ninochka, and Eileen O' Brien. 2017. "Seeking Liberation, Facing Marginalization: Asian Americans and Pacific Islanders' Conditional Acceptance in Hip-Hop Culture." *Sociological Inquiry* 87 (4): 634–658.

McWhorter, John. 2003. "How Hip-Hop Holds Blacks Back." *City Journal* 13 (3) (Summer): 66–75.

Merton, Robert. 1972. "Insiders and Outsiders: A Chapter on the Sociology of Knowledge." *American Journal of Sociology* 78: 9–47.

MF DOOM. 2009. "Gazillion Ear." *Born Like This.* Lex.

Michaels, Sean. 2010. "Outkast's Record Label Blocks Big Boi and Andre 3000 Collaboration." Retrieved January 1, 2018. https://www.theguardian.com/music/2010/jun/09/outkast-big-boi-andre-3000.

Miller-Young, Mireille. 2008. "Hip-Hop Honeys and Da Hustlaz: Black Sexualities in the New Hip-Hop Pornography: Feminism, Race, Transnational Feminism, Race Transnationalism." Special Issue, *Meridians* 8 (1): 261–292.

Mills, Brad. 2000. "Binary Star: Masters of the Universe, AllMusic Review." Retrieved April 15, 2016. www.allmusic.com/album/masters-of-the-universe-mw0000106803.

Mitchell, Tony. 1996. *Popular Music and Local Identity: Rock, Pop and Rap in Europe and Oceania.* Leicester: Leicester University Press.

Mitchell, Tony. 2000. "Doin' Damage in My Native Language: The Use of "Resistance Vernaculars" in Hip Hop in France, Italy, and Aotearoa/New Zealand." *Popular Music and Society* 24 (3): 41–54.

Mitchell, Tony. 2003. "Australian Hip-Hop as a Subculture." *Youth Studies Australia* 22 (2): 40–47.

Moore, Jacob. 2013. "How to Start an Independent Record Label." Retrieved April 15, 2016. www.pigeonsandplanes.com/2013/03/how-to-start-an-independent-record-label/s/be-careful-with-your-cash/.

Moore, Marcus. 2015. "MURS: Have a Nice Life." Retrieved April 15, 2016. http://pitchfork.com/reviews/albums/20622-have-a-nice-life/.

Moore, Ryan. 2007. "Friends Don't Let Friends Listen to Corporate Rock: Punk as a Field of Production." *Journal of Contemporary Ethnography* 36 (4): 438–474.

Morgan, George, and Andrew Warren. 2011. "Aboriginal Youth, Hip Hop and the Politics of Identification." *Ethnic and Racial Studies* 34 (6): 925–947.

Morgan, Marcyliena, and Dionne Bennett. 2011. "Hip-Hop & the Global Imprint of a Black Cultural Form." *Dædalus: The Journal of the American Academy of Arts & Sciences* 140 (2): 176–196.

Myer, Letrez, and Christine Kleck. 2007. "From Independent to Corporate: A Political Economic Analysis of Rap Billboard Toppers." *Popular Music and Society* 30 (2): 137–148.

Nathan S. 2015. "Your Favorite Indie Rapper is Secretly Signed to a Major Label." Retrieved April 15, 2016. http://djbooth.net/news/entry/indie-rapper-secretly-signed-major-label.

The NE Hip-Hop. 2013. "Immortal Technique on Being Independent." Retrieved April 15, 2016. www.youtube.com/watch?v=gRrlBwOBRJA.

The NE Hip-Hop. 2015. "Aesop Rock & Rob Sonic Talk Soundset, Indy Hip-Hop Today, Upcoming Solo Projects & More!" Retrieved April 15, 2016. https://www.youtube.com/watch?v=Z8Pf2eBDR-8.

Negus, Keith. 2002. "The Cultural Work of Intermediaries and the Enduring Distance Between Production and Consumption." *Cultural Studies* 16 (4): 501–515.

Newman, Michael. 2005. "Rap as Literacy: A Genre Analysis of Hip-Hop Cyphers." *Text* 25 (3): 399–436.

Nguyen, Hao. 2015a. "How Tech N9ne Became the Top Independent Hip-Hop Artist in The Game Today." Retrieved April 15, 2016. http://www.stopthebreaks.com/independent-case-studies/how-tech-n9ne-became-top-independent-hip-hop-artist-game-today/.

Nguyen, Hao. 2015b. "Independent Hip-Hop Record Label Profile: 300 Entertainment." Retrieved April 15, 2016. http://www.stopthebreaks.com/independent-case-studies/independent-hip-hop-record-label-profile-300-entertainment/.

Nielson, Erik. 2012. "'Here Come the Cops': Policing the Resistance in Rap Music." *International Journal of Cultural Studies* 15 (4): 349–363.

Ogbar, Jeffrey. 2007. *Hip-Hop Revolution: The Culture and Politics of Rap.* Lawrence: University Press of Kansas.

Oh, Minya. 2002. "Ludacris Barks Back at Pepsi, O'Reilly; P-Roach Antics Not an Issue for Soda Giant." Retrieved April 15, 2016. http://www.mtv.com/news/1457357/ludacris-barks-back-at-pepsi-oreilly-p-roach-antics-not-an-issue-for-soda-giant/.

Ollison, Rashod. 2008. "MURS Goes Mainstream." Retrieved April 15, 2016. http://articles.baltimoresun.com/2008-10-30/entertainment/0810280109_1_murs-for-president-rapper-major-label.

Omi, Michael, and Howard Winant. 1994. *Racial Formation in the United States: From the 1960s to the 1990s.* New York: Routledge.

Omoniyi, Tope. 2006. "Hip-Hop Through the World Englishes Lens: A Response to Globalization." *World Englishes* 25 (2): 195–208.

Ostrove, Geoffrey. 2014. "The Political Economy of Financially Successful Independent Artists." *Class, Race and Corporate Power* 2 (1): 1–22.

Ostrow, Jonathan. 2010. "Indie vs. Major: Which Record Label Contract Is Right for You?" Retrieved April 15, 2016. www.musicthinktank.com/mtt-open/indie-vs-major-which-record-label-contract-is-right-for-you.hml.

Oware, Matthew. 2011. "Brotherly Love: Homosociality and Black Masculinity in Gangsta Rap Music." *Journal of African American Studies* 15: 22–39.

Oware, Matthew. 2014. "(Un)conscious (Popular) Underground: Restricted Cultural Production and Underground Rap Music." *Poetics* 42: 60–81.

Oware, Matthew. 2016. "'We Stick Out Like a Sore Thumb …': Underground White Rappers' Hegemonic Masculinity and Racial Evasion." *Sociology of Race and Ethnicity* 2 (3): 372–386.

Paine, Jake. 2013. "Logic Signs to Def Jam Records, NO I.D. to Executive Produce Album." Retrieved April 15, 2016. http://hiphopdx.com/news/id.23588/title.logic-signs-to-def-jam-records-no-i-d-to-executive-produce-debut-album/.

Peisner, David. 2015. "Why the Rap Veterans Behind Atlanta Indie Label Quality Control Music Are the Smartest Guys in Hip-Hop." Retrieved April 15, 2016. http://www.billboard.com/articles/news/6443743/quality-control-smartest-guys-in-hip-hop.

Pennycook, Alastair. 2007. "Language, Localization, and the Real: Hip-Hop and the Global Spread of Authenticity." *Journal of Language, Identity, and Education* 6 (2): 101–115.

People Under the Stairs. 2002a. "Acid Raindrops." *OST*. Om Records.
People Under the Stairs. 2002b. "Keepin' It Live." *OST*. Om Records.
Perkins, William. 1996. *Droppin' Science: Critical Essays on Rap Music and Hip-Hop Culture*. Philadelphia: Temple University Press.
Perry, Imani. 2004. *Prophets of the Hood: Politics and Poetics in Hip Hop*. Durham, NC: Duke University Press.
Petchauer, Emery. 2010. "Sampling Practices and Social Spaces: Exploring a Hip-Hop Approach to Higher Education." *Journal of College Student Development* 51 (4): 359–372.
Petchauer, Emery. 2015. "Starting with Style: Toward a Second Wave of Hip-Hop Education Research and Practice." *Urban Education* 50 (1): 78–105.
Peters, Mitchell, and Chris Martins. 2016. "Watch Dr. Dre Welcome Anderson. Paak to Aftermath Roster." Retrieved April 15, 2016. http://www.billboard.com/articles/columns/hip-hop/6859424/dr-dre-anderson-paak-compton-malibu-aftermath-entertainment.
Phillips, Amy. 2017. "Chance the Rapper Explains How He's Still Independent, Despite Apple Music Deal." Retrieved January 1, 2018. https://pitchfork.com/news/71701-chance-the-rapper-explains-how-hes-still-independent-despite-apple-music-deal/.
Platon, Adelle. 2017. "Chance the Rapper Talks Fatherhood, Dealing with Anxiety, Record Labels & Possibly Selling His Next Album." Retrieved January 1, 2018. https://www.billboard.com/biz/articles/7720954/chance-the-rapper-talks-fatherhood-dealing-with-anxiety-record-labels-possibly.
Potter, Russell. 1995. *Spectacular Vernaculars: Hip-Hop and the Politics of Postmodernism*. Albany: State University of New York Press.
Pough, Gwendolyn. 2004. *Check It While I Wreck It: Black Womanhood, Hip-Hop Culture, and the Public Sphere*. Boston, NH: Northeastern University Press.
Prindle, Gregory. 2003. "No Competition: How Radio Consolidation Has Diminished Diversity and Sacrificed Localism." *Fordham Intellectual Property, Media, and Entertainment Journal Law* 14 (1): 279–325.
Rapsody. 2012a. "Kind of Love." *The Idea of Beautiful*. Jamla.
Rapsody. 2012b. "The Cards." *The Idea of Beautiful*. Jamla.
Rapsody. 2012c. "Believe Me." *The Idea of Beautiful*. Jamla.
Rapsody. 2012d. "Non-Fiction." *The Idea of Beautiful*. Jamla.
Raymer, Miles. 2013. "Cakes da Killa: The Eulogy." Retrieved April 15, 2016. http://pitchfork.com/reviews/albums/17684-the-eulogy/.
Rebollo-Gil, Guillermo, and Amanda Moras. 2012. "Black Women and Black Men in Hip Hop Music: Misogyny, Violence and the Negotiation of (White-Owned) Space." *The Journal of Popular Culture* 45 (1): 118–132.

Resnikoff, Paul. 2014. "Why Major Labels Are the Best Thing That Happened to Artists..." Retrieved April 15, 2016. www.digitalmusicnews.com/2014/09/19/major-labels-best-thing-happened-artists/.

Resnikoff, Paul. 2017. "How to Get Signed by Spotify Records." Retrieved January 1, 2018. https://www.digitalmusicnews.com/2017/03/20/get-signed-spotify-records/.

Reyna, Christine, Mark Brandt, and Tendayi Viki. 2009. "Blame It on Hip-Hop: Anti-Rap Attitudes as a Proxy for Justice. *Group Processes and Intergroup Relations* 12 (3): 361–380.

Reynolds, Daniel. 2015. "The Exclusive Interview with Mykki Blanco You've Been Waiting For." Retrieved April 15, 2016. http://www.hivplusmag.com/people/2015/10/08/mykkis-mad-genius.

Rodriquez, Jason. 2006. "Color-Blind Ideology and the Cultural Appropriation of Hip-Hop." *Journal of Contemporary Ethnography* 35 (6): 645–668.

Rose, Tricia. 1994. *Black Noise: Rap Music and Black Culture in Contemporary America*. New York: Wesleyan University Press.

Rose, Tricia. 2008. *The Hip Hop Wars: What We Talk About When We Talk About Hip Hop—And Why It Matters*. New York: Basic Civitas.

Sanchez, Deborah. 2010. "Hip-Hop and a Hybrid Text in a Post-Secondary English Class." *Journal of Adolescent & Adult Literacy* 53 (6): 478–487.

Saunders, Tanya. 2016. "Towards a Transnational Hip-Hop Feminist Liberatory Praxis: A View from the Americas." *Social Identities* 22 (2): 178–194.

Scholtes, Peter. 2007. "Rhymesayers Sign Deal with Warner." Retrieved April 15, 2016. http://www.citypages.com/music/rhymesayers-sign-deal-with-warners-6620729.

Schwartzberg, Lauren. 2014. "Lesbian Hip-Hop Hits Primetime." Retrieved April 15, 2016. https://www.vice.com/en_us/article/out-comes-the-lesbian-rap-ballad-456.

Seghal, Kabir. 2018. "Spotify and Apple Music Should Become Record Labels so Musicians Can Make a Fair Living." Retrieved January 1, 2018. https://www.cnbc.com/2018/01/26/how-spotify-apple-music-can-pay-musicians-more-commentary.html.

Shabazz, Rashad. 2014. "Masculinity and the Mic: Confronting the Uneven Geography of Hip-Hop." *Gender, Place, & Culture* 21 (3): 370–386.

Shusterman, Richard. 1992. "Challenging Conventions in the Fine Art of Rap." In *That's the Joint! The Hip-Hop Studies Reader*, edited by Murray Forman and Marc Anthony Neal, 459–480. New York: Routledge.

Simmel, Georg, and Kurt Wolff. 1950. *The Sociology of George Simmel*. New York: Free Press.

Sköld, David, and Alf Rehn. 2007. "Makin' It, by Keeping It Real Street Talk, Rap Music, and the Forgotten Entrepreneurship from 'the Hood.'" *Group & Organization Management* 32 (1): 50–78.

Smalls, Shante Paradigm. 2011. "The Rain Comes Down: Jean Grae and Hip Hop Heternonormativity." *American Behavioral Scientist* 55 (1): 86–95.
Smith, Christopher. 1997. "Method in the Madness: Exploring the Boundaries of Identity in Hip-Hop Performativity, Social Identities." *Journal for the Study of Race, Nation and Culture* 3 (3): 345–374.
Smith, Clyde. 2012. "The Heist: Macklemore & Ryan Lewis Take DIY Route to iTunes #1." Retrieved April 15, 2016. http://www.hypebot.com/hypebot/2012/10/the-heist-macklemore-ryan-lewis-take-diy-route-to-itunes-1.html.
Smith, Clyde. 2013. "The Major 'Exposure' of Macklemore and the Myth of the Indie Artist." Retrieved April 15, 2016. http://www.hypebot.com/hypebot/2013/02/the-exposure-of-macklemore-and-the-myth-of-the-indie-artist.html.
Söderman, Johan. 2013. "The Formation of 'Hip-Hop Academicus'—How American Scholars Talk About the Academisation of Hip-Hop." *British Journal of Music Education* 30 (3): 369–381.
Söderman, Johan, and Goran Folkestad. 2004. "How Hip-Hop Musicians Learn: Strategies in Informal Creative Music Making." *Music Education Research* 6 (3): 313–326.
Stahl, Matt, and Leslie Meier. 2012. "The Firm Foundation of Organizational Flexibility: The 360 Contract in the Digitalizing Music Industry." *Canadian Journal of Communication* 37: 441–458.
Stapleton, Katina. 1998. "From the Margins to Mainstream: The Political Power of Hip-Hop." *Media, Culture & Society* 20: 219–234.
Steiner, B.J. 2014. "Rap Albums That Got Shelved into Oblivion." Retrieved January 1, 2018. http://www.complex.com/music/2014/11/rap-albums-that-never-came-out/.
Stern, Bradley. 2016. "Mykki Blanco Is Right: Gay Media Has an Inclusivity Problem." Retrieved April 15, 2016. http://popcrush.com/mykki-blanco-gay-media-inclusivity-problem/.
Stovall, David. 2006. "We Can Relate: Hip-Hop Culture, Critical Pedagogy, and the Secondary Classroom." *Urban Education* 41 (6): 585–602.
Strachan, Robert. 2007. "Micro-Independent Record Labels in the UK." *European Journal of Cultural Studies* 10 (2): 245–265.
Strauss, Anselm, and Juliet Corbin. 1994. "Grounded Theory Methodology: An Overview." In *Handbook of Qualitative Research*, edited by Norman Denzin and Yvonna Lincoln, 273–285. Thousand Oaks, CA: Sage.
Suhr, Hiesun. 2011. "Understanding the Hegemonic Struggle Between Mainstream Vs. Independent Forces: The Music Industry and Musicians in the Age of Social Media." *International Journal of Technology, Knowledge and Society* 7 (6): 123–136.
Sullivan, Nikki. 2003. *A Critical Introduction to Queer Theory*. New York: New York Press.

Sullivan, Rachel. 2003. "Rap and Race: It's Got a Nice Beat, but What About the Message?" *Journal of Black Studies* 33 (5): 605–622.
Swollen Members. 2002a. "Long Way Down." *Monsters in the Closet*. Battle Axe.
Swollen Members. 2002b. "Act on It." *Monsters in the Closet*. Battle Axe.
Swollen Members. 2002c. "Breathe." *Monsters in the Closet*. Battle Axe.
Tanner-Smith, Emily, Damian Williams, and Denise Nichols. 2006. "Selling Sex to Radio Program Directors: A Content Analysis of *Radio and Records Magazine*." *Sex Roles* 54 (9/10): 675–686.
Taviano, Stefania. 2016. "The Global Imaginary of Arab Hip Hop: A Case Study." *Im@go: A Journal of the Social Imaginary* 5 (7): 183–199.
Taylor, Carl, and Virgil Taylor. 2007. "Hip-Hop Is Now: An Evolving Youth Culture." *Reclaiming Children and Youth* 15 (4): 210–213.
Tech N9ne. 2008a. "Like Yeah." *Killer*. Strange Music.
Tech N9ne. 2008b. "Crybaby." *Killer*. Strange Music.
Terkourafi, Marina. 2010. *Languages of Global Hip Hop*. London: Continuum.
Tickner, Arlene. 2008. "Aqui en el Ghetto: Hip-Hop in Colombia, Cuba, and Mexico." *Latin American Politics and Society* 50 (3): 121–146.
Trapp, Erin. 2005. "The Push and Pull of Hip-Hop: A Social Movement Analysis." *American Behavioral Scientist* 48 (11): 1482–1495.
Tucker, Nichole. 2015. "Tech N9ne Tells the Breakfast Club He 'Will Never Go Mainstream.' Here's Why." Retrieved April 15, 2016. www.inquisitr.com/1991886/tech-n9ne-says-real-music-is-supposed-to-spread-and-shine-but-he-will-never-go-mainsream-heres-why/.
Villegas, Mark, DJ Kuttin' Kandi, and Roderick Labrador. 2013. *Empire of Funk: Hip-Hop and Representation in Filipina/o America*. San Diego, CA: Cognella Academic Publishing.
Vito, Christopher. 2015a. "Who Said Hip-Hop Was Dead?: The Politics of Hip-Hop Culture in Immortal Technique's Lyrics." *International Journal of Cultural Studies* 18 (4): 395–411.
Vito, Christopher. 2015b. "Can We Keep Independent Hip-Hop Lowkey?: Using Content Analysis to Analyze Glocalization in Lowkey's Lyrics." *Studies in Media and Communication* 3 (2): 109–116.
Wang, Oliver. 2014. *Legions of Boom: Filipino American Mobile DJ Crews in the San Francisco Bay Area*. Durham, NC: Duke University Press.
Warren, Andrew, and Rob Evitt. 2010. "Indigenous Hip-Hop: Overcoming Marginality, Encountering Constraints." *Australian Geographer* 41 (1): 141–158.
Watkins, S. Craig. 2005. *Hip Hop Matters: Politics, Pop Culture, and the Struggle for the Soul of a Movement*. Boston, MA: Beacon Press.
Weitzer, Ronald, and Charis Kubrin. 2009. "Misogyny in Rap Music: A Content Analysis of Prevalence and Meanings." *Men and Masculinities* 12 (1): 3–29.

Wells-Wilbon, Rhonda, Nigel Jackson, and Jerome Schiele. 2010. "Lessons from the Maafa: Rethinking the Legacy of Slain Hip-Hop Icon Tupac Amaru Shakur." *Journal of Black Studies* 40 (4): 504–526.

Williams, Paul. 2008. "Twenty-First-Century Jeremiad: Contemporary Hip-Hop and American Tradition." *European Journal of American Culture* 27 (2): 111–132.

XXL Staff. 2008. "The #6 Biggest Moment: Cash Money Signs with Universal." Retrieved April 15, 2016. http://www.xxlmag.com/xxl-magazine/2008/02/the-6-biggest-moment-cash-money-signs-with-universal/.

YONAS. 2011. "I Could." *The Proven Theory*. City of Dreams.

Zafar, Aylin. 2013. "What It's Like When a Label Won't Release Your Album." Retrieved January 1, 2018. https://www.buzzfeed.com/azafar/what-happens-when-your-favorite-artist-is-legally-unable-to?utm_term=.ux0Ew82pe#.guldxWo63.

Index

0–9

3:16 The 9th Edition, 27. *See also* MURS
300 Entertainment, 120, 136. *See also* Fetty Wap; Migos; Quality Control
360 Degree contracts, 74, 76–80, 83, 84, 87, 89, 90
50 Cent, 113

A

A&R. *See* Artist & Repertoire (A&R)
Activism, 9, 13, 21, 23–25, 91. *See also* Social movements
ADA. *See* Alternative Distribution Alliance (ADA)
Adams, Teri, 8, 20
Adorno, Theodor, 6
Advances, 29, 34, 35, 78, 80, 85, 92, 101, 113, 114, 118, 124, 133, 134
Advertising, 35, 77, 78, 81, 83, 84, 92, 133, 136. *See also* Media and Press
Aesop Rock, 27, 59, 62, 63, 106, 119
Affiliating, 113, 121, 133
African-American
 culture, 15, 16, 19, 24, 136
 youth, 24
Aftermath Entertainment, 114. *See also* Anderson Paak; Dr. Dre; Eminem
AGC Productions, 102, 106. *See also* Colon, Anthony
Alim, Samy, 19, 22, 111
Alridge, Derrick, 3, 8, 10, 23
Alternative Distribution Alliance (ADA), 27, 121, 122
American Society of Composers, Artists, and Publishers (ASCAP), 81
Anderson Paak, 114
Andrews, Catherine, 114, 119, 124
Androutsopoulos, Jannis, 5, 18, 35, 134
ANTI-/Epitaph, 27. *See also* Sage Francis
A Piece of Strange, 27. *See also* Cunninlynguists
Apple Music Inc., 122

AD Deals. *See* Artist Development Deals (AD Deals)
Artist & Repertoire (A&R), 34, 78, 81–83, 92, 120, 133
Artist Development Deals (AD Deals), 72, 75, 92
Artistic direction and relations. *See* Artist & Repertoire (A&R)
Asante, Molefi Kete, 15, 63
ASCAP. *See* American Society of Composers, Artists, and Publishers (ASCAP)
Atlantic Records, 116. *See also* Big Three
Atmosphere, 27, 53, 59, 62, 77
A-Trak, 99, 100
Authenticity, 5, 14, 17–19, 34, 62, 63, 100–102, 104, 107, 108, 110, 111, 124, 132, 133

B

Babygrande Records, 27. *See also* Jean Grae
Bad Boy Records, 12, 73. *See also* Notorious B.I.G.; Puff Daddy; Ma$e; The Lox
Balaji, Murali, 4, 8, 10, 20
Ball, Jared, 3, 5, 12, 14, 35, 50, 55, 91, 134
Barber shops, 139
Bars, 28, 29
Battle Axe, 27, 61, 88, 90. *See also* Swollen Members
Beats by Dre. *See* Dr. Dre
Below the Heavens, 27. *See also* Blu and Exile
Bennett, Dionne, 3, 5, 9, 10, 14, 18, 21, 106, 134, 136
Bettie Rubble: The Initiation, 27. *See also* Mykki Blanco
Big Daddy Kane, 62

Big Three
 Sony Music Entertainment, 26
 Universal Music Group, 26
 Warner Bros. Music Group, 26
Billboard, 27, 85, 87, 88, 115, 123
Binary Star, 27, 47, 48, 50, 51, 54, 57, 63, 74, 76, 77, 81–83, 91
Biz Markie, 62
Blackalicious, 27, 48
Black culture, 16
Black Panthers, 11, 62. *See also* Social movements
Blair, Elizabeth, 6
Blavatnik, Len, 117
Blazing Arrow, 27. *See also* Blackalicious
Bling-Bling Era, 47
Blu and Exile, 27, 48, 52, 57, 77, 80, 82, 86
Blue Scholars, 27, 63, 86, 131
Blues music, 87
Blurry lines of Hip-Hop, 5
Bobby Shmurda, 114
Born Like This, 27. *See also* MF Doom
Brandt, Mark, 16
Breakdancing, 10, 25, 61. *See also* Dance
Brother Ali, 27, 60, 62, 119, 121
Bush, G.H.W., 16, 55
Butts, Reverend Calvin, 16

C

Cakes the Killa, 27
California, 31, 32, 100, 136, 138
Capitalism, 6, 10, 29, 60, 135
Carris, Lauren Mason, 19
Cash Money Records, 121. *See also* Big Three
Chance the Rapper, 120, 122
Chang, Jeff, 10, 12, 24, 73
Chief Keef, 114
Choc Quib Town, 18

Ciphers, 11, 21, 23, 56
City of Dreams, 27. *See also* Yonas
Clark Gable, 76, 77
Clay, Andreana, 10, 25
Clear Channel. *See* Iheart Music
Clinton, Bill, 16
Collins, Patricia Hill, 7–9, 20
Colon, Anthony, 102
Common, 3, 33, 51, 115
Complex, 90, 114
Connell, Raewyn, 7, 8
Conscious Rap, 13, 14
Content analysis, 1, 4, 5, 19, 24, 25, 31, 33, 34, 132. *See also* Methodology
Copyright, 5, 12, 73, 78, 81
Corporate control, 5, 55, 77, 82, 83, 92, 105
  of the Hip-Hop industry, 113
  of the music industry, 78
Corporations, 2, 5, 11–14, 16, 25, 29, 34, 45–48, 50, 51, 53, 54, 58, 59, 61, 64, 72–74, 76, 77, 80, 81, 84–92, 101, 102, 104, 106, 113, 114, 117, 118, 121–123, 132, 133, 136, 139
Cosigns, 86, 120
Critical Hip-Hop, 22. *See also* KRS-One
Critical Race Theory, 1, 6, 132. *See also* Theory
Cunninlynguists, 27

D
Dance, 11, 107
DatPiff, 89, 120
Davey D., 2
Dead Prez, 14, 91
Death Row Records, 73. *See also* Tupac Shakur
Dedman, Todd, 25

Definitive Jux, 27, 59, 115. *See also* Aesop Rock; MURS
Def Jam Records, 113. *See also* Logic
Del the Funky Homosapien, 115
Dennis, Christopher, 11, 18, 19, 135
DeVault, Marjorie, 33
Diaspora of Hip-Hop, 135
Dimaggio, Paul, 17
DIY (Do It Yourself) ethic, 55, 88, 89, 120, 121, 123
DJ(ing), 10, 18, 51, 52, 59, 61, 99
Dr. Dre, 73, 102, 110, 114
Dyson, Michael Eric, 2, 8, 15, 54, 137

E
Elektra Records, 52. *See also* Del the Funky Homosapien; KMD; MF Doom
Elektrik, 112
Eminem, 17, 21, 73, 136
Envy, 112
Esoteric, 17
The Eulogy, 27, 112. *See also* Cakes the Killa
The Evil Jeanius, 27. *See also* Jean Grae
Exploitation, 5, 29, 34, 35, 46, 72, 74, 78, 83, 84, 87, 89, 91, 92, 132, 133
  economic, 5, 6, 29, 34, 35, 72, 78, 87, 91, 92, 132, 133

F
Facebook, 119, 120
Fetty Wap, 120
Fil-Ams. *See* Filipino-Americans
Filipino-Americans, 138, 139
Folami, Akilah, 108
Fools Gold Records, 99, 115. *See also* Killer Mike

Forbes magazine, 89
Forman, Murray, 10, 16, 18, 25, 62, 87–89, 102, 109
Forwards. *See* Advances
Fox, Mark, 104, 118
Fraley, Todd, 17
Frank Ocean, 135
Full Circle, 27, 55. *See also* Hieroglyphics
Fuller, Douglas, 8, 14, 20
Funk Volume, 123. *See also* Ritter, Damien

G
Gangster rap, 13, 47, 48, 50
Gender, 2–10, 15, 19, 21, 31, 33–36, 100, 101, 108, 111, 112, 124, 132–135, 138
 black stereotypes, 15
Generation Z, 134, 136, 138
George, Nelson, 11, 12, 24, 73, 87, 137
Glocalization, 18, 19, 135
Glory Boyz Entertainment, 114. *See also* Chief Keef
God-des and She, 112
God Loves Ugly, 27, 53. *See also* Atmosphere
Golden Era, 12, 46–48, 55, 72, 117, 136
Golden Era of Hip-Hop, 1, 14, 25, 34, 35, 46, 64, 72, 73, 87, 88, 100, 132–134
Goodfellas Barbershop Shave Parlor, 139
Graffiti, 10, 61, 62. *See also* Taki 183
Grainge, Lucian, 117
Gramsci, Antonio, 6, 7, 9, 10, 22
Grind Time Official, 115. *See also* Killer Mike
Griswold, Wendy, 26
Grouch and Eligh, 118

Grounded theory, 28, 29, 33. *See also* Theory
Gupta-Carlson, Himanee, 20, 111

H
Harkness, Geoff, 2, 3, 8, 15, 20, 55, 91, 107, 112, 132, 135
Harrison, Anthony, 3, 5, 11, 13, 35, 59, 86, 106, 115, 134
Hegemonic masculinity, 7, 8, 19, 111. *See also* Collins, Patricia Hill
The Heist, 2, 27, 61, 86. *See also* Macklemore and Ryan Lewis
Hesmondhalgh, David, 18, 19, 55, 135
Hess, Mickey, 15, 17, 56, 114, 115
Heteronormativity, 7, 101, 108, 135
Hibbett, Ryan, 59, 103
Hidden transcripts, 22, 56
Hieroglyphics, 27, 47, 48, 55, 57, 79, 90
Hieroglyphics Imperium Recordings, 115. *See also* Hieroglyphics
Hill, Marc Lamont, 15, 22, 23, 25, 33, 56
Hip-Hop
 activism, 23, 24
 Afro-Columbian, 18
 artists, 4, 6, 8, 23, 28, 31, 32, 34–36, 46, 64, 72, 87, 91, 133
 Bay Area and San Francisco, 25
 commercialization of, 14
 commodification of, 56, 101, 133
 cooptation and resistance of, 134, 135
 corporatization of, 46, 51, 63, 72
 culture, 1, 4, 6, 8, 9, 17, 18, 22, 25, 29, 31, 35, 47, 48, 51, 62, 100–102, 108, 110, 112, 124, 132, 138

European, 135
Hong-Kong, 18
music, 1–3, 10, 12, 18, 24, 25, 27, 29, 31, 33, 58, 60, 61, 73, 100, 111, 137
Muslim, 21
Nigerian, 18
origins, 10, 15, 34, 61, 64, 132
Philadelphia, 33
popular culture and music, 7
UK (Grime), 25, 88, 135
Hip-Hop Lives, 27. *See also* KRS-ONE
Hip-Hop Matters, 2, 102. *See also* Watkins, S. Craig
Hodgman, Matthew, 17, 62, 63
Homogenization of Hip-Hop Music, 46
Hopson, 136
Horkheimer, Max, 6
Hunter, Margaret, 20, 111

I
Ice-T, 16
The Idea of Beautiful, 27. *See also* Rapsody
Iheart Music, 85
Immortal Technique, 16, 27, 45, 50, 52, 56, 57, 75, 80–84, 89, 91, 107, 109, 118, 124
Independent (indie) hip-hop albums, 1, 4, 5, 26–28, 31, 33, 46
alternative culture, 29, 58, 60
cultural politics, 5
culture, 3–5, 10, 15, 34
economic politics, 5
movements, 21
Instagram, 119
Internal colonialism, 24. *See also* Mansbridge, Jane; Morris, Aldon
Interscope Records, 2, 73, 114. *See also* Dr. Dre; Iovine, Jimmy; Macklemore and Ryan Lewis; Mos Def
Intersectional Feminist Theory, 6. *See also* Theory
Interviews, 1, 4–6, 25, 29, 31–33, 35, 81, 100, 101, 103, 105–108, 110, 112, 124, 132, 133. *See also* Methodology
Iovine, Jimmy, 2, 53, 73, 79, 84
iTunes, 51, 76, 85, 87, 118. *See also* Apple Music Inc.
Iwamoto, Derrick, 8, 19

J
J. Cole, 135
Jackson, Nigel, 13, 47
Jamla, 27, 74, 85, 91. *See also* Rapsody
Jay-Z, 83, 110
Jean Grae, 20, 27
Jedi Mind Tricks, 27
Johnson, Christopher, 11, 12, 46, 72
Jones, Quincy, 52
Jones, Steve, 55, 105, 119
Juice Crew, 62

K
Kandi, DJ Kuttin, 137
Kanye West, 21
Karubian, Sara, 15, 76, 89, 113, 114, 119, 124
Kazaa, 76
Keeping (Keepin') it Real, 19, 61–63. *See also* Authenticity
Kelow, 112
Kendrick Lamar, 135
Kevin Gates, 123
Killer, 27. *See also* Tech N9ne
Killer Mike, 115
Kitwana, Bakari, 3
Klatch, Rebecca, 32

180   INDEX

Kleck, Christine, 2, 3, 11, 12, 46, 51, 73, 104, 110, 132, 135
KMD, 52, 53. *See also* MF Doom
Koch Records, 27. *See also* KRS-ONE
KRS-ONE, 22, 27, 48, 56, 88
Kubrin, Charis, 3, 19, 26, 27, 132, 135

L
Labor Days, 27, 59. *See also* Aesop Rock
Lady Gaga, 76
Lashua, Brett, 23, 56
Leard, Diane, 23, 56
Lee, Jooyoung, 19
Lesbian, Gay, Bisexual, Transgender, and Queer (LGTBQ), 5
Lex, 52. *See also* MF Doom
LGBTQ. *See* Lesbian, Gay, Bisexual, Transgender, and Queer (LGBTQ)
Li(f)e, 27. *See also* Sage Francis
Lin, Angel, 18, 135
Live Nation, 83, 123
Living Legends, 118
Logic, 84, 113, 123
The Long March, 27, 86. *See also* Blue Scholars
Lopes, Paul, 15, 87, 89, 117
Love of the Music, 59, 61, 63, 64. *See also* Authenticity
Low, Bronwen, 23
Lowkey, 135
The Lox, 73
Ludacris, 84
Lupe Fiasco, 116

M
Ma$E, 73
Mac Dirrty. *See* Sanchez, Carlos
Macklemore and Ryan Lewis, 2, 27, 53, 61, 73, 74, 79, 84, 86, 87, 90, 111, 120–122, 136

Macklemore LLC-ADA, 27. *See also* Macklemore and Ryan Lewis
Mac Miller, 89, 114
Madonna, 76, 83
MadVillain, 27
Madvillainy, 27. *See also* MadVillain
Maher, George Ciccariello, 3, 14, 21, 24, 55, 59, 91, 136
Mainstream Hip-Hop
  culture, 1, 2, 5, 8, 10, 12–14, 16, 17, 22, 24, 34, 45, 46, 48, 50, 55, 56, 62, 64, 87, 106, 132
  major corporations, 5, 13
  major radio stations, 46
  major record label artists, 46
  major record labels, 2
  popular culture, 6, 13, 59
Mansbridge, Jane, 1, 4, 6, 9, 22, 24, 112, 132
Marginalization, 8, 50, 57
  of urban youth, 23
Marlon Craft, 136
Martinez, Theresa, 2, 3, 21, 27, 132, 135
Masculinity, 7, 17, 19
  hegemonic masculinity, 7
  hyper-masculinity, 8, 19
  whiteness, 17
Massline, 27. *See also* Blue Scholars
Master P, 110
Masters of the Universe, 27, 47. *See also* Binary Star
MC Angel, 112
MCA Records, 27. *See also* Blackalicious
McLaren, Malcolm, 12
McTaggart, Ninochka, 137
McWhorter, John, 25
Media and Press, 78
Merchandise, 77, 78, 83, 84, 89
Merton, Robert, 33
Method. *See* Methodology
Methodology, 1, 25

MF Doom, 15, 21, 52, 53
Migos, 120
Millennial generation, 134, 138
Mindie rappers, 123
Minor leagues, 15, 114
Mishka Records, 112. *See also* Cakes the Killa
Misogyny, 21, 63, 110, 135. *See also* Gender
Mixed methods. *See* Methodology
Mixed space, 112, 117, 123, 124. *See also* Blurry Lines
Mixtapes, 14, 16, 89, 91, 113, 136
Monsters in the Closet, 27, 61. *See also* Swollen Members
Moore, Ryan, 55, 104, 116
Moras, Amanda, 16, 19
Morgan, Marcyliena, 9, 10, 14, 18, 21, 62, 106, 136
Morris, Aldon, 1, 4, 6, 9, 22, 24, 112, 132
Morris, Doug, 117
Mos Def, 117
Mr. Life, 16
Multiple Rights Deals. *See* 360 Degree Contracts
MURS, 27, 116, 118
Music industry, 3, 11, 13, 15, 18, 26, 34, 46, 47, 51, 54, 55, 58, 60, 64, 74–76, 78, 80, 85, 87–92, 101, 110, 119, 121, 122, 124, 133
Myer, Letrez, 2, 3, 11, 12, 46, 51, 73, 104, 110, 132, 135
Mykki Blanco, 27, 111
MySpace, 119

N
Napster, 76
Nas, 115
National Public Radio (NPR), 121
Neal, Marc Anthony, 18

Neo-Marxist, 1, 6, 9, 132. *See also* Theory
New School Hip-Hop, 138
Nichols, Denise, 20
Nielson, Erik, 25, 119
Nipsey Hussle, 105
No Limit Records, 121
Notorious B.I.G., 73
NPR. *See* National Public Radio (NPR)
NVivo, 28, 33

O
Objectification of women, 19, 101, 108. *See also* Gender
Old School Hip-Hop, 62
Omi, Michael, 7, 8
Omoniyi, Tope, 18, 135
Om Records, 27, 57, 60. *See also* People Under the Stairs
Oppositional consciousness, 1–6, 9, 10, 22, 25, 35, 36, 112, 132–134, 138. *See also* Mansbridge, Jane; Morris, Aldon
Organic intellectuals, 9, 10, 22. *See also* Gramsci, Antonio
OST, 27. *See also* People Under the Stairs
Ostrove, Geoffrey, 15, 76, 80, 83, 89, 114, 115, 123
Oware, Matthew, 10, 13, 15, 17, 28, 110, 114, 115, 132, 137

P
Pandora, 76, 118
Paramore, 76
Patriarchy, 13, 19, 135. *See also* Gender
Pay for Play, 12. *See also* Payola
Payola, 50, 84–86
Pennycook, Alastair, 19

People Under the Stairs, 60
Perkins, William, 11, 87
Perry, Imani, 2, 3, 5, 16, 17, 35, 55, 134
Petchauer, Emery, 23, 137
The Pirate Bay, 76
Pitchfork, 86
Post-Golden Era, 1, 2, 4, 5, 12–16, 34, 35, 46, 47, 54, 64, 72, 73, 82, 87, 88, 100, 102, 110, 132–134. *See also* Golden Era
Prison industrial complex, 11, 62
The Proven Theory, 27. *See also* Yonas
Puff Daddy, 73, 110
Punk music, 88
Pussycat Dolls, 76

Q
QN5/L.A. Underground, 27, 80. *See also* Cunninlynguists
Quality Control, 120
Quayle, Dan, 16
Queen Latifah, 24, 110
Queen Pen, 112
Queer Theory, 7, 8. *See also* Theory

R
Race, 2–10, 15–19, 21, 25, 31, 33–36, 52, 62, 87, 100, 101, 108–112, 124, 132–135, 137, 138
Racism, 11, 15–18, 21, 23, 52, 56, 107–109, 117, 135
Radio and Records, 20
Radio stations, 12, 14, 34, 35, 46, 50, 51, 64, 85, 89, 91, 92, 119, 132, 133
Rainbow Noise, 112. *See also* Lesbian, Gay, Bisexual, Transgender, and Queer (LGBTQ)
Rap, 10, 13, 17, 20, 28, 47, 48, 50–55, 57, 59–61, 63, 74–77, 79–82, 86–88, 90, 104–107, 112, 115, 119, 121, 124
Rap Genius, 57
Rapsody, 27, 51, 63, 74, 85, 91
Rawkus Records, 117. *See also* Mos Def
Reagan, Ronald, 24
"Real" or "Straight" Talk, 22. *See also* Authenticity
Rebollo-Gil, Guillermo, 16, 19
Recording Industry Association of America (RIAA), 27, 76
Record labels, 2, 3, 6, 12, 26, 34, 35, 45, 46, 52, 54–56, 58, 63, 64, 72, 74, 80, 83, 85–87, 90, 91, 110, 113, 123, 132, 133, 136, 139
Religion, 21
REMember Music, 114. *See also* Mac Miller
Resistance to domination, 22, 132. *See also* Social movements
Revolutionary Vol. 2, 27. *See also* Immortal Technique
Reyna, Christine, 16
Rhymesayers Group, 27. *See also* Atmosphere, Brother Ali
RIAA. *See* Recording Industry Association of America (RIAA)
Rick Ross, 72
Ritter, Damien, 123
Roc-A-Fella Records, 121. *See also* Jay-Z
Rock the Bells, 118
Rose, Tricia, 136, 137
Rostrum Records, 114. *See also* Mac Miller
RoxXxan, 112
Royalty(ies), 77, 80, 81, 83, 85, 90

Ruben, Rick, 12
Run the Jewels, 115. *See also* Killer Mike; Ruthless Records
Ruthless Records, 88

S
Sage Francis, 27
Sanchez, Carlos, 22, 103
San Diego, CA, 31, 32, 102, 139
Schiele, Jerome, 13, 47
Scholz, Arno, 5, 18, 35, 134
"Selling out", 50, 91, 106, 118, 153. *See also* Authenticity
Sex, 20, 104, 111
Sexism, 17, 19, 111, 135. *See also* Gender
Sexuality, 3–7, 9, 10, 16, 20, 21, 34–36, 100, 111, 124, 133–135, 138
Sexual orientation. *See* Sexuality
Shazam, 118
"Shelved", 52–54
Shusterman, Richard, 6, 28
Silverman, Tom, 12
Simmons, Russell, 110
Sistah Souljah, 16
Skizzy Mars, 123
Social media, 11, 21, 27, 56, 83, 84, 90, 118–120, 123, 124, 135, 136, 138, 139
Social movements
 Black Lives Matter, 139
 Civil Rights Movement, 8, 10, 11, 23, 24, 62
 Day without Immigrants, 139
 Feminist Movement, 24
 Los Angeles Riots of 1992, 25
 Occupy Wall Street, 10, 139
 Women's March, 139
Söderman, Johan, 23, 137
SoundCloud, 89, 118–120
Sound in Color, 27, 77, 80, 82, 86. *See also* Blu and Exile

Soundscan, 31, 88
The Source, 86
Spotify, 76, 118, 122, 123
Stapleton, Katina, 2, 3, 10, 20, 22, 62, 132, 135
Stones Throw, 27. *See also* MadVillain
Strachan, Robert, 88, 103
Strange Music, 27, 89, 120. *See also* Tech N9ne
Street Team(s), 84, 89, 119
Subculture, 2, 3, 6, 15, 25, 55, 62, 64, 132, 135
Subterraneous Records, 27, 63. *See also* Binary Star
Suhr, Hiesun, 15, 121, 123
Sullivan, Nikki, 7, 8
Sullivan, Rachel, 8, 16
Superegular Records, 27. *See also* Jedi Mind Tricks
Swollen Members, 27, 61, 88, 90

T
Taki 183, 62
Talib Kweli, 3, 119
Tanner-Smith, Emily, 20
Tech N9ne, 27, 52, 53, 57, 86, 89, 108, 109, 116, 120
Technology and Media
 cassettes, 11
 CD, 11, 89, 136
 digital downloads, 76
 P2P, 76, 89, 136
 technological advancements, 87, 119, 121
 technological changes, 4, 89, 92
 the Internet, 11, 119, 120, 124, 135, 136
Telecommunications Act of 1996, 85
Theory, 1, 7, 19, 29
Tickner, Arlene, 13, 17–19, 22
Tommy Boy, 88
Torrentz, 76

Touring, 5
Trapp, Erin, 24
Tucker, Deloris, 16, 53
Tunecore, 76
Tupac Shakur, 13, 16, 19, 24, 73
Twitter, 89, 119, 120

U
Underground Hip-Hop, 3, 14, 33, 87, 91, 115, 117. *See also* Independent Hip-Hop
UNO Records, 27. *See also* Mykki Blanco
Us, 60. *See also* Brother Ali

V
Vibe Magazine, 86, 106
Viki, Tendayi, 16
Violent by Design, 27. *See also* Jedi Mind Tricks
Viper Records, 27, 50, 56, 57, 75, 80–84, 89, 91, 109. *See also* Immortal Technique
Visionary Music Group, 113. *See also* Logic
Voodoo SoulJahs, 18

W
Watkins, S. Craig, 2, 11, 24, 47, 54–56, 131, 135
Waves of commodification in Hip-Hop, 101, 124, 133
Weitzer, Ronald, 19, 27
Wells-Wilbon, Rhonda, 13, 47
White(s), 7, 8, 12, 16–20, 31, 47, 51, 60, 62, 73, 108–110, 112, 136
  color-blindness, 8, 17
  whiteness, 17
Williams, Damian, 20
Williams, Robbie, 76
Winant, Howard, 7, 8
Wiz Khalifa, 113, 115

X
XXL, 86, 121

Y
YG, 105
Yo Majesty, 112
Yonas, 27
Young Lords, 11, 62
Young Ma, 135
Young Thug, 114
YouTube, 29, 119, 122